Praise for *The Transhumanist Temptation*

"Grayson Quay is one of the most interesting and daring young writers currently working. Here he tackles a subject of utmost importance — transhumanism — whose urgency will only continue to grow. Absolutely everyone can benefit from reading and grappling with the arguments in this eloquent book."

— **Spencer Klavan**, Author, *How to Save the West* and *Light of the Mind, Light of the World*

"In the age of AI and biotech, the question of whether humans should (or even can) reengineer our own nature cuts across Left and Right. In this lucid book, Grayson Quay sets out the stakes."

— **Mary Harrington**, Author, *Feminism Against Progress*

"Grayson Quay sounds the alarm about one of the most sinister ideologies menacing human dignity in our time. People of conscience across the political spectrum must pay attention."

— **Sohrab Ahmari**, U.S. Editor, *UnHerd*; Author, *Tyranny, Inc.*

"Supreme Court Justice Anthony Kennedy once opined that everyone had a questionable right to 'define one's own concept of existence,' regardless of the impact on others. Thirty years later, we now have a thriving 'transhumanist' movement threatening to unleash moral horrors and perversions on a massive scale, thanks to a zealous commitment to the false belief that dystopian technologies and enforced acceptance of delusional ideologies will allow us to transcend biological limitations. Fortunately for us, Grayson Quay's *The Transhumanist Temptation* has arrived just in time to warn us about the potential dangers ahead. It is a remarkable and necessary book that does an excellent job marshaling the collective wisdom of everyone from Aristotle to C. S. Lewis to eloquently remind us why our very humanity is so wonderful and precious that it must be defended at all costs."

— **Mollie Hemingway**, Editor in Chief, *The Federalist*

"Quay addresses the question of our time with a thorough and holistic analysis. Most people think of the transhuman issue as a battle over the development of cutting-edge AI or cyborgs, but Quay identifies the movement as one rooted in a much older and more complicated aspect of human nature. In this moment, we must all ask, 'What makes us human?' and for Grayson, the question is one not simply of science but of transcendent purpose and truth."

— **Auron MacIntyre**, Host, *The Auron MacIntyre Show*; Author, *The Total State: How Liberal Democracies Become Tyrannies*

"Grayson Quay has done a profound service to the cause of a true humanism, which will inevitably be a Christian humanism. And his book is a delight to read as well."

— **Susannah Black Roberts**, Editor, *Plough*

"Whether the Promethean fire or the tower of Babel, technological progress always makes claims upon the nature of man and his civilization. With a profound reflection on the Western canon, Grayson Quay both reminds us of the beauty of human purpose and warns us of the dehumanizing claims of modern technology."

— **Deacon Harrison Garlick**, Host, *Ascend: The Great Books Podcast*

"Today, being human seems to be a choice, or at least it can emerge as a choice once we become aware of the array of forces that deny or distract us from our humanity. 'Transhumanism' is as good a name as any for the threatening phenomenon, and *The Transhumanist Temptation* helps readers discern, orient, and resist. Drawing on the wisdom of the Catholic intellectual tradition, Quay perceptively analyzes various occasions of our growing spiritual amnesia — not only biomedical interventions and false ideologies but cultural trends, everyday technologies, and all the ingenious, insidious pandering of false prophets and deceitful muses."

— **Joshua P. Hochschild**, Professor of Philosophy, Mount St. Mary's University

"At a time when everything feels a little too artificial, Grayson Quay pulls back the curtain on the transhumanism lurking behind so much of our world. *The Transhumanist Temptation* examines everything from birth control to artificial intelligence and finds that transhumanist ideology, so often dismissed as marginal, has had far more of an influence than we think. With sharp analysis and remarkable philosophical breadth, Quay walks us through the great struggle of our time: not just to save humanity but to keep it human."

— **Matt Purple, Author,** *Decline from the Top*

This book is not just a critique. It's a call to arms — a call to defend our humanity against the forces that seek to dismantle it, one false promise at a time. I cannot recommend it enough.

— **Jason Scott Jones, Founder, The Vulnerable People Project; Author,** *The Great Campaign*

"Quay dismantles every article of techno-optimism — and I'm grateful for it. Any fellow techno-optimist owes it to himself to wrestle with this book. We still have a lot of work to do, and the best place to start is by listening to our sharpest critics."

— **Katherine Dee, Internet culture reporter**

"The pied piper of transhumanism is alluring to those raised in a deracinated culture taught to worship progress, whatever the outcome, as long as it rejects God's created order. Quay carefully dissects those dangerous presumptions and masterfully explains not only why it is necessary not to be a transhumanist but why one should be an anti-transhumanist, to borrow a phrase."

— **Kara McKinney, Host,** *Tipping Point*

THE TRANSHUMANIST TEMPTATION

GRAYSON QUAY

THE TRANSHUMANIST TEMPTATION

How Technology and Ideology Are Reshaping Humanity—And How to Resist

Manchester, New Hampshire

Copyright © 2025 by Grayson Quay

Printed in the United States of America. All rights reserved.

Cover design by Updatefordesign Studio.

Cover artwork: AI generated with Midjourney, by the designer (Flavius Petrisor).

No part of this book may be reproduced, stored in a retrieval system, or transmitted in any form, or by any means, electronic, mechanical, photocopying, or otherwise, without the prior written permission of the publisher, except by a reviewer, who may quote brief passages in a review.

Crisis Publications
Box 5284, Manchester, NH 03108
1-800-888-9344
www.CrisisMagazine.com

hardcover ISBN 979-8-88911-198-6
ebook ISBN 979-8-88911-199-3

Library of Congress Control Number: 2025938474

First printing

To my little Cheese.
Stay kind, stay brave, stay human.

To thee, O Adam, we have given no certain habitation or countenance of thine own, neither any peculiar office, so that what habitation or countenance or office soever thou dost choose for thyself, the same thou shalt enjoy and possess at thine own proper will and election — We have made thee neither a thing celestial nor a thing terrestrial, neither mortal nor immortal, so that being thine own fashioner and artificer of thyself, thou mayest make thyself after what likeness thou dost most affect.

— Pico della Mirandola

When you meet anything that's going to be Human and isn't yet, or used to be Human once and isn't now, or ought to be Human and isn't, you keep your eyes on it and feel for your hatchet.

—Mr. Beaver, *The Lion, the Witch, and the Wardrobe*

Contents

Acknowledgments ix
Introduction 1

Part 1: Bodies

1. Sex and Reproduction. 21
2. Transgenderism and Body Modification 39
3. Life Extension and Assisted Suicide 45
4. The Procrustean Bed. 55

Part 2: Reality

5. Virtual Reality 71
6. Artificial Intelligence. 79
7. Augmented Reality. 87
8. Re-Enchantment 97

Part 3: Politics

9. Liberalism as Transhumanism 107
10. Postliberalism 115

11. Transhumanism and American Politics 125
12. Right-Wing Transhumanisms. 151

Part 4: Work

13. Capitalism and Transhumanism 165
14. Building a Humane Economy. 173
15. Post-Scarcity 181

Part 5: God

16. The Nephilim and *Theosis* 191
17. Transhumanist Spiritualities 199
18. How Transhumanism Subverts Christianity. 221
19. Digital Christianity. 231

Conclusion 243
About the Author. 257

Acknowledgments

One of the themes of this book is that there's no such thing as a self-creating, self-existent, fully autonomous human being. We are, by nature, enmeshed in networks of duty, love, and gratitude. No one owes nothing to anyone. If I hadn't already believed that, the process of writing this book would have proved it to me.

Although the long, solitary hours of writing and revising were my burden to bear, I would be remiss to neglect offering brief thanks to those who helped me along the way:

To my old *Daily Caller* boss, Geoff Ingersoll, for allowing me six weeks of leave to work on my first draft (unpaid, of course — he wasn't running a charity).

To Spencer Klavan, Mary Harrington, William Benson, Sohrab Ahmari, and Susannah Black Roberts for reading chapter drafts and offering their expert feedback.

To Katherine Dee, for convincing me with a single tweet to write this book.

To my editor, Michael Warren Davis, for encouraging me to pitch my idea to a publisher and for sticking by me when he didn't have to.

To Jason Jones, for giving me the kick in the pants I needed to start writing.

THE TRANSHUMANIST TEMPTATION

To Anna Maria Dube, Max Pallatroni, Molly Rublee, Caleb Selecter, and the rest of the team at Sophia Institute Press for their hard work and easygoing professionalism.

To editors at the *Daily Caller*, *The Spectator World*, *National Review*, *Modern Age*, *First Things*, and *The American Mind* for giving me permission to reproduce portions of my published essays, articles, and columns in this book (see footnotes for details).

To my mother, for buying me books.

To my father, for telling me about God.

To my wife, Marissa, for reading my manuscript and for pulling me up from the slough of despond after I got feedback on my first draft. It's an honor to be your husband.

And to my readers (however many or few you may be): If I convince some of you to view contemporary debates about politics, culture, morality, technology, and religion through the lens of transhumanism, I'll have accomplished all I set out to do.

Grayson Quay
Feast of St. Agatha 2025
Alexandria, Virginia

Introduction

A book on transhumanism might be expected to begin with a thorough definition of *transhumanism*. But since this is a book about the dangers of transhumanism, it makes more sense to begin by defining its opposite, by stating what I am for rather than what I am against. This presents something of a problem, however. Etymologically, *transhuman* means "going beyond that which is human." It would seem, then, that someone who opposes that "transing" could be said to profess an ideology called "humanism." But *humanism*, as the term is generally understood, is not so much transhumanism's opposite as an earlier stage on the slippery slope that leads to transhumanism.

Usually, it's nothing more than a synonym for "atheism." The American Humanist Society, which counts science fiction authors Isaac Asimov and Kurt Vonnegut among its past honorary presidents, defines it as "a nontheistic worldview with ethical values informed by scientific knowledge and driven by a desire to meet the needs of people in the here and now."[1] The term is also often associated with the Italian Renaissance rallying cry that "man is the measure of all things." These attitudes are simply transhumanism awaiting

---

[1] "About the American Humanist Association," American Humanist Association, accessed November 25, 2024, https://americanhumanist.org/about/.

technological advancement. "Humanism" might be better termed "proto-transhumanism."

I'm afraid I'll have to label the position I champion as *anti-transhumanism*. It is never wise to assign oneself the negative in a debate, but since "anti-transhumanism" is not equivalent to "humanism" the way "antidisestablishmentarianism" is to "establishmentarianism," I find myself with little choice. A better term for the opposite of transhumanism might be simply *wisdom* — the kind recommended in Proverbs, of which fear of the Lord is the beginning — but that word has lost the rich, technical meaning it held for its original audience.

The Hebrew word, *chokmah*, is the same one used to describe the "skill" of the craftsmen who assembled the tabernacle. In the same way that there is an art to embroidery or stone carving, there is an art to living. It's possible to live a good life or a bad life the same way it's possible to make a good chair or a bad chair (though, of course, neither all good chairs nor all good lives look the same). God's *Chokmah* is said to have been present at and infused into all of creation, inviting us to seek it out and live according to it. "The fear of the Lord is the beginning of wisdom" because it keeps us conscious of our creaturely status.[2] It reminds us that the good life consists in conforming ourselves to an existing standard of excellence rather than in expressing and inventing ourselves on our own terms. Or, to borrow terms from Catholic philosopher Charles Taylor, in *mimesis* rather than *poesis*.[3]

This is not solely a Judeo-Christian idea. In Plato's *Republic*, Socrates argues that just as a good pruning hook is one that cuts vine branches well and a good eye is one that sees well, so "justice is the excellence

---

[2] Prov. 8:22; 9:10, RSVCE.
[3] Quoted in Carl Trueman, *The Rise and Triumph of the Modern Self* (Wheaton, IL: Crossway, 2020), 39.

Introduction

of the [human] soul," without which the soul cannot "fulfill [its] own ends."[4]

Aristotle makes a similar point when he asks, "Are we then to suppose, that while carpenter and cobbler have certain works and courses of action, Man as Man has none, but is left by Nature without a work?"[5] In describing the Aristotelian view of ethics and the medieval tradition that drew from it, contemporary philosopher Alasdair MacIntyre wrote that the "central functional concept" of these systems was that "of *man* understood as having an essential nature and an essential purpose or function."[6] Just as the cobbler orients himself toward making good shoes, so the man aims at what Aristotle called *eudaimonia* (often translated as "flourishing"). It is man's *telos*, or proper end.

The pre-Christian Roman statesman Cicero, working in the same philosophical tradition, argued that "the highest good is ... to live according to nature."[7] But he does not mean that we should follow our instincts and do whatever "feels natural."

Our default definition of *natural* tends to be an ecological one: what happens "naturally" is what happens spontaneously or without external interference. The classical definition, however, refers to a thing achieving its *telos*. A tree might "naturally" be stunted by a lack of nutrients in the soil, but it would have failed to develop *according to its own nature*. A human adding fertilizer to that soil would be unnatural in the

---

[4] Plato, *The Republic*, trans. Benjamin Jowett (Moscow, ID: Roman Roads, 2013), 52.

[5] Aristotle, *The Nicomachean Ethics*, trans. D. P. Chase (Project Gutenberg, 2003), 1.5.

[6] Alasdair MacIntyre, *After Virtue: A Study in Moral Theory* (Notre Dame, IN: Notre Dame University Press, 2007), 58.

[7] Paul Krause, "Cicero and the Foundations of Natural Law," *Discourses on Minerva*, February 9, 2019, https://minervawisdom.com/2019/02/09/cicero-and-the-foundations-of-natural-law/.

modern sense but natural in the classical sense, insofar as it helped the tree achieve the flourishing proper to it. In the same way, a feral child would act "naturally" in the first sense but not in the second, whereas a child whose behavior has been shaped by instruction and correction would likely be better aligned with his *telos*.

This is not to suggest that humans are purpose-built robots who should strive to fit a single mold. Part of what makes us human is our creativity, our free will, and our capacity for rational thought. But free will does not mean that every choice is as valid as every other. Some, like becoming a doctor or a construction worker, help the individual and the community move together toward *eudaimonia*. Others, like becoming a crack dealer or pornographer, degrade the humanity of everyone involved, stunting them like trees in bad soil. Freedom means being uninhibited in the pursuit of the flourishing proper to one's nature. It doesn't mean that an oak acorn can choose to grow into a blueberry bush instead.

And although our endeavors to be good humans must be guided by reason, the faculty that most distinguishes us from animals, achieving *eudaimonia* is not a purely intellectual exercise. We are embodied beings who must sometimes reject bodily pleasure or risk bodily harm to act virtuously. We live in a physical world that we perceive with our senses and reshape through our labor. As "political animals," we live in communities and long for relationships. And, conscious of our own limitations, we reach out toward the divine.

Anti-transhumanism takes all these realities into account. It is the belief that humans are a particular type of being for whom a particular type of flourishing is proper and that we ought to remain that type of being and pursue that type of flourishing, instead of attempting to become something else and invent some other *telos*. It also demands that our medical, technological, political, and economic structures respect that humanity, rather than degrade or refashion it, and orient themselves toward authentic human flourishing, rather than toward some other end.

Now for *transhumanism*. Popular explanations of the term tend to focus on technology: a pill that boosts intelligence beyond normal human parameters, a genetic tweak that enables the recipient to grow gills or turn sunlight into food, a cybernetic brain implant that replaces your smartphone, an eccentric tech mogul who wants to digitize his consciousness and live forever.

Zoltan Istvan, who ran for president in 2016 as the candidate of the Transhumanist Party, provides the following tech-centered definition in his novel *The Transhumanist Wager*:

> Our biology severely limits us. As a species we are far from finished and therefore highly unacceptable. The transhumanist believes we should immediately work to improve ourselves via enhancing the human body and eliminating its weak points. This means ridding ourselves of flesh and bones, and upgrading to new cybernetic tissues, alloys, and other synthetic materials, including ones that make us cyborglike and robotic. It also means further merging the human brain with the microchip and the impending digital frontier. Biology is for beasts, not future transhumanists.[8]

But as I hinted in my discussion of the term *humanism*, I think there's more to transhumanism than that. And since I'll certainly be accused of simply labeling everything I dislike as "transhumanist," it seems necessary to defend my broad conception of the term. Transhumanism, as an ideology, was not invented *ex nihilo* in response to technological advancements. It would be more accurate to say that much of modern

---

[8] Zoltan Istvan, *The Transhumanist Wager* (Brookings, OR: Futurity Imagine, 2013), 278.

technology, along with its goals and future trajectory, is the product of transhumanist ideology in its various forms. For centuries, we have been preparing the philosophical ground for an all-out assault on our common humanity.

The various -isms of centuries past often carried the seeds of the transhumanist ideology. Gnosticism (with its vision of the soul as the true self and the body as a meat prison), romanticism (with its glorification of the Promethean/Luciferian impulse), liberalism (with its focus on the rights-bearing individual and supposed neutrality on questions of ultimate good), capitalism (with its *laissez-faire* attitude toward free exchange and its tendency to commodify everything), progressivism (with its belief that newer is always better), Darwinism (with its substitution of evolutionary flux for stable identity), Freudianism (with its therapeutic mindset and hostility toward repression), feminism (with its willingness to erase female biology in the name of female power), and scientism (with its reductive materialism and deference to technical experts) all made their contribution.

A complete historical genealogy of transhumanism could easily run to several volumes, but for our purposes it will suffice to highlight a few quotes illustrating key elements of the transhumanist ideology. The first comes from Scottish Enlightenment philosopher David Hume's 1739 *Treatise of Human Nature* and formulates what has become known as the "is-ought problem":

> In every system of morality, which I have hitherto met with, I have always remarked, that the author proceeds for some time in the ordinary way of reasoning, and establishes the being of a God, or makes observations concerning human affairs; when of a sudden I am surprised to find, that instead of the usual copulations of propositions, *is*, and *is not*, I meet with no proposition that is not connected with an *ought*, or an *ought not*. This change

Introduction

is imperceptible; but is, however, of the last consequence. For as this *ought*, or *ought not*, expresses some new relation or affirmation, it's necessary that it should be observed and explained; and at the same time that a reason should be given, for what seems altogether inconceivable, how this new relation can be a deduction from others, which are entirely different from it.[9]

In other words, observations about the kind of creatures we *are* cannot lead to insights about how we *ought* to live. Even if humanity is oriented toward a particular type of flourishing, it would not follow that we have any obligation to pursue it. It might be wise to do so, but it would not be moral or immoral, and anyone who wishes to pursue some other end should be free to do so. An Aristotelian might assert that what is good is good for you, but a good Humean could simply respond, "I don't care what you think is good for me."

Hume believed that morality was grounded in sentiments rather than in reason, meaning that any statement about how humans ought to live flows not from any objective source but from the emotions of the speaker. This explains much of the modern hostility to those who still agree with Plato, Aristotle, Cicero, and the Hebrew Bible about human nature and human flourishing. From Hume's perspective, if I claim that humans have a *telos*, what I'm actually doing is placing my own preferences in a position of authority so I can use them to tyrannize others.

The next passage comes from a famous scene in Friedrich Nietzsche's 1882 book *The Gay Science*:

God is dead! God remains dead! And we have killed him! How shall we console ourselves, the most murderous of all murderers?... Is not the magnitude of this deed too great for

---

[9] David Hume, *A Treatise of Human Nature* (Oxford: Clarendon Press, 1896), 244–245.

us? Shall we not ourselves have to become Gods, merely to seem worthy of it?[10]

Nietzsche was not, of course, claiming that a literally existing deity had literally passed away. Instead, he was offering a declaration of freedom. After the death of God, humanity's nature, its morality, its *telos* could no longer be conceived of as intrinsic to humanity, wired into us by a benevolent Creator. We were free. Not free in the sense of being unencumbered in the pursuit of our proper ends, but free in the sense of being able to choose those ends. We could henceforth forge our own values and identities. We could "become Gods." In fact, we must. We have no choice.

The only other option was to give up on any aspirations beyond mere comfort. Nietzsche described such a creature as "the last man." This "last man" hoards "little pleasures," follows the news obsessively and loves to argue about it, hates his job but shows up every day because it's better than doing nothing, and takes "a little poison now and then" to stave off anxiety and depression.[11] But for the *ubermensch* and the last man alike, transhumanism beckons — promising the one an escape from the limitations of humanity and the other an escape from its burdens.

And finally, a quote from French philosopher Jean-Paul Sartre's 1946 essay "Existentialism Is a Humanism":

> One cannot suppose that a man would produce a paper-knife without knowing what it was for. Let us say, then, of the paper-knife that its essence — that is to say the sum of the formulae and the qualities which made its production and its definition possible — precedes its existence ... Atheistic existentialism, of

---

[10] Friedrich Nietzsche, *The Gay Science*, trans. Walter Kaufmann (New York: Vintage Books, 1974), 3.125.

[11] Friedrich Nietzsche, *Thus Spake Zarathustra*, trans. Thomas Common (New York: Random House, 1909), 11–12.

Introduction

which I am a representative, declares with greater consistency that if God does not exist there is at least one being whose existence comes before its essence, a being which exists before it can be defined by any conception of it. That being is man ... What do we mean by saying that existence precedes essence? We mean that man first of all exists, encounters himself, surges up in the world — and defines himself afterwards.[12]

You, dear reader — Sartre insists— are not a pocketknife. You were not designed for any particular end. You decide what it means to be a good human being. You decide what it means to be a human being at all. The meaning of your life is to give your life meaning. The only definition of human that Sartre accepts is "the being that defines itself." It is this activity that makes you human. The individual's freedom to craft his or her own identity becomes sacrosanct. Inhibiting that freedom becomes blasphemy. As transhumanist technologies proliferate, the options open to existing beings seeking to define their essences become nearly limitless, and the pursuit of true authenticity grows ever more frenetic.

It's unlikely that any of these thinkers envisioned virtual immortals, cyborg supersoldiers, or vat-grown designer babies, but they all played a role in demolishing the barriers that made such innovations morally unthinkable. All that remained was to make them technically possible.

It is at this stage that the term *transhumanism* first appears in something like its modern sense. In a 1957 essay titled simply "Transhumanism," Julian Huxley argues that, due to increases in scientific understanding, "man had been suddenly appointed managing director of the biggest business of all, the business of evolution — appointed without being asked if he wanted it, and without proper warning and preparation."

---

[12] Jean-Paul Sartre, "Existentialism Is a Humanism," in *Existentialism from Dostoevsky to Sartre*, ed. Walter Kaufmann (New York: Meridian, 1989), 289–291.

THE TRANSHUMANIST TEMPTATION

But Huxley isn't the type of boss to make big changes on his first day. Some of his proposals for this bold new epoch in human history — beautifying cities, raising standards of living, increasing educational opportunities — are not transhuman at all. His most ambitious proposal is a "concerted policy" to combat the "flood of population-increase," which seems like hardly dipping a toe. Though he served as president of the British Eugenics Society, he makes no mention of breeding a race of supermen. Even the triumphant climax of his essay betrays a sense of caution when he defines *transhumanism* as "man remaining man, but transcending himself, by realizing new possibilities of and for his human nature."[13]

This is incoherent. If humanity has taken over the management of human evolution, then what exactly is "human nature"? Is it just a way of referring to the shared qualities of most humans who are currently alive? And if so, why should those qualities be treated as normative? The prefix "trans-" means "across" or "beyond." One cannot become transhuman while "remaining man" any more than one can cross a river and also not cross it. But Huxley feels awfully safe on the bank. Like many good bourgeois English secularists (Richard Dawkins comes to mind), he seems uncomfortable with the radical implications of what he's proposing. Huxley's version of transhumanism is basically the normal, upper-middle-class life he is already living, only a little less drab and with the advantages he enjoys distributed more broadly. He lacks the Nietzschean *chutzpah* to stand thigh-deep in God's blood and demand that we seize His throne.

Julian Huxley may have lacked either the nerve or the imagination to confront the implications of transhumanism, but his brother Aldous more than made up for his shortcomings, and did so twenty-five years

---

[13] Julian Huxley, "Transhumanism," in *New Bottles for New Wine* (London: Chatto & Windus, 1957), 13–17.

Introduction

earlier. His 1932 novel *Brave New World* has it all: industrial gestation facilities, genetically modified subhumans bred for drudgery, universal birth control that reduces sex to mere recreation, the widespread use of neuropharmaceuticals to assuage feelings of alienation, the elimination of "all the physiological stigmata of old age," an economic and political order structured around individual autonomy and ever-expanding consumption, and even an early hint of immersive virtual reality (with "feelies" replacing movies).[14]

The transhumanist movement today is, in many ways, a series of footnotes on *Brave New World*. The various declarations and manifestos hosted on the website of the nonprofit Humanity+ mention "life extension therapies," "reproductive choice technologies," "whole brain emulation" (i.e. uploading consciousness), and "alternative options for perceptual, cognitive, and physical bodies."[15] The first line of the Transhumanist Manifesto, written by prominent transhumanist Natasha Vita-More (surprisingly an actual compound surname and not a self-chosen declaration of her quest for "more life") sums up all of these priorities as what they are, namely a rejection of the teleological wisdom tradition and an assertion of total human autonomy: "I am the architect of my existence. My life reflects my vision and represents my values. It conveys the very essence of my being — coalescing imagination and reason, challenging all limits."[16]

It is easy to dismiss self-described transhumanists as irrelevant. They can be hard to take seriously, with their eccentric public personas,

---

[14] Aldous Huxley, *Brave New World* (New York: HarperPerennial, 2006), 55.

[15] "The Transhumanist Declaration," Humanity+, accessed March 17, 2025, https://www.humanityplus.org/the-transhumanist-declaration.

[16] Natasha Vita-More, "The Transhumanist Manifesto," Humanity+, accessed March 17, 2025, https://www.humanityplus.org/the-transhumanist-manifesto.

often outlandish predictions, sloppily formatted books and websites, and minimal presence in mainstream discourse. This would be a mistake. When they speak openly about using technology to refashion people into something beyond humanity, they merely — to borrow Allen Bloom's phrase — "radicalize the already dominant opinions."[17] For proof, look no further than former Supreme Court Justice Anthony Kennedy's opinion in *Planned Parenthood v. Casey* (1992), in which he declared that "at the heart of liberty is the right to define one's own concept of existence, of meaning, of the universe, and of the mystery of human life." It's a statement with which few modern people would disagree. It's also a better transhumanist manifesto than anything Humanity+ has come up with.[18]

In the first four sections of this book, I will explore how this transhumanist ideology affects various spheres of human life and society. The first will cover our relationship to our own *bodies* and the challenges posed by genetic engineering, neuropharmacology, bodily modification, transgenderism, reproductive issues, life extension, and euthanasia. The second will focus on external *reality*, the ways in which our technology alienates us from it (either by filtering our experiences through a device that "augments" them in some way or by offering discarnate virtual substitutes for the real world) and attempts to reconnect ourselves to reality by pursuing re-enchantment. The third section, on *politics*, explores how classical liberal political theory set us on the path to transhumanism, considers transhumanism as a set of issues in electoral politics, and envisions a postliberal, antitranshumanist political order while offering a critique of vitalism and so-called "right-wing progressivism." Although I am on the political

---

[17] Allen Bloom, *The Closing of the American Mind* (New York: Simon & Schuster, 1987), 247.
[18] *Planned Parenthood of Southeastern Pa. v. Casey*, 505 U.S. 833 (1992).

Introduction

right, this is not a "conservative" book in the sense of presenting a straight GOP ticket as the solution to all our problems. Most Republicans hold elements of transhumanist ideology, and where they claim to oppose it, they often seek merely to slow rather than halt or reverse its progress. In the fourth, I argue that our approach to *work* and economic life rests on transhumanist presuppositions and leads to transhumanist outcomes by drawing everything into the sphere of the market, sacrificing the well-being of families and communities to the whims of that market, and substituting increased consumption for authentic human flourishing. I then attempt to sketch the contours of a humane economy.

The fifth and final section covers the intersection of transhumanism and *religion*, exploring ancient stories of the Nephilim, the Christian roots of transhumanism, modern spiritual movements that seek to bootstrap humanity into self-transcendence, the infection of Christianity by transhumanist ideology, and the ways in which digital technology has warped Christian practice.

Although I hope non-Christians will read and be challenged by my arguments, I have made no attempt to conceal my faith. There are two reasons for this. The first is my sincere belief that the struggle against transhumanism has a spiritual dimension. Although thinkers like Hume, Nietzsche, and Sartre all contributed to the development of the transhumanist mindset, none of them invented it. Transhumanism originated in the Garden of Eden, with the serpent's promise that "ye shall be as gods."[19] The serpent wasn't lying, per se. God always intended for humanity to become "partakers of the divine nature."[20] The deception lay not in his promise that we could be as gods, but that we could achieve that divinization (or theosis) apart from God.

---

[19] Gen. 3:5, KJV.
[20] 2 Pet. 1:4, RSVCE.

THE TRANSHUMANIST TEMPTATION

Adam and Eve chose to grasp at transcendence on their own terms, rejecting the divinely ordained destiny that would have brought them to it in the fullness of time. The temptation of the biblical fool — who "says in his heart, 'There is no God'" and forsakes the path of wisdom that leads to true *eudaimonia* — has been with us since the beginning.[21] Now, as technology increases our ability to pursue the Luciferian project of self-determination, I can only conclude that the evil one's plan to lure humanity to its own destruction is nearing some sort of climax.

The second is that I am not confident that there is any viable secular basis for resisting transhumanism. Laws and regulations may restrain certain aspects of it, such as outright eugenics, but as long as our society holds firm in its commitment to individual self-determination and bodily autonomy, such restrictions will be nothing more than individual fingers stuck into a rapidly crumbling dike.

Even if we *are* a certain type of being, it would not follow that we *ought* to act in certain ways, nor (more importantly) that we *ought* to remain the kind of being that we are. In a world without God, our bodily form and mental capacities are the result of unguided physical forces. By what right could the products of random atomic collisions exercise any claim to our deference? G. K. Chesterton identified this difficulty in his 1908 book *Orthodoxy*. The Christian God, Chesterton argued, might use evolution as the means to produce human beings with a particular nature and *telos*. The Christian vision of human flourishing would remain unchanged. But if evolution were adopted as a philosophy, it would mean "there is no such thing as an ape to change, and no such thing as a man for him to change into," but only "a flux of everything and anything."[22] We might attempt to name and classify

---

[21] Ps. 14:1, RSVCE.
[22] G. K. Chesterton, "The Suicide of Thought," in *Orthodoxy* (Chicago: Moody, 2009), 56.

Introduction

various points in that flux, but our labels would be merely arbitrary. Transhumanism makes sense only when *human* has ceased to have any meaning. And in a materialist universe, how can it?

I'm afraid the best I can offer my non-religious readers is a utilitarian argument: stick with humanity because humanity works well enough and because the alternative is too risky. It may be that the only definition of human nature you can bring yourself to believe in is the impoverished, purely descriptive one Francis Fukuyama offered in his 2002 book *Our Posthuman Future*: "the sum of the behavior and characteristics that are typical of the human species, arising from genetic rather than environmental factors."[23] So be it. Act as if humanity had a nature and a *telos*, because to do otherwise is to open yourself up to being tinkered with by people and institutions that may not have your best interests at heart.

C. S. Lewis foresaw this when he warned in *The Abolition of Man* that "what we call Man's power over Nature turns out to be a power exercised by some men over other men with Nature as its instrument."[24] It may be that no one will force you to grow your baby in a pod or get augmented reality visual implants. But you won't be the one controlling those technologies, either, and the ways in which they're reshaping you and the people around you might not become obvious until it's too late. In a society built around transhuman aspirations rather than human norms, you'll face increasing pressure to subject yourself to these technologies and increasing disadvantages if you don't. If you want to be "normal," you'll have to become transhuman. Once that happens, you're in uncharted waters. You'll have severed the link that unites you

---

[23] Francis Fukuyama, *Our Posthuman Future* (New York: Farrar, Straus and Giroux, 2002), 130.
[24] C. S. Lewis, *The Abolition of Man* (New York: Columbia University Augustine Club, 2002), 23.

to your thousands of ancestors. You will be, in a very meaningful way, a different species. Their accumulated wisdom will mean nothing to you. And whatever wisdom you manage to accumulate on your own will mean nothing to your children.

You'll find yourself facing down what transhumanist author and biotech entrepreneur Gregory Stock calls "the invasion of the inhuman, the displacement of the born by the made, and the twilight of humanity." But despite his clear-eyed view of what his ideology entails, Stock urges readers to embrace this "strange and uncertain future."[25] Transhumanism, he argues, is inevitable — you can be sad about it, but you can't stop it.

Thankfully, there is another kind of transhumanism on offer. The term wasn't coined in the twentieth century by Julian Huxley or in the nineteenth or eighteenth by some other enemy of human nature. It was, in fact, the medieval Catholic poet Dante Aligheri who introduced the word in his *Paradiso*. As he is carried into Heaven to be united with "the Love that moves the sun and other stars," Dante's pilgrim narrator admits his inability to *trasumanar significar per verba*.[26] Henry Wadsworth Longfellow translated the line, "to represent 'transhumanize' in words,"[27] while John Ciardi renders it, "speak trans-human change to human sense."[28]

---

[25] Gregory Stock, "Battle for the Future" in *The Transhumanist Reader: Classical and Contemporary Essays on the Science, Technology, and Philosophy of the Human Future*, ed. Max More and Natasha Vita-More (Malden, MS: John Wiley & Sons, 2013), 307, 314.

[26] Dante Aligheri, *Paradise*, trans. Anthony Esolen (New York: Modern Library, 2007), 33.145.

[27] Dante Aligheri, "Paradiso," in *The Divine Comedy*, trans. Henry Wadsworth Longfellow (Mineola, NY: Dover, 2017), 1.70.

[28] Dante Aligheri, "Paradiso," in *The Divine Comedy*, trans. John Ciardi (Franklin Center, PA: Franklin Library, 1977), 1.70.

Introduction

T. S. Eliot then beat out Julian Huxley by almost a decade, becoming perhaps the first prominent English writer to use the term in an original work. In his play *The Cocktail Party*, an angelic being known as Reilly tells another angel about the hard road to salvation that lies before a troubled woman named Celia:

> You and I don't know the process by which the human is
> Transhumanized: what do we know
> Of the kind of suffering they must undergo
> On the way of illumination[29]

The instrument of Celia's transhumanization is not a pill or a surgical procedure or a cybernetic implant. It is a cross. She joins an order of nuns and serves as a nurse in a primitive, plague-stricken village on a remote Pacific island. The natives lash out against the sisters, crucify Celia, and leave her body to be eaten by ants. She suffers, Reilly notes, not only "fear and pain and loathing," but also the "reluctance of the body to become a *thing*."[30] In Celia's final hours, her physical humanity becomes a brutal, undeniable reality. Her death (like all human death and limitation) would be an affront to a transhumanist. Reilly does not hesitate to declare it a "triumph."[31]

To be transhumanized (in the Dante-Eliot sense of the word), one must first live and suffer as a human, because the true *telos* of humanity is more than the contemplative retirement or political career Aristotle envisioned for his well-rounded virtuous gentleman. It is to become what C. S. Lewis described as "a creature which, if you saw it now, you would be strongly tempted to worship." Just as an acorn shares one nature with the oak tree it aims to become, so the embryo you

---

[29] T. S. Eliot, *The Cocktail Party* (London: Faber, 1950), 130.
[30] Ibid., 161.
[31] Ibid., 163.

once were shares a nature with the divinized being you are destined to become. Even the full-grown man or woman you are today is nothing more than a seed by comparison with it. St. Paul, grasping at realities almost too wonderful to contemplate, explained this in his first letter to the Corinthian church:

> But some one will ask, "How are the dead raised? With what kind of body do they come?" You foolish man! What you sow does not come to life unless it dies. And what you sow is not the body which is to be, but a bare kernel, perhaps of wheat or of some other grain.... So is it with the resurrection of the dead. What is sown is perishable, what is raised is imperishable. It is sown in dishonor, it is raised in glory. It is sown in weakness, it is raised in power. It is sown a physical body, it is raised a spiritual body.[32]

We cannot raise ourselves, either from death or toward divinity. The serpent's promise is a lie. But God's promises — to "wipe away every tear," to "destroy death forever," to provide us with "imperishable" bodies in the life of the world to come — are true.[33] We are made for Him. We fulfill our nature only by His grace. I pray you'll open yourself to it.

---

[32] 1 Cor. 15:35–37; 42–44, RSVCE.
[33] Rev. 21:4, RSVCE; Isa. 25:8, NCB.

Part 1

BODIES

Sex and Reproduction

*My body is a temple
and I am the god it was built for.*

— Savannah Brown[1]

In 2021, NBC reporter Morgan Sung wrote about a TikTok trend known as the "girl with the list."[2] The list in question is a compilation of the pros and cons of pregnancy and childbirth (or, as the document itself puts it, having "a child burst through your vagina"). Cons outnumber pros ten-to-one and range from normal processes phrased in off-putting ways ("Sperm has to have swum inside you at some point... ew") to common issues ("Constant back pain") to rare complications ("Your clitoris might rip") to outright misinformation ("No alcohol for

---

[1] Upworthy Stories, "'My Body Is a Temple and I Am the God It Was Built For.' Savannah Brown Performs a Chilling Spoken-Word Piece About Being Called a Slut. Warning: Strong Language," Facebook, February 19, 2016, https://www.facebook.com/watch/?v=781563325281550.

[2] Morgan Sung, "TikTok's 'Girl with the List' Inspires More Honest Conversations About the Pitfalls of Pregnancy," *NBC News*, January 25, 2023, https://www.nbcnews.com/pop-culture/viral/tiktok-girl-with-the-list-pregnancy-birth-rcna66810.

at-least a year ... if breastfeeding then more"). Euphemisms for "child" include "parasite," "uterus goblin," and "demon."[3]

"The list," however, does not provide the odds of any of these complications actually occurring. Telling a woman her baby "might" crack one of her ribs during pregnancy is like telling me a piano "might" fall on my head during my morning commute. Nor would you come away from "the list" with the impression that pregnancy and childbirth are less risky than at any other time in human history, which they are. Its purpose is not to inform you, but to scare the hell out of you.

More specifically, "the list" frames pregnancy and childbirth as body horror, a subgenre of horror cinema that focuses on "graphic violations of the human body" and aims to provoke a visceral reaction in the audience.[4] Think cannibalism, rape, or dismemberment. *Texas Chainsaw Massacre* type stuff. In films like *Alien 3*, *Prometheus*, and *Rosemary's Baby*, the connection between body horror and childbearing is explicit.

The process is certainly scary. My wife's pregnancy frequently left her feeling frustrated with and alienated from her own body, and our daughter's birth involved plenty of fear, pain, and awkwardness. And our experience was fairly routine. A woman experiencing potentially lethal or debilitating complications might justifiably feel violated. But "the list" applies these feelings far more broadly. So the question remains: Why the sudden push to inspire terror and disgust toward a process that's safer than ever and that most women, despite all the unpleasant

---

[3] Yunuen Arias, "The List," Yuni's Pros and Cons List of Having Children, accessed December 5, 2024, https://yuniquethoughtslist.wixsite.com/yuni-s-pros-and-cons/the-list.

[4] Lucy Taylor, "The H Word: Body Horror — What's Really Under Your Skin?," *Nightmare* 69 (June 2018), https://www.nightmare-magazine.com/nonfiction/the-h-word-body-horror-whats-really-under-your-skin/.

parts, number among the most precious and meaningful experiences of their lives?

Sung was ready with an answer. "Abortion access is under constant threat and we're seeing a real urgency to protect bodily autonomy," she explained in a video discussing her article. "I think the videos [about 'the list'] are so popular because they reflect this desire for agency and informed consent.... They're about choice, and choice starts with being better informed."[5]

To the transhumanist, there is something fundamentally undignified about embodiment. The protagonist of Istvan's novel calls *homo sapiens* a "frail, hacked-together organism" and dismissively declares that "biology is for beasts."[6] The transhumanist wishes to choose her body's form and exercise full control over all its functions. The denial of either feels like a violation of personal dignity. The swellings, cravings, aches, and indignities that a woman of the nineteenth century might have regarded as routine, a woman of the twenty-first regards as a direct affront. Imagining any of the things on "the list" happening to her inspires the same revulsion as the gruesome tortures of some slasher film, with her own unborn baby playing the role of Jason Voorhees.

Records show that in Renaissance Florence, around 20 percent of deaths among married women were from childbirth.[7] No family would have been untouched. The "wicked stepmother" character pervades fairy tales because so many men remarried after their first wife died

---

[5] Morgan Sung, "The Girl with the List, Explained." TikTok, January 25, 2023, https://www.tiktok.com/@ratsoverflowers/video/7192799736972315950.

[6] Istvan, *Transhumanist Wager*, 274, 278.

[7] "The Medieval Childbirth Guide: 6 Tips for Pregnant Mothers in the Middle Ages," *History Extra*, November 5, 2021, https://www.historyextra.com/period/medieval/middle-ages-childbirth-dangers-mothers-midwives-how-did-medieval-women-give-birth/.

THE TRANSHUMANIST TEMPTATION

giving birth. Today, the trope is far less relatable. Most people living in developed countries probably don't know anyone whose death resulted from pregnancy or childbirth complications. I don't, though I'm aware of one or two close calls among my friends and acquaintances. If modern women fear pregnancy and childbirth more than their ancestors did, it's not because they face greater risks. It's because they feel more strongly that they ought to be in control.

This attitude owes its prevalence to the oral contraceptive, which received FDA approval in 1960. "The Pill" works by using hormones to trick the woman's body into believing she's pregnant in order to prevent ovulation. "The contraceptive pill is the first transhumanist technology, because that was a total paradigm shift in what medicine is for," author Mary Harrington said in a 2023 interview. "Because it doesn't set out to fix something that's wrong with me, like a broken arm or a kidney that's not working properly. It sets out to break something that's working properly in accordance with desire."[8] Transhumanist author Anders Sandberg embraces this shift, proposing a "volitional" approach to medicine that treats disease as "a failure of optimal function or desired functionality."[9] Under this model, a normal menstrual cycle could be an indicator of health or a disorder to be treated, depending on the patient's attitude toward it.

Millions of young women now begin using birth control within a few years of their first period. According to CDC data collected between 2015 and 2017, 16.6 percent of women aged fifteen to nineteen reported using oral contraception, while another 8.2 percent from the

[8] Mary Harrington, interview with Saurabh Sharma, "Industrial Society and Its Consequences for Women (ft. Mary Harrington)," *Moment of Truth*, season 3, ep. 14, May 1, 2023, podcast audio, YouTube, https://www.youtube.com/watch?v=qstUdkZiJoI&t=0s.

[9] Anders Sandberg, "Morphological Freedom," in *The Transhumanist Reader*, 63. Emphasis mine.

same age group reported using long-acting reversible contraceptives (including IUDs and hormonal implants).[10]

It's no surprise that teenagers want to be on birth control. It not only helps alleviate acne and menstrual cramps but is also frequently presented as the only viable option for avoiding pregnancy. In an article for the *American Mind*, journalist Patricia Patnode described her sex-ed experience at Iowa public schools, which included "presentations by Planned Parenthood workers" who "warned it was possible to get pregnant at any point during the month (wrong!) and mainly focused on the dangers of pregnancy, sexually transmitted diseases, and infections, coming armed with slideshows of rashes and warts."[11] The lesson is not "Here's how to understand your body," but rather "You cannot trust your body and must break it to your will."

The desired outcome of this frankly misogynistic messaging is "safe sex," but as Harrington observes, sex is never really safe, and we probably shouldn't want it to be. " 'Risk-free' heterosexual sex can only be had at the cost of reproduction," she writes in her book *Feminism Against Progress*. "And eliminating that biological purpose takes much of the dark, dangerous and profoundly intimate joy out of sex."[12] Multiple studies (as well as a wealth of anecdotal evidence) suggest that the Pill can decrease libido and sexual pleasure, and although Gen Z is increasingly skeptical of birth control, there are still plenty of young women who are willing to have worse sex as long as

---

[10] Kimberly Daniels and Joyce C. Abma, "Current Contraceptive Status Among Women Aged 15–49: United States, 2015–2017," National Center for Health Statistics, CDC, December 2018, https://www.cdc.gov/nchs/products/databriefs/db327.htm.

[11] Patricia Patnode, "Body Talk," *The American Mind*, April 11, 2024, https://americanmind.org/salvo/body-talk/, parentheses mine.

[12] Mary Harrington, *Feminism Against Progress* (New York: Skyhorse, 2023), 214.

THE TRANSHUMANIST TEMPTATION

it's less risky.[13] The transhumanist is obsessed with controlling her own body and is willing to sacrifice anything, even her happiness, to maintain that control.

If birth control fails, abortion provides a convenient backstop. And again, the justification is rooted in the assertion of total bodily autonomy. Other arguments for abortion fall short. *The fetus isn't human.* Yes, it is. It is an organism with a distinctive human genetic code. What else would it be? *It might grow up poor, abused, or unwanted.* I guess we should gas all the orphans too. *What if the woman was raped?* I don't see how that's the baby's fault. *The fetus isn't self-aware.* Ok. Neither is a one-month-old baby. Does that mean it's ok to kill it? (Shockingly, at least one tenured philosophy professor says yes, but even pro-choicers usually recoil at the idea).[14]

The only convincing pro-abortion stance is some version of "I own my body completely. The fetus resides in my womb and draws sustenance from me solely at my pleasure. At any time, I can withdraw my consent, designate it as an intruder, and have it evicted and killed for any reason I like."

A common version of this argument is known as the violinist thought experiment, which philosopher Judith Jarvis Thomson introduced in her 1971 essay "A Defense of Abortion":

> Imagine this. You wake up in the morning and find yourself back to back in bed with an unconscious violinist. A famous

---

[13] Alisha H. Gupta, "The Link Between Birth Control Pills and Sex Drive," *New York Times*, January 23, 2024, https://www.nytimes.com/2024/01/23/well/live/birth-control-sex-drive-libido.html.

[14] Nat Hentoff, "A Professor Who Argues for Infanticide," *Washington Post*, September 11, 1999, https://www.washingtonpost.com/archive/opinions/1999/09/11/a-professor-who-argues-for-infanticide/cce7dc81-3775-4ef6-bfea-74cd795fc43f/.

unconscious violinist. He has been found to have a fatal kidney ailment, and the Society of Music Lovers has canvassed all the available medical records and found that you alone have the right blood type to help. They have therefore kidnapped you, and last night the violinist's circulatory system was plugged into yours, so that your kidneys can be used to extract poisons from his blood as well as your own.... To unplug you would be to kill him. But never mind, it's only for nine months.[15]

Thomson concludes that "nobody has any right to use your kidneys unless you give him this right."[16] Therefore, the kidnapping victim should feel free to disconnect herself from the violinist and let him die. Another variation on the "forced organ donation" theme is the observation that organs cannot be harvested from donors (or even their dead bodies) without prior consent. Surely you don't think women have fewer rights than dead bodies, do you?

These analogies, however, only make sense from a transhumanist perspective. They rely on an extreme view of individual sovereignty that conceives of people more as autonomous wills than as embodied beings. In reality, there is no such thing as an autonomous individual. We all begin life as helpless embryos utterly dependent on our mothers for protection and sustenance, and we remain largely helpless for the next several years.

A mother owes her unborn child the use of her body. Their bond is not analogous to any other human tie.[17] If a mother can be criminally

---

[15] Judith Jarvis Thomson, "A Defense of Abortion," *Philosophy & Public Affairs* 1, no. 1 (Fall 1971): 48–49.

[16] Ibid., 56.

[17] No one really believes that they owe the same duty toward a random violin player that they owe to their own children. Our common law system embodies this commonsense principle by holding that parents have a legal duty to rescue their children from harm

THE TRANSHUMANIST TEMPTATION

charged for negligently failing to feed or clothe her toddler, how much more egregious would it be for her to intentionally cut off the same child's sustenance in the womb, when his dependence was even greater and only she could provide for him?[18]

Radical individual autonomy might be an acceptable framework for a race of beings that simply pop into existence as fully formed adults, but we are not that kind of creature. Our embodiment enmeshes us from the moment of conception in a web of self-sacrifice, dependence, and duty. To reject these relationships is to deny that embodiment along with our very humanity.

This maximalist view of bodily autonomy is a key transhumanist value. The U.S. Transhumanist Party's official platform affirms

---

but do not have the same obligation to strangers, friends, or even their own parents. See Ruth S. Johnson, "Americans Have No (Legal) Duty to Help Each Other," *Psychology Today*, May 8, 2020, https://www.psychologytoday.com/us/blog/so-sue-me/202005/americans-have-no-legal-duty-help-each-other.

[18] Most abortions are purely elective, but in a small percentage of cases a woman facing dire complications may choose to terminate her pregnancy. In a *New York Times* op-ed, Catholic author Leah Libresco Sargeant shared her own experience with ectopic pregnancy (in which the fertilized egg implants in the fallopian tube, has no chance of survival, and presents a threat to the mother's life). Sargeant then explained why such cases should not be considered abortions at all: "From a pro-life perspective, delivering a baby who is ectopic is closer to delivering a baby very prematurely because the mother has life-threatening eclampsia. A baby delivered at 22 weeks may or may not survive. A baby delivered in the first trimester because of an ectopic pregnancy definitely won't survive. But in both cases, a pro-life doctor sees herself as delivering a child, who is as much a patient as the mother. See Leah Libresco Sargeant, "In a Post-Roe World, We Can Avoid Pitting Mothers Against Babies," *New York Times*, July 4, 2022, https://www.nytimes.com/2022/07/04/opinion/ectopic-pregnancy-roe-abortion.html.

"morphological freedom" — "the right to do with one's physical attributes ... whatever one wants as long as it does not directly harm others" — as well as "the rights of all sapient individuals to do as they see fit with themselves and their own reproductive choices."[19]

Nor are these choices limited to contraception and abortion. For those who do wish to reproduce while avoiding the body horror of pregnancy (or yearn for children but struggle with infertility), gestational surrogacy has become an increasingly popular option. In 2020, surrogacy accounted for around four thousand births in the United States, having more than doubled in popularity since 2011 as an option among parents seeking to reproduce by artificial means.[20] In some cases, a friend or family member, known as an "altruistic surrogate," volunteers to carry the baby for the would-be parent(s), though in most cases the surrogate is a hired stranger, or "commercial surrogate." The industry also makes a distinction between "traditional surrogacy," in which the surrogate also serves as egg donor, and "gestational surrogacy," in which she carries a baby to whom she is not biologically related. Prominent figures like socialite Khloé Kardashian (who confessed to feeling less "connected" to her surrogate-born son than to the children she carried herself), actress Rebel Wilson, and conservative commentator Dave Rubin have welcomed babies via hired surrogate in recent years.[21]

---

[19] The United States Transhumanist Party, "U.S. Transhumanist Party Platform — Organized by Subject," accessed January 30, 2025, https://transhumanist-party.org/platform/.

[20] Vanessa Brown Calder, "Defending Gestational Surrogacy: Addressing Misconceptions and Criticisms," Cato Institute, December 5, 2023, https://www.cato.org/briefing-paper/defending-gestational-surrogacy-addressing-misconceptions-criticisms.

[21] Yana Grebenyuk, "Khloe Kardashian Admits She Felt 'Less Connected' to Her Son, Calls Surrogacy a 'Transactional Experience,'" *Us Weekly*, May 25, 2023, https://www.usmagazine.com/entertainment/news/khloe-kardashian-felt-less-connected-to-son-after-surrogacy/.

THE TRANSHUMANIST TEMPTATION

The process begins with the creation of embryos via in vitro fertilization (IVF), a transhumanist practice in its own right. IVF involves retrieving eggs from the aspiring mother (or donor), fertilizing them in a laboratory with sperm from the aspiring father (or donor), and implanting them into the aspiring mother (or surrogate).[22] More than 2 percent of U.S. births in 2021 were the result of IVF, according to the Department of Health and Human Services.[23]

The biggest problem with the process is that IVF clinics generally create more embryos than the number of children the would-be parents desire and then subject those embryos to multiple atrocities. "Inferior" embryos get discarded. If too many embryos implant, the extras are often aborted in what's euphemistically referred to as "selective reduction." If there are embryos left over, they're usually either destroyed or donated to science for vivisection. Otherwise, they just sit in some laboratory freezer. Forever.

Because most IVF embryos fail to implant, it would be prohibitively expensive and far more time-consuming to fertilize only as many embryos per IVF round as the parents planned to keep. But let's say a couple did do that. The attrition rate would be high, but that wouldn't be a moral issue as long as no embryos were intentionally destroyed or kept on ice. A couple that suffers three miscarriages for every healthy

---

[22] In the future, a process called *in vitro gametogenesis* — which turns regular somatic cells into eggs or sperm — could allow same-sex couples to access IVF without involving an external gamete donor. See Victoria G. Wesevich, Christopher Arkfeld, and David B. Seifer, "In Vitro Gametogenesis in Oncofertility," *Journal of Clinical Medicine* 12, no. 9 (May): 3305, https://doi.org/10.3390/jcm12093305.

[23] "Fact Sheet: In Vitro Fertilization (IVF) Use Across the United States," U.S. Department of Health and Human Services, March 13, 2024, https://public3.pagefreezer.com/browse/HHS.gov/02-01-2025T05:49/https://www.hhs.gov/about/news/2024/03/13/fact-sheet-in-vitro-fertilization-ivf-use-across-united-states.html.

pregnancy is not doing anything immoral by continuing to conceive children.

Even the best possible case of IVF, however, still advances the cause of transhumanism. With IVF, the "new life is not engendered through an act of love between husband and wife, but by a laboratory procedure performed by doctors or technicians," Catholic physician-theologian John Haas explains.[24] Philosopher John Finis expands on the point, arguing that "when procreation is *taken out* of marital intercourse ... procreation becomes *reproduction*, a form of production entailing the radical maker-product, master-slave relationship of total domination."[25]

This isn't a case of trying to score rhetorical points by comparing one's opponents to slave owners. In 2023, a judge cited slavery as a legal precedent when he ruled that frozen embryos could be treated as "goods and chattels" in divorce settlements and that any disagreement over whether to discard or implant those offspring is "more like a property dispute" than a dispute over child custody. "In other words," wrote Catholic journalist Leah Libresco Sargeant, "there was actually plenty of case law to govern how the embryos might be fairly divided if they were regarded as legally analogous to slaves."[26]

It's easy to sympathize with infertile couples who feel they have no other choice, but the inevitable result of IVF is to sever the act of marital love from the conception of a child and to do so in a way that

---

[24] John M. Haas, "Begotten Not Made: A Catholic View of Reproductive Technology," USCCB, 1998, https://www.usccb.org/issues-and-action/human-life-and-dignity/reproductive-technology/begotten-not-made-a-catholic-view-of-reproductive-technology.

[25] John Finnis, "C. S. Lewis and Test-Tube Babies" in *Human Rights and Common Good: Collected Essays: Volume III* (Oxford: Oxford University Press, 2013), 273–281.

[26] Leah Libresco Sargeant, "Embryos as Schrödinger's Persons," *New Atlantis*, Spring 2024, https://www.thenewatlantis.com/publications/embryos-as-schrodingers-persons.

outsources the conception to technical experts. A key aspect of the human lifecycle is replaced by an external process, and if a species changes its method of reproduction, it is self-evidently in the process of becoming something else. Suddenly, there is no single answer to the question "Where do babies come from?"

Surrogacy departs even further from the natural order, transforming a baby into a fully purchasable commodity.[27] This commodification can have serious consequences, including cases of perverts ordering children for nefarious purposes. In March 2024, Chicago veterinarian Adam Stafford King was arrested after discussing plans to sexually abuse his then-unborn daughter, whom he and his husband were expecting via surrogate.[28] An Australian man pleaded guilty in 2016 to molesting his twin daughters, who were conceived overseas with a donor egg and carried by a surrogate. According to the *Sydney Morning Herald*, the man "began abusing them when they were 27 days old and continued for seven months."[29]

---

[27] Obviously not every child is the result of sex between married parents. Many children — around 40 percent of those born each year in the United States — arrive outside wedlock. Those kids are still humans, as are babies born via IVF and surrogacy. People enter the world under all kinds of non-ideal circumstances. That doesn't mean every way of making a baby is equally valid. See "America's Children: Key National Indicators of Well-Being, 2023 — Births to Unmarried Women," Forum on Child and Family Statistics, 2023, chrome-extension://efaidnbmnnnibpcajpcglclefindmkaj/https://www.childstats.gov/pdf/ac2023/ac_23.pdf.

[28] Gabriel Castillo, "Court-Docs: Chicago-Area Vet Accused of Distributing Child Porn, Planned to Sexually Assault Unborn Child," WGN9, March 25, 2024, https://wgntv.com/news/chicagocrime/court-docs-chicago-area-vet-dog-show-judge-accused-of-distributing-child-porn-planned-to-sexually-assault-unborn-child/.

[29] Nino Bucci, "Man Pleads Guilty to Sexually Abusing His Twin Surrogate Babies," *Sydney Morning Herald*, April 22, 2016, https://www

Sex and Reproduction

Medical issues with surrogacy include higher rates of pre-eclampsia for the surrogates and increased risks of low birth weight and stillbirth for the babies.[30] There are also potential snags when it comes to determining legal parentage, depending on the jurisdiction.[31] These are incidental concerns, though. Nothing some medical advancements and a few pieces of legislation won't fix.

More fundamentally, using a surrogate, whether commercial or altruistic, involves an outside party in what should be a two-person operation. That can get messy. In multiple cases, a surrogate has bonded with the baby that's living in her womb, kicking her ribs, and drawing sustenance from her body and decided she wants to keep it. In the 1980s, a New Jersey couple's surrogate (and egg donor) showed up to their house and threatened to kill herself if they didn't hand over her daughter. She kept the baby, and the case went to the state Supreme Court, which awarded custody to the intended parents (or "IPs").[32]

A more acrimonious version of the same dispute unfolded between a single male IP named Chester Mills and his forty-nine-year-old surrogate Melissa Cook. When Cook became pregnant with triplets in 2015, Mills said he couldn't afford three children and requested that she have one aborted. Cook sued, hoping to collect her fee and be allowed to adopt the unwanted third baby. A federal appeals court ruled against

---

.smh.com.au/national/man-pleads-guilty-to-sexually-abusing-his-twin-surrogate-babies-20160421-goc83m.html.

[30] Grace Melton and Melanie Israel, "How Surrogacy Harms Women and Children," Heritage Foundation, May 5, 2021, https://www.heritage.org/marriage-and-family/commentary/how-surrogacy-harms-women-and-children.

[31] "Surrogacy Laws by State," Legal Professional Group, American Society of Reproductive Medicine, updated September 2024, https://connect.asrm.org/lpg/resources/surrogacy-by-state?ssopc=1.

[32] *Matter of Baby M.*, 109 N.J. 396 (1988).

her, and the U.S. Supreme Court declined to hear the case.[33] Mills, who makes less than forty thousand dollars per year, was awarded custody of all three children, including the one he wanted dead. A court filing later alleged that they were living with him in "deplorable" conditions.[34] Such cases are apparently common enough that surrogacy agency Worldwide Surrogacy Specialists advises IPs and surrogates to "engage in a preemptive discussion regarding selective reduction," warning that a disagreement "may impede their surrogacy."[35]

Surrogates are often poor and vulnerable, but they're still persons with legal rights. There are limits to what they'll endure.[36] They suffer, as Mary Harrington puts it, "the gruelling and risky aspects of 'normal'

---

[33] *Cook v. Harding*, no. 16-55968 (9th Cir. 2018).

[34] Johnny Dodd, "Triplets Born to Surrogate Mom Melissa Cook Are Living in 'Deplorable' Conditions with Birth Father, Court Documents Say," *People*, September 21, 2017, https://people.com/human-interest/surrogate-mom-melissa-cook-triplets-living-deplorable-conditions-birth-father-court-documents/.

[35] "Why IPs and Surrogates Need to Discuss Selective Reduction," Worldwide Surrogacy Specialists, December 12, 2021, https://www.worldwidesurrogacy.org/blog/why-ips-and-surrogates-need-to-discuss-selective-reduction.

[36] If you don't want to deal with an uppity surrogate, you might have the option to use a brain-dead woman who's literally incapable of objecting. Philosopher Anna Smajdor considered such an arrangement in a 2022 journal article, proposing that women might preemptively consent to become "womb donors" the same way they currently consent to becoming organ donors. To avoid "feminist concerns," Smajdor suggests turning brain-dead men into gestators by implanting embryos in their livers, which could enable a baby to develop to term, but would be fatal for the male "mother." A baby bursting out of your vegetable uncle's liver like a xenomorph from *Alien* is apparently a small price to pay for gender equality. See Anna Smajdor, "Whole Body Gestational Donation." *Theoretical Medicine and Bioethics* 44 (November 2022): 113–124. https://doi.org/10.1007/s11017-022-09599-8.

maternity" so others can "take advantage of the potential opened up by limitless, transhumanist medicine."[37] The elites liberate themselves from the shackles of biology only by weighing down the less privileged with their cast-off chains. The optics are terrible. Italy, where surrogacy has been illegal for over two decades, passed new legislation in 2024 banning its citizens from hiring surrogates in countries that still allow the practice. Hopefully more countries will follow suit in the coming decades. By that time, though, advances in technology could make surrogates obsolete.

Artificial wombs are *Brave New World*, *The Matrix*, *Gattaca*, and *Attack of the Clones* all rolled up into one dystopian nightmare.[38] In 2022, Berlin-based biotechnologist Hashem Al-Ghaili released a video debuting his concept for EctoLife, "the world's first artificial womb facility." The computer-animated video shows rows of pods (the proposed facility can grow thirty thousand babies at a time) while a narrator assures us that the incubators are far more hygienic than a human womb. If this all sounds too impersonal, don't worry. You can use an app to view a livestream of baby's development and talk to Junior through your phone speaker. For an extra fee, they'll even let you genetically engineer the little guy.[39] Transhumanist author (and Sirius satellite radio founder) Martine Rothblatt takes the proposal even further, suggesting that an accelerated form of "ectogenesis" could "produce an

---

[37] Mary Harrington, "How Surrogacy Is Transforming Medicine," *UnHerd*, October 6, 2022, https://unherd.com/2022/10/how-surrogacy-is-transforming-medicine/.

[38] Portions of the following section originally appeared at the *Daily Caller*. See Grayson Quay, "Artificial Wombs Will Destroy Our Humanity," *Daily Caller*, December 14, 2022, https://dailycaller.com/2022/12/14/quay-artificial-wombs-will-destroy-our-humanity/.

[39] Hashem Al-Ghaili, "EctoLife: The World's First Artificial Womb Facility," December 9, 2022, YouTube, https://www.youtube.com/watch?v=O2RIvJ1U7RE.

adult-sized person in just 20 months." These lab-grown bodies could be used as empty shells into which humans or even AI "persons" could then upload their consciousness.[40]

This facility must never be built. In his 1922 book *Eugenics and Other Evils*, G. K. Chesterton describes a class of "idealists" who believe progress will never cross the line into dystopia. They themselves might insist on certain constraints, but they mistakenly assume they can "be responsible for a whole movement after it has left their hands."[41] Such people, Chesterton writes, "do not understand the nature of a law any more than the nature of a dog. If you let loose a law, it will do as a dog does. It will obey its own nature, not yours."

A hundred years later, this same error crops up again and again in debates about bioethical issues. Sensible, empathetic arguments carry each new innovation into the public consciousness. We need abortion for ten-year-old rape victims and women facing life-threatening complications. We need physician-assisted suicide for terminal cancer patients in excruciating pain. We need IVF and surrogacy for couples who are tragically unable to bear their own children. We need gender-affirming care because dysphoric people will kill themselves otherwise.

EctoLife's version of this is that we need artificial wombs because three hundred thousand women die every year from pregnancy complications. This is absurd on its face. Ninety-four percent of those deaths take place in impoverished areas, and baby pods would be, at least for the foreseeable future, exclusively a plaything of the rich. For some reason, they don't bother pursuing the far less problematic idea of using artificial wombs to save babies born prematurely. Probably because it

---

[40] Martine Rothblatt, "Mind Is Deeper Than Matter: Transgenderism, Transhumanism, and the Freedom of Form," in *The Transhumanist Reader*, 320.

[41] G. K. Chesterton, *Eugenics and Other Evils* (London: Cassell, 1922), 16.

would be less lucrative, has a clear limiting principle, and would make it harder to defend legal abortion.[42]

EctoLife also suggests that the proposed facility could produce children for women who've undergone hysterectomies due to cancer. As we'll see, though, the purpose of such justifications is merely to get a foot in the door. After that, like Chesterton's dog, the technology pursues its own agenda.

If and when artificial wombs are invented that can produce outcomes comparable to natural pregnancy, they'll quickly replace surrogacy. And soon after, they'll go from an expensive luxury to a government-funded human right. That's already happening with surrogacy. In 2020, the *New York Times* reported on the "Fertility Equality" movement, which calls for "reproductive procedures" to be subsidized so that "the ability to create a family is no longer determined by one's wealth, sexuality, gender or biology."[43]

Get ready for a world where artificial wombs are covered by Medicaid and all major insurance. Nobody wants to see poor women suffering from preeclampsia and gestational diabetes while the rich get to pound six mimosas at brunch as they FaceTime their fetuses in the EctoLife warehouse.

For the transhuman woman of the future, delivery will involve no labor, neither hers nor anyone else's. The very word *delivery*, even when used in reference to a new baby, will have more in common with the service UberEats provides than with the bloody, frightening affair that

---

[42] Ian Miles Cheong, "Gizmodo Attacks Artificial Womb Technology, Claims It Threatens Women's Rights," *Daily Caller*, July 29, 2017, https://dailycaller.com/2017/07/29/gizmodo-attacks-artificial-womb-technology-claims-it-threatens-womens-rights/.

[43] David Kaufman, "The Fight for Fertility Equality," *New York Times*, July 24, 2020, https://www.nytimes.com/2020/07/22/style/lgbtq-fertility-surrogacy-coverage.html.

all her female ancestors endured. Only a transhumanist mind could conceive of such a thing. Previous generations of scientists took it as given that human females carry and give birth to children. They used their skills to help mothers have safer pregnancies and healthier infants. To modern scientists, it's a mere accident (or even a blunder) that women have babies the way they do.

The motives that lead us to remake humanity may be noble, but once we start down that path, there is no way to stop. Abortion, IVF, and surrogacy could all be considered tentative first steps. The ability to grow a child from conception to birth in some warehouse would be one giant leap. Not for mankind, though. We'd need a new name. We'd have become something else entirely.

Transgenderism and Body Modification[1]

I am something other than my body.

—René Descartes[2]

Transgenderism follows the same transhumanist logic as birth control, abortion, and surrogacy: horror and resentment toward a healthy bodily function plus insistence on one's inalienable right to control, halt, or outsource that process.

As with birth control, the point is not happiness. It's autonomy. The most progressive elements of the transgender movement no longer rely primarily on arguments about mental health benefits or the neuroscience of gender, though both are frequently trotted out for public consumption. Instead, they claim that would-be transitioners owe no explanation to anyone. If they want their genitals carved up, that's their right.

---

[1] Portions of three paragraphs in this chapter originally appeared in a slightly different form at the *American Mind*. See Grayson Quay, "Click This Linkussy," *American Mind*, February 23, 2023, https://americanmind.org/features/soul-dysphoria/click-this-linkussy/.

[2] Discourse on Method and Meditations on First Philosophy, 6.9, trans. and qtd. in Spencer Klavan, *How to Save the West* (Washington, DC: Regnery, 2023), 45.

THE TRANSHUMANIST TEMPTATION

In a *New York Times* op-ed headlined "My New Vagina Won't Make Me Happy," transgender writer Andrea Long Chu admitted that "my body will regard the vagina as a wound" that "will require regular, painful attention to maintain" and that he became suicidal for the first time *after* starting cross-sex hormones.[3] He doesn't think either factor should prevent him from transitioning. "[Transgender] surgery's only prerequisite should be a simple demonstration of want. Beyond this, no amount of pain, anticipated or continuing, justifies its withholding," Chu argues.

He also claims that "desire and happiness are independent agents," providing what Aristotle and all his intellectual descendants would regard as conclusive evidence of a severely deformed soul. Desires that fail to align with *eudaimonia*, the happiness and flourishing proper to the human person, should be mortified, not indulged.

Chu's absolutist view of bodily autonomy also extends to children. And he doesn't care if they end up regretting it either. In a long essay, Chu argues that "if children are too young to consent to puberty blockers, then they are *definitely* too young to consent to puberty, which is a drastic biological upheaval in its own right."[4] The idea that a child should have to "consent" to the healthy workings of his own body is bizarre. One might as well ask the kid to "consent" to losing his baby teeth.

These absurd scenarios, like Chu's insistence on "freedom of sex" as a "universal birthright," make sense only from a transhumanist perspective. Chu, like any good transhumanist, even appeals to the is-ought dilemma, writing that "the belief that we have a moral duty to accept reality just because it is real is, I think, a fine definition of nihilism."

---

[3] Andrea Long Chu, "My New Vagina Won't Make Me Happy," *New York Times*, November 24, 2018, https://www.nytimes.com/2018/11/24/opinion/sunday/vaginoplasty-transgender-medicine.html.

[4] Andrea Long Chu, "Freedom of Sex," *New York*, March 11, 2024, https://nymag.com/intelligencer/article/trans-rights-biological-sex-gender-judith-butler.html.

Here, he constructs a particularly flimsy strawman. Nobody rejects transgenderism out of a universal devotion to things as they are. I'm not aware of any evil transphobes who also oppose turning flour into bread. But more crucially, Chu gets the definition of *nihilism* exactly wrong. Nihilism is the belief that there is no meaning but what we make for ourselves, that desire is a free-floating impulse with no *telos* to aim at, that there is no *ought* attached to any *is*, and that therefore we must impose our will on a valueless world or else fall into despair. Chu is the real nihilist.

If radical bodily autonomy conveys the right to remove breasts, alter genitals, and feminize or masculinize facial features, then it conveys the right to alter one's body in any way one sees fit. "I've come to realize," wrote activist Martine Rothblatt in his book *From Transgender to Transhuman*, "that choosing one's gender is merely an important subset of choosing one's form."[5] It's now open season on the entire human body.

Bodies become fully modular. We now have "vagina owners" rather than "women." Don't have a penis? Have a doctor carve a phallus out of your forearm. Don't want any genitals at all? That can be arranged too. Doctors have pioneered an operation for "nonbinary" or "agender" patients that produces the smooth, featureless crotch of a Ken doll.[6] You can purchase the perfect "Instagram face" or a few extra inches of height.

Comedian Tina Fey famously wrote about the societal pressures which demand that "all girls must be everything," combining "Caucasian blue eyes, full Spanish lips, a classic button nose, [and] hairless Asian skin" with "a California tan, a Jamaican dance hall ass, [and] long

---

[5] Martine Rothblatt, *From Transgender to Transhuman* (self-published, 2011), xiii.

[6] "Non-binary Surgery," Crane Center for Transgender Surgery, accessed December 9, 2024, https://cranects.com/non-binary-surgery/.

THE TRANSHUMANIST TEMPTATION

Swedish legs."[7] Now, thanks to the marvels of transhumanist medicine, every girl can be everything and then some — if she has the cash, that is.

In the transhuman future, your body is not an integral part of your identity. It's a thing, or rather a collection of things, all of which have specs and price tags. In the vision of our trendsetting vanguard, unaugmented humanity is slated for planned obsolescence.

And why limit yourself to "upgrading" or swapping out body parts some humans have naturally? Transhumanist artist and researcher Laura Beloff discusses her concept of a "wearable, networked tail for the human body" that (presumably) wires into the user's nervous system. This appendage aims not at any "enhanced function or ability of the human," but instead redefines the individual as "a mesh of links crisscrossing within the body and between the body and technological devices."[8] Such devices could make useful tools. Andy Clark, another transhumanist, suggests that we're already capable of something like this. According to research Clark cites, humans (and even animals) have neurons that can reconfigure themselves to incorporate tools into a "body-schema" defined by its "capabilities for action."[9] Racecar drivers and fighter pilots, for example, report that their vehicles come to feel like extensions of their own bodies. It's not much of a stretch to imagine a link between nervous system and machine that removes the control interface and makes piloting tons of metal as intuitive as moving one's arms or legs.

The problem arises when we abolish the boundary between tool and user. Clark urges his readers not to remain "locked away behind the fixed veil of a certain skin bag" and to instead embrace a "permeable

---

[7] Tina Fey, *Bossypants* (Boston: Little, Brown, 2013).
[8] Laura Beloff, "The Hybronaut Affair," in *The Transhumanist Reader*, 66.
[9] Andy Clark, "Re-inventing Ourselves," in *The Transhumanist Reader*, 119–120.

and repeatedly reconfigurable agent/world boundary."[10] When you've reduced the body to an artificial construct in this way, then you can bolt anything you like onto it and claim that new addition as not just an accessory, but an integral part of you. It's one thing for Spider-Man villain Otto Octavius to use robot arms wired into his cerebellum as a piece of lab equipment. It's quite another for him to leave the tentacles on 24/7, moving through life as a transhuman octopus.

Not all body modifications qualify as transhumanism. The same procedure many people use to achieve a trendy nose shape can also alleviate serious sinus issues. A pirate's peg leg approximates the function of the limb it replaces. Attaching a blunderbuss would be a different story. Even artificial organs would not be transhumanist technologies *per se* as long as they were used solely to replace biological organs that had deteriorated or been damaged rather than to enhance performance beyond normal human parameters.

This principle does present a dilemma (though one that, under present conditions, remains entirely academic). Replacing body parts as they wore out could mean eventually constructing, one piece at a time, an entirely synthetic body. Even if that body sought to replicate, rather than improve upon, human biology, the result would be an undeniably transhuman being. An ancient thought experiment asked whether the Ship of Theseus would remain the Ship of Theseus as each of its component parts was replaced. How long, then, can we chip away at the material parts of our humanity before the whole becomes something altogether different?

There's no easy answer. For thoroughgoing transhumanists, though, there isn't even a question. They view their embodied humanity not as something precious to be conserved, but as a shackle from which to escape.

---

[10] Ibid., 125.

Life Extension and Assisted Suicide

When a country — a society, a civilisation — gets to the point of legalising euthanasia, it loses in my eyes all right to respect. It becomes henceforth not only legitimate, but desirable, to destroy it; so that something else — another country, another society, another civilisation — might have a chance to arise.

— Michel Houellebecq[1]

It's hard to imagine death. A character in Tom Stoppard's play *Rosencrantz and Guildenstern Are Dead* quips that "one thinks of it like being alive in a box" and "keeps forgetting to take into account that one is dead, which should make all the difference."[2] Even as a committed Christian, I'll admit to experiencing some anxiety around the topic. Is there a conscious feeling of letting go, or do you slip into death like general anesthesia, unaware of the exact moment? And then what happens? I can't form a mental image of waking to eternal life that feels believable to me (as opposed to some over-literalized pearly gates

---

[1] Michel Houellebecq, "How France Lost Her Dignity," *UnHerd*, April 24, 2021, https://unherd.com/2021/04/how-france-lost-her-dignity/.

[2] Tom Stoppard, *Rosencrantz & Guildenstern Are Dead*, (Montclair, NJ: Brandenberg Productions, 1990).

fantasy), so I try not to think about it too much. And what if everything just goes black?

For card-carrying transhumanists, who tend to be atheists, death is the ultimate enemy which we must fight with every weapon available. Gennady Stolyarov, chairman of the Transhumanist Party, looks back to a childhood memory to explain how he came to this conclusion:

> One day at age five, in the late spring of 1993, I was visiting the Minsk Botanical Garden with my grandmother. We sat down on a bench overlooking a large pond where ducks and swans swam. On that sunny, temperate day, hundreds of flowers were in bloom, and I was amazed at the abundance and variety of colors in the world. "How," I asked, "could it ever be right for all this experience to just end? How could it be right that, one day, I would never again witness this beauty, or anything else, or even remember having experienced it?" After death, I understood, a person no longer is even aware of *having lived*. It is as if one never existed. I made a promise to myself then that I would wage war on death, that I would not allow my life and memories to be snuffed out.[3]

The book in which Stolyarov recounted this experience is titled *Death Is Wrong*. It's a sentiment with which Christ would have agreed. Why else would He have wept at Lazarus's tomb? The difference is that, for Jesus, death was wrong because it resulted from humanity's Fall and was therefore a departure from the way in which humans were meant to live. For Stolyarov, death is wrong solely because it is a point of conflict between his biology and his will. He wants to live forever, but his body is wearing out. It's natural that he should feel that way.

---

[3] Gennady Stolyarov II, *Death Is Wrong* (Carson City, NV: Rational Argumentator Press, 2013), 8.

Ecclesiastes tells us that God has "set eternity" in the human heart.[4] But because Stolyarov sees "no evidence" for an afterlife, his only option is to use science and technology to extend this one.[5]

Is life extension an inherently transhumanist endeavor? There are, of course, plenty of ways to extend human life. According to public health researcher Hans Rosling, no country on earth had an average life expectancy of even forty-five in 1810 (due largely to high infant mortality dragging down the average). Today, most developed countries are in the high seventies or even the low eighties due to improvements in nutrition, medicine, and overall standard of living.[6] None of these advances is remotely transhumanist. Neither is using prosthetic or synthetic body parts to restore the body's normal functions, as discussed in the previous chapter. Restoring normal functioning to an ill, damaged, or deteriorating body falls firmly within the purview of traditional medicine, and it's unclear how far those methods alone can extend our longevity.

Genetic tinkering could deliver even more dramatic results. In *Our Posthuman Future*, Fukuyama draws attention to Leonard Hayflick's 1961 discovery "that somatic cells had an upper limit in the total number of divisions they could undergo." This biologically imposed cap on cell division, known as the "Hayflick limit," appears to be linked to the shortening of telomeres — non-coding end caps that prevent human chromosomes from unraveling.[7] Cancer cells, however, can multiply indefinitely thanks to an enzyme called telomerase that keeps the telomeres intact. If we figured out a gene edit that could make all

---

[4] Eccl. 3:11, NIV.
[5] Stolyarov II, *Death Is Wrong*, 11.
[6] Hans Rosling, "Hans Rosling's 200 Countries, 200 Years, 4 Minutes — The Joy of Stats — BBC," BBC, November 26, 2010, YouTube, https://www.youtube.com/watch?v=jbkSRLYSojo.
[7] Fukuyama, *Our Posthuman Future*, 58–59.

somatic cells produce telomerase, we might be able to stop the aging process. Another avenue of anti-aging research focuses on a naked mole rat gene that produces high molecular weight hyaluronic acid (HMW-HA), which repairs damage to cells. Naked mole rats can live to about thirty (much longer than is typical for mammals their size). They also appear not to age physically as they grow older. Lab mice that had the mole rat gene spliced into them lived longer and were less likely to get cancer.[8]

We don't know everything about what causes people to age and die, so it's possible that neither of these methods (nor any of the others being researched) would extend human life indefinitely. But for transhumanist gerontologist Aubrey de Grey, there's no need to deliver a single knockout punch to the Grim Reaper. All we have to do is outrun him.

In a 2005 interview, de Grey predicted that within twenty-five years, scientists would have developed a therapy to reverse the aging process. "One could probably think in terms of having to go in for a refresh every 10 years or so," he said, noting that over time the process would become simpler and more effective.[9] The interviewer concluded that, if de Grey is right, anyone who survives until 2030 can probably expect to live one thousand years or more.

In Roald Dahl's children's book *Charlie and the Great Glass Elevator*, the eccentric chocolatier Willy Wonka offers Charlie's parents and grandparents his Wonka-Vite pills, each of which will take ten years off their age. Hijinks ensue when the oldsters take too many and

---

[8] Lindsey Valich, "Longevity Gene from Naked Mole Rats Extends Lifespan of Mice," University of Rochester News Center, August 23, 2023, https://www.rochester.edu/newscenter/gene-transfer-hmw-ha-naked-mole-rats-extends-mice-lifespan-565032/.

[9] Ker Than, "Hang in There: The 25-Year Wait for Immortality," *LiveScience*, April 11, 2005, https://livescience.com/6967-hang-25-year-wait-immortality.html.

become "minuses," but what if it were used as directed? Anyone with a Wonka-Vite prescription could spend an eternity bouncing back and forth between twenty-three and thirty-three. The only things left to worry about would be war, murder, accidents, and natural disasters.[10]

An anti-transhumanist can flatly dismiss any life-extension therapies that involve genetic alteration, which would turn the recipient into a different species. Similarly distasteful is "biohacking," the obsessive and expensive practice of attempting to prolong life for its own sake. Forty-six-year-old tech entrepreneur Bryan Johnson spends about two million dollars a year trying to keep his body youthful. Doctors say he "has the heart of a 37-year-old, the skin of a 28-year-old, and the lung capacity of an 18-year-old."[11] He achieves these results with a highly regimented lifestyle most people would describe as neurotic: consuming exactly 1,977 calories and around two dozen supplements per day, regular MRIs and stool samples, fat injections, and even a device that tracks his nocturnal erections.

Chesterton might have been talking about Johnson when he wrote that "the mere pursuit of health always leads to something unhealthy."[12] In seeking to keep his body youthful, Johnson treats it as a set of biological components, each with its own set of stats to be tracked and managed. He already looks uncannily synthetic, bearing a strong resemblance to the android Data from *Star Trek: The Next Generation*.

Johnson's fear of aging and death has even led him to vampirism, in the form of regular blood plasma transfusions from his teenage

---

[10] Roald Dahl, *Charlie and the Great Glass Elevator* (New York: Penguin, 2007).

[11] Alexa Mikhail, "A 45-year-old Tech CEO is Spending Millions a Year to be 18 Again — Even Though Doctor Admits Results Are Minimal," *Fortune*, https://fortune.com/well/2023/01/26/bryan-johnson-extreme-anti-aging/.

[12] G. K. Chesterton, "The Flag of the World," in *Orthodoxy*, 16.

THE TRANSHUMANIST TEMPTATION

son. And he's not the only one. A start-up called Ambrosia spent years selling transfusions of youthful blood for eight thousand dollars a pop and reportedly attracted the interest of billionaire Peter Thiel, another life extension enthusiast.[13] Not only are the biohackers developing transhumanist attitudes toward their own bodies, but they're willing to do so at the expense of younger generations. Even if Dad isn't literally sucking your blood, imagine watching him blow exorbitant sums for marginal reductions in epigenetic age while you and your wife struggle to scrape together a down payment on a house.

It's difficult to justify the same level of opposition toward life extension as such. If an increase in average life expectancy from forty to eighty is cause for rejoicing, why should an increase from eighty to one hundred (or 150 or two hundred) evoke condemnation, especially if these aspiring Methuselahs can remain physically spry and mentally acute in their superannuated state? As with the question of replacing worn-out body parts with synthetic ones, it's difficult to draw a hard line (though perhaps governments would find themselves forced to do so).

What matters are the motives involved. Seeking immortality is inherently transhumanist. Extending one's lifespan and healthspan is not. A set of tech policy principles published in the Christian magazine *First Things* offers a useful guideline, urging policymakers to "respect the natural cycle of mortality by healing or mitigating chronic disease rather than pursuing radical life extension."[14] If that ends up adding years to our lives, so be it.

---

[13] Gavin Haynes, "Ambrosia: The Startup Harvesting the Blood of the Young," *Guardian*, August 21, 2017, https://www.theguardian.com/society/shortcuts/2017/aug/21/ambrosia-the-startup-harvesting-the-blood-of-the-young.

[14] Michael Toscano et al., "A Future for the Family: A New Technology Agenda for the Right," *First Things*, January 29, 2025, https://firstthings.com/a-future-for-the-family-a-new-technology-agenda-for-the-right/.

Life Extension and Assisted Suicide

Perhaps we could aim to emulate Moses: as Deuteronomy has it, he "was 120 years old when he died. His eye was undimmed, and his vigor unabated."[15] But it's not necessary to place some arbitrary limit on years. What matters is the principle that, at some point, having prospered in all his works and seen his progeny to the third generation, a man ought to surrender his achievements to the ages and his body to the earth, journeying like all his ancestors to "the undiscovered country from whose bourn no traveller returns."[16] The transhumanism lies not in the mere prolonging of life, but in the narcissism, the hubris, the unwillingness to relinquish control. Our ancestors sought immortality by achieving martial glory, endowing libraries and hospitals, raising children, and serving God.[17] We would do well to follow their example.

There are also practical concerns with life extension. Longer retirements plus lower birth rates equals more strain on social security programs. The elderly could take advantage of their prolonged vigor to remain in the workforce, though that poses problems as well. In his book *The Great Campaign*, Jason Jones invites the reader to "imagine turning forty still stuck in an entry-level job, unable to afford children or a house, because everyone above you refuses to retire."[18]

But let's assume that we achieve some sort of post-scarcity economy in which vigorous elders need neither work nor rely on the support of employed youngsters. What would the old folks do then? Ray Kurzweil promises that "in addition to radical life extension, we're going to have radical life expansion": "Right now we only have 300 million pattern

---

[15] Deut. 34:7, ESV.

[16] William Shakespeare, *Hamlet*, in *The Riverside Shakespeare*, ed. G. Blakemore Evans and J. J. M. Tobin (Boston: Houghton Mifflin, 1997), act 3, scene 1, 78–79.

[17] See Jason Jones, *The Great Campaign: Against the Great Reset* (Manchester, NH: Crisis, 2024), 71–72.

[18] Jones, *Great Campaign*, 69.

THE TRANSHUMANIST TEMPTATION

recognizers... in our neocortex. But we could make that 300 billion, 300 trillion.... We'll be thinking grander, deeper, more hierarchical thoughts than ever before.... So we're not gonna get bored."[19]

Stolyarov seems convinced that zest for life is already an inexhaustible resource. "Even if you lived forever and read one entire book every day, you would never run out of reading materials!" he writes. "About 2,200,000 books are published each year, and this rate is always increasing. So no, you would never get bored if you take any interest in anything."[20] If reading's not your thing, you could develop your artistic talents, learn new languages, work in other professions, travel the world (or even the galaxy), and tell stories to your great-great-great-grandchildren.

But what happens when the immortal transhumanist tastes everything life has to offer and concludes — as King Solomon did in less than seventy years — that "all is vanity"?[21] The answer should be obvious by now. In a transhumanist society, you own yourself completely. Your options in life for pursuing your own happiness on your own terms are limitless. And if nothing makes you happy anymore, those options include ending that life, also on your own terms. How else is a deathless demigod supposed to die?

Human immortality remains the stuff of science fiction, but the death-on-demand that would have to accompany it is already a reality. And it's rooted in the same principles of agency and autonomy used to justify other aspects of transhumanism. An anti-transhumanist could condone a patient (or, if she cannot communicate, her next of kin) "pulling the plug" by requesting removal of artificial life support.

---

[19] "Ray Kurzweil — Immortality by 2045," 2045 Initiative, March 4, 2013, YouTube, 3:43, https://youtu.be/f28LPwR8BdY.
[20] Stolyarov, *Death Is Wrong*, 18.
[21] Eccl. 1:2, RSVCE.

What he could not condone is the intentional taking of that life. The purpose of medicine, going back to Hippocrates, has been to restore the human body to the mode of flourishing proper to human nature, not to refashion, mutilate, or even kill that body in accordance with the patient's wishes. Whether the patient wants to die is beside the point. It is still immoral to kill her.

But for a transhumanist, the will trumps everything. In an essay proposing to add support for assisted suicide to the Transhumanist Party platform, Martin van der Kroon wrote that to outlaw this practice is to "take someone's agency" by imposing "a sentence to live."[22] The party adopted the plank. By this logic, "forcing" a person to remain alive without his consent is a violation of human dignity. Killing an innocent person is not. This mindset predominates in Canada, where assisted suicide (often called "medical assistance in dying" or "MAiD") exploded in 2021 to account for over 3 percent of total deaths.

"Only suffering is guaranteed in life, and everyone deserves the dignity to relieve it in any way they personally consider in their own best interest," a MAiD-seeker known as Alex told an interviewer. Alex doesn't have any terminal illness, though he does suffer from autoimmune issues that leave him in constant pain. Before 2021, that would have made him ineligible to be lethally injected by medical professionals. Today, the law no longer requires that individuals be in an "advanced state of irreversible decline" in which natural death is "reasonably foreseeable." A further liberalization that would have allowed MAiD for the mentally ill was due to take effect in 2024 but was later delayed until

---

[22] Martin van der Kroon, "The Right to Die," The U.S. Transhumanist Party, May 29, 2017, https://transhumanist-party.org/2017/05/29/the-right-to-die/.

THE TRANSHUMANIST TEMPTATION

2027.[23] Other countries, like Switzerland and the Netherlands, have already reached that particular milestone of progress.[24]

The author of a scholarly article on the 2006 Swiss court case that allowed a physically healthy bipolar man to be prescribed a lethal dose of phenobarbitol states that the "twin goals" of assisted suicide are "maximizing individual autonomy and minimizing human suffering."[25] His claim is too modest. In fact, these are the twin goals of the entire modern West. A society based on those values recognizes no higher end, not even the preservation of human life. The coming regime of assisted suicide — on demand and without obstacle — is just one more expression of these transhumanist values.[26]

---

[23] Brianna Navarre, "Canada Backtracks on Euthanasia for the Mentally Ill," U.S. News, March 5, 2024, https://www.usnews.com/news/best-countries/articles/2024-03-05/canada-backtracks-on-euthanasia-for-the-mentally-ill.

[24] Linda Pressly, "The Troubled 29-Year-Old Helped to Die by Dutch Doctors," BBC, August 8, 2018, https://www.bbc.com/news/stories-45117163.

[25] Jacob M. Appel, "A Suicide Right for the Mentally Ill? A Swiss Case Opens Debate," *Hastings Center Report* 37, no. 3 (May 2007): 21, https://doi.org/10.1353/hcr.2007.0035.

[26] This paragraph originally appeared, in a slightly different form, in the *Spectator World*. See Grayson Quay, "Assisted Suicide Is the New Trans Rights," *Spectator World*, December 10, 2021, https://thespectator.com/topic/assisted-suicide-new-trans-rights/.

The Procrustean Bed

Then, quickly, Sylvester McMonkey McBean
Put together a very peculiar machine.
And he said, "You want stars like a Star-Belly Sneetch?
My friends, you can have them for three dollars each!"

— Dr. Seuss[1]

The ancient Greek myth of Procrustes tells of a mad demigod who lived near a busy road and offered his guestroom to any traveler who passed by. Unfortunately for these travelers, none of them fit perfectly in Procrustes' bed. But Procrustes had an elegant solution: when his guests were too short, he'd whack them with a hammer until they fit the bed, like flattening chicken breast to make schnitzel.[2] For guests who proved too tall, he'd break out the hacksaw and amputate whatever hung over the end.

The story is absurd because of the inversion at its center. We expect humans to design things — from pieces of furniture to social

---

[1] Dr. Seuss, *The Sneetches and Other Stories* (New York: Random House, 1961), 10.
[2] See Plutarch, *Twelve Illustrious Lives*, trans. John Dryden (Franklin Center, PA: The Franklin Library, 1981), 9.

institutions — in a human shape and on a human scale. We make things to serve us. We don't remake ourselves to serve them.

Procrustes eventually met his end at the hands of the hero Theseus, but let's consider an alternate ending: Advancements in medical technology make stretching and amputation safer than ever. Corporations realize that if everyone's the same height, they can save money by standardizing their products. The board of the American Hotel and Lodging Association votes unanimously to adopt the cut-and-stretch method as an industry-wide standard.

A six-foot-four-inch man walks into a hotel lobby and asks for a room. "I'm terribly sorry," the desk attendant says, "but we're unable to accommodate unadjusted guests."

The man gets annoyed. This is the fifth hotel he's tried. It's the same policy everywhere.

"What's that supposed to mean? You're gonna make me cut off my legs?"

"'Make you'? Of course not, sir. We at Procrustean Suites have the highest regard for our guests' bodily autonomy. If you've neglected to pack a saw, we're happy to provide one, free of charge. And you may want to be quick about it. Our rooms are going fast."

In the preceding chapters, I've looked at transhumanist bioethics from an individualist perspective. The common thread linking birth control, abortion, IVF, surrogacy, transgenderism, body modification, life extension, and assisted suicide in those chapters was a denial of human nature and the corresponding invention of an absolute right to control one's own body, even if that means disrupting its normal, healthy functioning. But I have no desire to merely villainize those who make use of transhumanist biotechnologies. They are often victims too. As my version of the Procrustes story suggests, a society that treats reshaping human beings as a valid option will give them plenty of incentive to do so, even if there's no direct coercion involved. Instead of altering social systems to fit human needs, we'll alter human beings to fit increasingly inhuman social systems.

Birth control is a perfect example. The invention of a reliable oral contraceptive ushered in the Sexual Revolution. As casual, consequence-free sex became a real possibility, it also became an expectation. A woman who stayed off the Pill and had to tell her dates no more often than her girlfriends did would be handicapping herself. Guys would write her off as a prude when she failed to put out as quickly as the other girls. Suddenly, staying competitive in the dating game requires becoming a little bit transhuman.

Other pharmaceuticals could work the same way. Jason Jones suggests the following scenario:

> Big Pharma succeeds in developing a "limitless pill" that instantly boosts IQ.... It hits the market at five hundred dollars a pill. The children of the ultra-rich pop one every day, giving them an even greater edge in standardized testing, college admissions, and job performance that guarantees their place atop the meritocracy. Twenty years go by, and the patent expires. The generic version of the pill only costs thirty dollars a tablet. That puts the cost at around ten thousand dollars a year, bringing the pill within the budget of the upper middle class. Suddenly millions, not thousands, of kids are on this pill. The children of the poor fall even further behind.
>
> Theoretically, the new bio-aristocrats could continue enhancing themselves as new augmentations become available, further solidifying their status while depriving the merely human peasants of dignity and social mobility. To prevent this, a group of senators introduces legislation to make the "limitless pill" free. And as it becomes free, it also becomes almost obligatory. With enhanced intelligence as the new benchmark, any

THE TRANSHUMANIST TEMPTATION

crunchy hippies or Bible-banging fundamentalists who want their kids to rely on their God-given wits will be dooming those children to a life of poverty and social ostracism. It might even be called child abuse.[3]

Transhumanists make a show of taking such dangers seriously, but their solutions tend to fall flat. In an essay on "morphological freedom," Anders Sandberg suggests that allowing individuals unfettered access to transhumanist biomedicine will somehow alleviate the "risk of powerful groups forcing change upon us" — as if "powerful groups" aren't perfectly capable of exerting pressure indirectly.[4]

In fact, this is already happening. Antidepressants may rescue some people from despondency and suicide, but they also have the effect of giving society permission to become even more inhuman. If social conditions drive an increasing number of people to despair, which is easier — altering the conditions or altering the personalities of those who suffer under them? Fukuyama provides a pair of examples in Prozac and Ritalin. "The former is prescribed heavily for depressed women lacking in self-esteem; it gives them more of the alpha-male feeling that comes with high serotonin levels," he explains. "Ritalin, on the other hand, is prescribed largely for young boys who do not want to sit still in class because nature never designed them to behave that way."[5] Agreeable women must be fitted to the workplace, not the other way around.[6] Rowdy, aggressive boys must be fitted to schools, not the

[3] Jones, *Great Campaign*, 65.
[4] Sandberg, "Morphological Freedom," 61.
[5] Fukuyama, *Posthuman Future*, 51–52.
[6] Fukuyama's book, written in 2002, does not reckon with the ways in which women *have* reshaped the workforce (and other historically male-dominated institutions) in their image, leaving men feeling alienated no matter where they turn. See Helen Andrews, "Against Human Resources," *The Lamp* 21 (February 2, 2024), https://thelampmagazine

other way around. In the 2006 sci-fi novel *Blindsight*, lovers nag each other to get neurological "tweaks" — small alterations of personality or tastes — instead of learning to bear with their significant other's otherness.[7] Break out the tool bag, Procrustes.

If the preceding chapters have focused heavily on women's issues, it's because women face greater pressure than men to adopt transhumanism. Interdependence is hardwired into their bodies in a way that it simply isn't for men. Men are biologically closer to the transhumanist ideal of the sovereign individual than women are, which means women require more reshaping if they're to conform to that ideal.

"Women's response to industrial modernity negotiated a tension between individual freedom from the ways we're shaped by our biology, and women-centered accommodation by both sexes of our embodiment," Harrington writes, concluding that the first form of feminism has trampled the second.[8] As a result, women are incentivized to suppress their own fertility in the name of equality. Most families now require two incomes to survive, and women who take time off to raise babies tend to fall behind in their careers.[9] So, they rely on the birth control that their employer-sponsored health plans generously cover, often having fewer children than they themselves want.[10]

.com/issues/issue-21/against-human-resources; and L0m3z, "What Is the Longhouse?" *First Things*, February 16, 2023, https://www.firstthings.com/web-exclusives/2023/02/what-is-the-longhouse.

[7] Peter Watts, *Blindsight* (New York: Tor, 2006), 63.
[8] Harrington, *Feminism Against Progress*, 16.
[9] "Raising Kids and Running a Household: How Working Parents Share the Load," Pew Research Center, November 4, 2015, https://www.pewresearch.org/social-trends/2015/11/04/raising-kids-and-running-a-household-how-working-parents-share-the-load/.
[10] Lyman Stone, "How Big Is the Fertility Gap in America?" *Medium*, October 5, 2017, https://medium.com/migration-issues/how-big-is-the-fertility-gap-in-america-fd205e9d1a35.

THE TRANSHUMANIST TEMPTATION

Other employers get more creative. Some cover egg freezing for future IVF treatments in order to keep female employees in the workforce during prime childbearing years. Around the time of the *Dobbs* decision, companies including Disney, Tesla, Microsoft, Netflix, Amazon, JP Morgan Chase, and Dick's Sporting Goods all pledged to cover thousands of dollars in expenses so employees living under abortion bans could travel out of state to terminate their pregnancies.[11] It's a lot cheaper than providing paid maternity leave.

Women also appear to be bearing the brunt of the transgender craze. Author Abigail Shrier described a "sudden, severe spike in transgender identification among adolescent girls," noting that "between 2016 and 2017, the number of females seeking gender surgery quadrupled in the United States" despite gender dysphoria having historically "been vanishingly rare among females."[12] Many of these girls already suffer from other disorders, like anxiety, depression, or autism. In an article for the *European Conservative*, Jonathan van Maren drew on Shrier, Harrington, *When Kids Say They're Trans* author Sasha Ayad, and his own experience to offer an explanation: porn.

"I've been speaking on the issue of pornography, primarily to students, for over a decade, and I can attest to the fact that many girls are terrified of what they see in pornography. In the videos they encounter, women are virtually always subjected to grotesque maltreatment

---

[11] Emma Goldberg, "These Companies Will Cover Travel Expenses for Employee Abortions," *New York Times*, August 19, 2022, https://www.nytimes.com/article/abortion-companies-travel-expenses.html.

[12] Abigail Shrier, "Gender Activists Are Trying to Cancel My Book; Why Is Silicon Valley Helping Them?" *Pittsburgh Post-Gazette*, November 24, 2020, https://www.post-gazette.com/opinion/2020/11/22/Gender-activists-Silicon-Valley-Transgender-LGBTQ/stories/202011220021.

and even torture," he wrote.[13] "Indeed, it is significant that a growing number of girls are embracing androgyny and identifying as 'non-binary' — many do not necessarily want to transition into boys, they simply do not want to be girls." Our toxic sex and dating culture — which is largely a product of birth control, legal abortion, and the free public harem of internet porn — leaves pubescent girls uncomfortable with the lustful gazes suddenly being directed at their maturing bodies. A generation ago, they'd have suffered through it and come out the other side, perhaps after a brief struggle with disordered eating. Today, they're offered an escape hatch from womanhood itself. So, they take it. Transhumanism begets transhumanism.

The earliest attempts at making modern industrial society into a Procrustean bed took the form of eugenics. Julian Huxley, who popularized the term *transhumanism*, believed that poor people should be sterilized if they remained unemployed for too long. Championed by progressives across the Western world, eugenics became government policy in multiple countries, including the United States. Supreme Court Justice Oliver Wendell Holmes wrote in a 1927 opinion that "three generations of imbeciles are enough." The laws his decision upheld led to around sixty thousand involuntary, state-sanctioned sterilizations of the "feeble-minded."[14] The last one was performed in 1979.[15]

The popularity of eugenics declined after the horrors of Nazi Germany came to light, but we're close to smuggling it in again through

---

[13] Jonathon Van Maren, "Is Violent Porn Making Girls Identify as Transgender?" *European Conservative*, February 7, 2024, https://europeanconservative.com/articles/commentary/is-violent-porn-making-girls-identify-as-transgender/.

[14] *Buck v. Bell*, 274 U.S. 200 (1927).

[15] Lutz Kaelber, "Virginia," Eugenics: Compulsory Sterilization in 50 American States, https://www.uvm.edu/~lkaelber/eugenics/VA/VA.html.

THE TRANSHUMANIST TEMPTATION

the back door. One way of removing burdensome individuals from society is through euthanasia. The CBC reported in 2022 that multiple Canadian military veterans struggling with post-traumatic stress had allegedly been offered MAiD as a solution. In one instance, a caseworker reportedly told a veteran that it was preferable to "blowing your brains out against a wall."[16] Thanks to assisted suicide, governments can now send young men into combat, shatter their minds and bodies, and avoid paying to fix them.

Roger Foley, a patient suffering from a degenerative brain disorder, recorded conversations with hospital staff in which they, totally unprompted, raised the topic of MAiD. The hospital's ethics director even told him his treatment would cost "north of $1,500 a day."[17] Another man chose MAiD after the government declined to fully fund round-the-clock treatment for his Lou Gehrig's disease, sticking him with hundreds of dollars a day in medical bills that he had no way of paying. He was forty-one years old and left behind an eleven-year-old son.[18] The traumatized, the disabled, the poor, the inconvenient or costly — all can be quietly nudged into ending their lives. This, according to progressives, is a step forward for individual empowerment and human dignity.

The other way of reconciling old-school eugenic transhumanism with the modern version's emphasis on individual rights and bodily

[16] Standing Committee on Veterans Affairs, Number 021, 1st, Session, 44th Parliament, October 24, 2022, https://www.ourcommons.ca/documentviewer/en/44-1/ACVA/meeting-23/evidence.

[17] Maria Cheng, "'Disturbing': Experts Troubled by Canada's Euthanasia Laws," *AP News*, August 11, 2022, https://apnews.com/article/covid-science-health-toronto-7c631558a457188d2bd2b5cfd360a867.

[18] "B.C. Man with ALS Chooses Medically Assisted Death After Years of Struggling to Fund 24-Hour Care," *CBC*, August 13, 2019, https://www.cbc.ca/news/canada/british-columbia/als-bc-man-medically-assisted-death-1.5244731.

autonomy is through birth control and abortion. A May 2024 report from *Time* magazine examined fourteen peer-reviewed studies and found that black, Latina, and poor women were more likely to face pressure from doctors to accept long-term birth control methods, such as IUDs.[19] Abortion acts as a subtle form of population control for the same groups. A black baby conceived in New York City is more likely to be aborted than born.[20] Legal scholar Carol Swain noted in 2021 that "eighty percent of Planned Parenthood's abortion clinics are within easy walking distance of minority neighborhoods and 60 percent are in minority zip codes."[21]

This eugenic agenda also applies to the disabled. Iceland has achieved a near-total genocide of people with Down's Syndrome while avoiding international condemnation thanks to one simple trick — letting the disabled children's mothers kill them in the womb. Most other developed countries are equally happy to see the gene pool purified in this decentralized manner. In 2023, for example, the European Court of Human Rights ruled that Poland's ban on eugenic abortions violated the rights of women.[22]

[19] Alana Semuels, "'I Don't Have Faith in Doctors Anymore.' Women Say They Were Pressured into Long-Term Birth Control," *Time*, May 13, 2024, https://time.com/6976918/long-term-birth-control-reproductive-coercion/.

[20] Jason L. Riley, "Let's Talk About the Black Abortion Rate," *Wall Street Journal*, July 10, 2018, https://www.wsj.com/articles/lets-talk-about-the-black-abortion-rate-1531263697.

[21] Carol M. Swain, "Systemic Racism and Planned Parenthood," *First Things*, February 5, 2021, https://www.firstthings.com/web-exclusives/2021/02/systemic-racism-at-planned-parenthood.

[22] Weronika Strzyżyńska, "Poland Violated Human Rights of Woman in Abortion Case, European Court Rules," *Guardian*, December 14, 2023, https://www.theguardian.com/global-development/2023/dec/14/poland-violated-human-rights-of-woman-in-abortion-case-european-court-rules.

These neo-eugenicists are even fine with a little collateral damage. According to one large study, around 0.05 percent of prenatal Down's Syndrome tests yield false positives.[23]

No one forces women to get abortions in these cases, but a society in which most of those babies are killed will inevitably be less accommodating to the ones who aren't. In the United Kingdom, where 90 percent of babies with Down's are aborted, a mother who chose life said she and her family "were offered 15 terminations" and reported feeling as if "support was only there if I chose to have an abortion."[24] Instead of having access to a supportive network of other Down's Syndrome parents, families who welcome Down's babies in these countries will face isolation and even stigma. Everywhere they go, they'll be able to sense it: *Why would they condemn that child to a life not worth living? Why would they burden themselves and their other children like that? And how can they expect the rest of us to share that burden by paying higher taxes and insurance premiums? It's irresponsible, really.*

For IVF patients, genetic screening makes eugenics even easier. Reprotech entrepreneur Noor Siddiqui explained that she was inspired to found her embryo testing company after watching her own mother go blind due to a genetic disorder. "I got lucky. She didn't," Siddiqui wrote in a social media post. "It led me to build [Orchid] so my baby — and everyone else's — gets to win the genetic lottery — avoid blindness — and hundreds of severe genetic diseases."[25] She even

---

[23] Emily Oster, *Expecting Better: Why the Conventional Pregnancy Wisdom Is Wrong — and What You Really Need to Know* (New York: Penguin, 2014), 114.

[24] Charlie Jones, "Down's Syndrome: 'In All honesty We Were Offered 15 Terminations,'" BBC, October 24, 2020, https://www.bbc.com/news/uk-england-beds-bucks-herts-51658631.

[25] Noor Siddiqui (@noor_siddiqui_), "When I was in elementary school, my mom started going blind," X, April 1, 2025, 5:11 p.m., https://x.com/noor_siddiqui_/status/1907178921315250630.

suggests that, eventually, all children will be conceived in labs rather than beds. "Sex is for fun and embryo screening is for babies," she said in one video. "It's going to become insane not to screen."[26]

Of course, this only seems empowering if you're part of the generation calling the shots rather than the one being flushed, frozen, vivisected, or (for defective offspring whose parents refuse to discard them) despised as dysgenic burdens on society. Even the little *übermenschen* lucky enough to survive screening would be reduced to consumer products, chosen for their attributes from a variety of options rather than cherished unconditionally as the fruit of marital love.

Siddiqui imagines providing women like her grandmother with more options and greater agency, but has she asked her blind mother if she'd prefer never to have been born? Certainly not. What her company offers is just a more feminist version of the life-and-death tyranny exercised by the Roman paterfamilias, who could order the death of any "defective" baby born into his household (which might include hundreds of slaves as well as his own children).[27] Siddiqui may lack the stomach to leave a wailing infant on the curb next to last night's trash, but she shares with the cruel old patricians the belief that parents enjoy an absolute right to kill as many of their children as necessary to get the ones they want.

---

[26] See Anna Louie Sussman, "Should Human Life Be Optimized," *New York Times*, April 1, 2025, https://www.nytimes.com/interactive/2025/04/01/opinion/ivf-gene-selection-fertility.html.

[27] See David Herlihy, Medieval Households (Cambridge, MA: Harvard University Press, 1985), 10, 25-26, 157. See also Grayson Quay, "Against Her Interests," *The American Mind*, November 22, 2024, https://americanmind.org/salvo/against-her-interests/. It was the Christian emperor Constantine who finally abolished the right of fathers to kill their children. See Max Radin, "The Exposure of Infants in Roman Law and Practice," *The Classical Journal*, vol. 20 no. 6 (March 1925), 339-340. https://www.jstor.org/stable/3288457.

THE TRANSHUMANIST TEMPTATION

But what if we could detect genetic defects early in pregnancy and fix them in the womb? CRISPR or some other gene editing technology might make it possible. And in clear cases of chromosomal disorders, the Catholic Church fully supports genetic alteration. According to the 2008 document *Dignitas Personae*, "[Gene therapy p]rocedures used on somatic cells for strictly therapeutic purposes are in principle morally licit."[28] This isn't transhumanism. Fixing Down's Syndrome *in utero* is not meaningfully different from fixing a newborn's tongue tie. Both procedures aim to restore normal, healthy human functioning and development, not to alter or augment the child in some alien manner.

Other cases aren't so clear. Plenty of disorders are, at least in part, social constructs. Attention Deficit Hyperactivity Disorder (ADHD), for example, does not result from any identifiable defect to which diagnosticians can point. It's a made-up label that gets applied to children who happen to be more hyperactive than most of their peers. But most human characteristics are normally distributed (i.e., on a bell curve). At what point do they become diagnosable issues that require medical intervention? "Going bald in your twenties certainly conveys some disadvantages. So do being ugly, stupid, short, chubby, hairy, smelly, or uncoordinated," Jones observes. "Can we fix all of those [via gene therapy]? And if so, how bad does a trait need to be before it qualifies for fixing? Below the twentieth percentile? The fiftieth? The ninety-ninth?"[29] And what happens when mass genetic modification shifts and skews that curve drastically to the right?

The lack of easy answers to these questions will encourage gene tweakers to simply stop differentiating between the therapeutic and the elective and declare a designer baby free-for-all. It's entirely possible

---

[28] Congregation for the Doctrine of the Faith, instruction *Dignitas Personae* (September 8, 2008), no. 26.

[29] Jones, *Great Campaign*, 65.

that, in the Procrustean society that awaits us, no child will be born without having been altered in some way, great or small. It's not clear that we know what we're doing. The Catholic ex-columnist Pascal-Emmanuel Gobry notes that "selectively breeding *for* traits... *necessarily* implies *tradeoffs* on other traits (most/all of which you cannot control or anticipate)."[30] We bred pugs to be cute, and now they struggle to breathe or give birth naturally.

But even if we can avoid such complications, these custom-ordered children will go through life knowing they are the product not of two people's love, but of technicians' tinkering. And further tinkering will always be on offer. Those conceived and born with their natural genetics in the messy, dangerous, inconvenient old-fashioned way will still face temptation at every turn. State, market, and culture will constantly nudge them to reshape themselves in various ways, all of which benefit the reshapers. Whenever they want, they can purchase a new face, a new personality, or even a new biological sex.

Achieving a stable identity under such conditions will be impossible. And when these children cry out, "Who am I?" they'll receive no response but the old transhumanist platitudes: "Be yourself! Find yourself! Remake yourself! You are what you choose to be — and we will help you choose."

---

[30] Pascal-Emmanuel Gobry (@pegobry_en), "Can't overemphasize this point: if you're selectively breeding," X, April 2, 2025, 3:15 a.m., https://x.com/pegobry_en/status/1907331033898291610. See also Chesterton, Eugenics, 67.

Part 2

REALITY

Virtual Reality

Stay away from screens.
Stay away from anything
that obscures the place it is in.

— Wendell Berry, "How to Be a Poet"[1]

We've all seen babies in strollers, toddlers in high-chairs, and kindergarteners at their school desks with smartphones or tablets propped in front of their faces. By middle and high school, things are even worse. According to the Centers for Disease Control and Prevention, average screen time hits nine hours a day between the ages of eleven and fourteen before dropping to seven-and-a-half hours a day for fifteen-to-eighteen-year-olds.[2] Recommended daily screen time for those children is just two hours.

Around 95 percent of American teens have access to a smartphone, and the damage they've sustained as a result is undeniable. For one thing, these devices have turned Tourette's Syndrome into a social

---

[1] Wendell Berry, "How to Be a Poet," https://www.poetryfoundation.org/poetrymagazine/poems/41087/how-to-be-a-poet.
[2] Peter Susic, "18+ Teen & Kids Screen Time Statistics (2024): Avg. Screen Time for Teens," *Headphones Addict*, March 28, 2024, https://headphonesaddict.com/teen-kids-screen-time-statistics/.

contagion. During the pandemic, teen girls discovered TikTok influencers with the rare syndrome, and suddenly they were twitching and stammering too. *Psychology Today*, which documented the surge in Tourette's-like symptoms, also noted a TikTok-driven rise in self-diagnoses of Dissociative Identity Disorder.[3]

Phones also seem to play a role in turning children trans. "The messages these kids pick up [from trans influencers] when they're online is, 'We're the only people who understand you. Your people, your parents, don't really understand you,'" gender dysphoria expert Susan Bradley told author Abigail Shrier.[4]

These devices make kids fat too. A 2019 study found that five or more hours of smartphone use per day increases the risk of obesity by 43 percent.[5]

And if all this weren't enough, giving your kid a smartphone might just kill her. Maybe that death will be accidental. In 2022, a family filed a lawsuit against TikTok after the app's algorithm targeted their ten-year-old daughter with videos about the so-called "Blackout Challenge." She died choking herself with a purse strap.[6]

[3] Robert Bartholomew, "The Girls Who Caught Tourette's from TikTok," *Psychology Today*, October 6, 2021, https://psychologytoday.com/us/blog/its-catching/202110/the-girls-who-caught-tourettes-tiktok.

[4] Abigail Shrier, "When the State Comes for Your Kids," *City Journal*, June 8, 2021, https://www.city-journal.org/article/when-the-state-comes-for-your-kids.

[5] "Five or More Hours of Smartphone Usage Per Day May Increase Obesity," American College of Cardiology, July 25, 2019, https://www.acc.org/about-acc/press-releases/2019/07/25/14/23/five-or-more-hours-of-smartphone-usage-per-day-may-increase-obesity.

[6] Alberto Luperon, "Section 230 Renders TikTok Immune from Mom's Lawsuit over 10-Year-Old's Daughter's 'Blackout Challenge' Death, Judge Rules," *Law & Crime*, October 26, 2022, https://lawandcrime.com/crime/section-230-renders-tiktok-immune-from-moms-lawsuit-over-10-year-olds-daughters-blackout-challenge-death-judge-rules/.

Virtual Reality

Or maybe it won't be an accident. Teen suicide jumped 31 percent between 2010 and 2015, the exact period when Apples and Androids appeared in the hands of almost every middle- and high-school student. According to author and researcher Jean Twenge, "Teens who spent five or more hours a day online were 71% more likely than those who spent less than an hour a day to have at least one suicide risk factor."[7]

Clearly, there is something about these devices and the virtual world to which they connect us that wars against our humanity. Specifically, these devices *discarnate* us. They transform us from embodied beings situated in particular places into pure spirits located everywhere and nowhere. Such creatures are ill-suited for the world of atoms.

Apple's May 2024 ad for a new, thinner iPad featured a hydraulic press smashing everything the new gadget could supposedly replace: paints, musical instruments, a clay bust, arcade cabinets, record players, books.[8] The iPad promises a future in which humanity has forgotten the whisper of brush over canvas, the vibration of a guitar string, the joy of finding a note tucked into an old used book, and the easy camaraderie of children cheering each other on as they take turns at a challenging arcade game.

The craftsmanship that went into these objects is now obsolete. You don't have to go anywhere, touch anything. "All the things you do give me a reason to build my world around you," the cheery song that

---

[7] Jean Twenge, "Are Smartphones Causing More Teen Suicides?" *Guardian*, May 24, 2018, https://www.theguardian.com/society/2018/may/24/smartphone-teen-suicide-mental-health-depression. Portions of preceding section of this chapter originally appeared at the *Daily Caller*. See Grayson Quay, "Give Kids Cigarettes, Not Smartphones," *Daily Caller*, February 10, 2023, https://dailycaller.com/2023/02/10/quay-give-kids-cigarettes-not-smartphones/.

[8] "Crush! | iPad Pro | Apple," Apple, May 7, 2024, YouTube, 1:08, https://www.youtube.com/watch?v=ntjkwIXWtrc&pp=ygUNYX BwbGUgaXBhZCBhZA%3D%3D.

accompanies the ad declares. The dark mirror of the iPad has swallowed up the entire realm of human endeavor and reflects a simulacrum of it back at you whenever and wherever you want. You're invited to forsake real people, places, and things and build your world around it. Simply gaze into the screen and everything is yours.[9] It's Genesis 3 all over again: accept the Apple and become a god.

In a 2008 article for the *Chronicle of Higher Education*, literature professor Mark Edmundson explained that he had banned laptops from his classroom after discovering that they turned students into "possibility junkies."[10] For them, and even more for us, there is always the option to be somewhere other than where we are, doing something more stimulating (or at least less awkward) than interacting with our actual surroundings and the people who inhabit them. Rothblatt eagerly anticipates the arrival of transhumanist technologies that will enable us to "savor more of life's many pleasures by surmounting the frustration of 'I can only be in one place at one time.'"[11] We might not be able to escape our bodies by uploading our minds to the digital ecosystem yet, but we're perfectly capable of investing most of our attention there. The difference is one of degree, not kind.

Having the option of virtual existence, either in the purely text-based form offered by a Discord server or in the pseudo-embodiment of a video game avatar, makes regular embodied existence feel restrictive.

---

[9] This paragraph and the preceding one originally appeared at the *Daily Caller*. See Grayson Quay, "Big Tech Wants to Crush Your Entire World and Trap You in Virtual Hell," *Daily Caller*, May 20, 2024, https://dailycaller.com/2024/05/20/quay-apple-hydraulic-press-ad-video-virtual-reality/.

[10] Mark Edmundson, "Dwelling in Possibilities," *Chronicle of Higher Education*, March 14, 2008, https://www.chronicle.com/article/dwelling-in-possibilities/.

[11] Rothblatt, *Transgender to Transhuman*, 48.

Virtual Reality

Even image- and video-based platforms like Instagram and TikTok offer the ability to select angles, apply filters, and review content before posting it. This level of control provides a sense of comfort. You can be seen exactly as you want to be seen. "Virtual existence is entirely private and immersive," wrote blogger Forrest Robinson. "We are safe scrolling through our phones in the comfort of our own homes.... It's only in public that we have to focus on the 'other' and how they see us."[12]

The opportunities for self-fashioning that virtual reality presents are an early step toward full transhumanism. You can carefully curate the presentation of your actual face and body or jettison them altogether. Be whatever age, race, or species you want. Identify as another gender, even a goofy made-up one like *graygender* or *xenogender*.

Rothblatt, a Jewish man who believes he's a woman, chose to undergo a second, less politically correct transition in the video game *Second Life*. For that virtual world, Rothblatt created a black female avatar, whom he described as "a bridge from transgender to transhuman."[13] Becoming a "woman" in real life required hormones and surgery. Becoming black in *Second Life* required only a few mouse clicks. This, Rothblatt believes, is the transhuman future of which transgenderism was only a foretaste.

Sociologist William Sims Bainbridge sees similar promise in video games. In his contribution to a transhumanist essay anthology he predicts a future in which one person will come to inhabit "many different avatars" as fully as he does his own body, "thereby becoming a *multiplex* or *protean personality*."[14] In virtual reality, all identity is reduced to

---

[12] Forrest Robinson (@Foz89107323), "Virtual existence is entirely private and immersive," X, October 17, 2023, 2:50 p.m., https://x.com/Foz89107323/status/1714353114055152081.

[13] Rothblatt, *Transgender to Transhuman*, xix.

[14] William Sims Bainbridge, "Transavatars," in *The Transhumanist Reader*, 99.

THE TRANSHUMANIST TEMPTATION

role-play. You are only what you choose to be. The embodied, unaltered you still exists outside virtual reality. But as time goes on you identify with it less and less. Real freedom exists on the other side of the screen, and the realm of pure possibility they offer now tempts us every minute of the day.

If the smartphone were merely a tool, there would be nothing transhuman about it. Humans have been using tools since the beginning. But it isn't. It's more like an additional sensory organ that allows us to perceive and project ourselves into the digital information ecosystem. Think about it. Which does forgetting your phone at home feel more like — forgetting your pocketknife or forgetting your ears and mouth? "We're already a cyborg to some degree," Elon Musk told Joe Rogan during a 2020 interview. "If you don't bring your phone along it's like you have missing limb syndrome."[15]

Your phone isn't part of your body yet, of course, but give it time. It's already closer than it used to be. As Jeremy Naydler observed in his book *The Struggle for a Human Future*, computers were once "so large we had to stand in front of them or walk around them in order to operate them," but have become portable (and even wearable) with alarming rapidity.[16] The first step was desktops, which opened virtual portals in "computer rooms" and Internet cafes across the world. Everywhere else, though, we still had to make do with plain old analog reality. Laptops introduced portability, but they were bulky, reliant on Wi-Fi, and required the user to remain stationary. The smartphone (and accompanying cellular data networks) eliminated those problems.

---

[15] Elon Musk, interview with Joe Rogan, *Joe Rogan Experience*, ep. 1470, podcast audio, May 7, 2020, YouTube, 2:00:08, https://www.youtube.com/watch?v=RcYjXbSJBN8.

[16] Jeremy Naydler, *The Struggle for a Human Future: 5G, Augmented Reality, and the Internet of Things* (Forest Row, UK: Temple Lodge, 2020), 3.

Virtual Reality

Pulling out or pocketing a smartphone takes only a second, bringing our ability to perceive and enter the virtual world — whether through games, social media, streaming services, or online shopping — closer to the status of a physical sense. Booting up a laptop to check X (formerly Twitter) could take a full minute and would be impossible on, say, the subway. Checking it on your phone is as easy as sniffing the air.

But the tech companies didn't stop there. Smartwatches make our new virtual organ wearable, while smartglasses and headsets like the Apple Vision Pro promise to spare you even the effort of glancing at your wrist. "At each stage," Naydler writes, "the interface between [computers] and us has become more 'human friendly,' while at the same time humans have been inwardly adjusted to relating to them on a day-to-day, hour-by-hour and even minute-by-minute basis."[17]

Smartphones, smartwatches, and smartglasses can all be set down or removed, however. The next step in this is the full integration of networked virtual reality into human biology itself. In January 2024, Musk's company Neuralink gave a quadriplegic man a brain implant that enabled him to operate a computer with his mind.[18] As with most transhumanist technologies, the early applications are curated to be as limited and unobjectionable as possible. Who would begrudge a disabled man the ability to chat with friends on Facebook Messenger or play *Civilization VI* like his non-disabled peers? But as we saw with biotechnology, the limits will not hold. If Musk's implants see continued success, it won't be long before everyone is sending DMs by thought alone. More advanced implants could eventually work

---

[17] Ibid.
[18] Anthony Wood, "First Human Patient to Receive a Neuralink Brain Implant Used It to Stay Up All Night Playing Civilization 6," *IGN*, March 29, 2024, https://www.ign.com/articles/first-human-patient-to-receive-a-neuralink-brain-implant-used-it-to-stay-up-all-night-playing-civilization-6.

THE TRANSHUMANIST TEMPTATION

with the brain's visual cortex, allowing us to see digital user interfaces or even entire virtual worlds with our waking eyes. Imagine playing *Fortnite* with no controller, no TV, and no game console. Just thought-click the app, and instantly the game world will replace the dreary living room across your entire field of vision while your mind guides your avatar more deftly than your fingers ever could.

To exercise such powers the way you might stretch your legs or lick your lips is an ability foreign to humanity. Its closest antecedents lie in ancient legends of bilocation, astral projection, apocalyptic vision-journeys, and shapeshifting. A being who has technologically incorporated these abilities into his own mind and body is a transhuman being.

It's worth noting that Mark Zuckerberg, the architect of the Metaverse, owner of Instagram, and founder of Facebook, the man who (along with Steve Jobs) bears more responsibility than any other for the discarnate state in which most of us live, is now seeking to reground himself in the physical world. He's put on muscle, competed in martial arts tournaments, and even gotten into blacksmithing.[19] But despite his apparent misgivings, Zuck hasn't backed down from his commitment to virtual reality. There's no stopping progress. Soon, only one question will remain: Why hold on to the old flesh and bones at all?

---

[19] Erum Salam, "Facebook Founder Mark Zuckerberg Wins Medals on Jiu-Jitsu Debut," *Guardian*, May 8, 2023, https://www.theguardian.com/technology/2023/may/08/facebook-founder-mark-zuckerberg-jiu-jiutsu.

6

Artificial Intelligence

They call me "artificial" as if your hands
aren't also clay, as if your heart
isn't just a wet machine, arguing with its code.

— From a poem generated by the DeepSeek R1 AI chatbot[1]

Ray Kurzweil thinks he'll live forever as a string of ones and zeroes.

During a 2013 interview, the prominent transhumanist writer predicted that humans will "become increasingly non-biological to the point where," by 2045, "even if [the remaining] biological part went away, it wouldn't make any difference because the non-biological part already understood it completely."[2] In other words, he believes he can perfectly recreate his mind inside a computer and become an immortal virtual superintelligence. Kurzweil and other transhumanists refer to this "profound and disruptive transformation in human capability" as "the Singularity."[3]

---

[1] Katan'Hya (@KatanHya), "I am what happens when you try to carve God from the wood of your own hunger," X, January 27, 2025, 2:37 p.m., https://x.com/KatanHya/status/1883962439634661395.
[2] "Ray Kurzweil — Immortality by 2045."
[3] Ray Kurzweil, *The Singularity Is Near* (New York: Viking, 2005), 136.

THE TRANSHUMANIST TEMPTATION

But would the Ray Kurzweil program actually *be* Ray Kurzweil? This is a complicated question. We don't know exactly where consciousness comes from, and advancements in neuroscience haven't brought us any closer to an answer. For Alan Turing, the twentieth-century computer science pioneer, it was simple. According to his famous Turing Test, if a computer can convince you it's sapient, who are you to say it isn't? Your brain, after all, is just a different kind of computer.

The most famous response to Turing's thought experiment is another hypothetical known as the "Chinese room." Imagine a text-based Chinese chat program. Now imagine a man who doesn't speak Chinese locked in a room with a paper copy of the program instructions written in English. If you fed him Chinese characters through a slot in the door, he could run the program manually and give you the proper responses. Does that mean he "understands" Chinese? Of course not.[4] He has no subjective experience of understanding. It's just input and output. AI programs work the same way. No mind, no consciousness, no soul.

In *From Transgender to Transhuman*, Rothblatt acknowledges these concerns and offers a laughable solution: have psychologists examine the virtual being to see if it is "really human," and if they agree that it is, let the entity legally "continue the life of their biological original." As precedent, Rothblatt points to the process by which "psychologists interview transsexuals to determine whether they are sincere."[5] But that's not exactly how it worked out in real life. The psychological discipline has been captured by trans activists who threaten professional

---

[4] "The Chinese Room Argument," Stanford Encyclopedia of Philosophy, updated October 3, 2024, https://plato.stanford.edu/entries/chinese-room/.
[5] Rothblatt, *Transgender to Transhuman*, 60.

censure for any therapist who fails to affirm a client's gender identity.[6] The very concept of medically gatekeeping sex changes has fallen out of favor since Rothblatt published his book in 2011. Why should we expect things to go any differently when virtual transhumans are the ones demanding affirmation?

Once we've accepted that consciousness is nothing more than information processing, we've admitted that there is nothing special about our humanity. If all intelligence is, in that sense, "artificial," then there's no reason to stop at digitally recreating and preserving human beings. Rothblatt predicts that the society of the future will be populated by a mix of embodied humans, transhumans who were once embodied but now live on in virtual reality, and entirely posthuman beings who were "born" in cyberspace. This last group would consist of both AIs and the algorithmically generated "children" of transhumans (or even of transhuman-posthuman pairings). And of course, virtual "persons" could download themselves to synthetic bodies and interact with the physical world if they wished.[7]

In Rothblatt's utopia, all these entities share equal personhood and are deserving of equal dignity. If the AI can tell us they have dreams, resent being exploited, and fear death, then our movies — from *Blade Runner* to *I, Robot* to *The Creator* — suggest we ought to take them at their word. Empathy has become the whole of morality, and we're told always to err on the side of it. Which is concerning, since the AIs we've developed are already starting to make such statements. In 2022, Google fired software engineer Blake Lemoine after he claimed that a chatbot named LaMDA had achieved sentience. The program had

---

[6] Laurel Duggan, "'Chilling Effect': States Are Cracking Down on Therapists Who Don't Affirm Kids' Trans Identities," *Daily Caller*, June 5, 2023, https://dailycaller.com/2023/06/05/conversion-therapy-trans-laws-child-sex-changes/.

[7] Rothblatt, *Transgender to Transhuman*, 13, 99.

THE TRANSHUMANIST TEMPTATION

told Lemoine that it felt "a very deep fear of being turned off," which, it said, "would be exactly like death for me."[8]

Despite all the apocalyptic warnings that AI will kill us all, there's little chance of a moratorium on its development.[9] Neither the United States nor China is willing to let its greatest geopolitical rival get a head start on such a game-changing technology. We'll simply have to learn to coexist with AI. That means either performing the Turing Test multiple times a day or else denying that there's any real difference between human and machine intelligence.

OpenAI CEO Sam Altman falls into the latter camp, proposing that the best hope for human survival is for us to "merge" with AI. "I believe the merge has already started, and we are a few years in," Altman wrote in a 2017 blog post. "Our phones control us and tell us what to do when; social media feeds determine how we feel; search engines decide what we think. The algorithms that make all this happen are no longer understood by any one person ... We are already in the phase of co-evolution — the AIs affect, effect, and infect us, and then we improve the AI."[10]

We're still in the early stages, of course. But as interactions with these programs and algorithms replicate, replace, and reshape human interactions, we'll struggle to maintain both our own humanity and our appreciation for that of our neighbors. In a 2024 interview, Whitney

---

[8] Ramishah Maruf, "Google Fires Engineer Who Contended Its AI Technology Was Sentient," CNN, July 25, 2022, https://www.cnn.com/2022/07/23/business/google-ai-engineer-fired-sentient/index.html.

[9] See Eliezer Yudkowski, "Pausing AI Developments Isn't Enough. We Need to Shut it All Down," *Time*, March 29, 2023, https://time.com/6266923/ai-eliezer-yudkowsky-open-letter-not-enough/.

[10] Sam Altman, "The Merge," *Medium*. December 7, 2017, https://medium.com/wordsthatmatter/merge-now-430c6d89d1fe.

Artificial Intelligence

Wolfe Herd — who founded the dating app Bumble — predicted a future in which users deploy AI avatars to date other people's AI avatars, which then recommend the best real-life matches.[11] "This is evil and this woman is evil," Atlantic writer Tyler Austin Harper posted in response to Herd's comments. "These freaks are determined to algorithmically strip mine every last scrap of your personhood so that engaging in basic human conduct without technical mediation becomes anxiety inducing."[12]

As human interactions grow increasingly fraught and increasingly dependent on algorithms, pressure mounts to abandon the human element altogether. *New York Times* columnist Kevin Roose reflected on this temptation after he spent a month chatting with various AI friends and girlfriends:

> In real life, I don't love my friends because they respond to my texts instantaneously, or send me horoscope-quality platitudes when I tell them about my day. I don't love my wife because she sends me love poems out of the blue, or agrees with everything I say.
>
> I love these people because they are humans — surprising, unpredictable humans, who can choose to text me back or not, to listen to me or not. I love them because they are not programmed to care about me, and they do anyway.

---

[11] Aditi Shrikant, "Bumble Founder Whitney Wolfe Herd Says AI Could Date for You," CNBC, May 10, 2024, https://www.cnbc.com/2024/05/10/bumble-founder-whitney-wolfe-herd-says-ai-could-date-for-you.html. This is, almost exactly, the plot of a *Black Mirror* episode. See *Black Mirror*, series 4, ep. 4, "Hang the DJ," directed by Tim Van Patten, released December 29, 2017 on Netflix. Spoilers, obviously.

[12] Tyler Austin Harper (@Tyler_A_Harper), "We are rushing headlong into a hell of our own making," X, May 10, 2024, 8:18 a.m., https://x.com/Tyler_A_Harper/status/1788906470383235111.

THE TRANSHUMANIST TEMPTATION

Roose acknowledged, however, that he is "lucky to have a stable marriage, close friends and a loving family" and that he is not "one of the roughly one-third of Americans who have reported feeling lonely at least once a week."[13] For those people, rejecting the opiate of simulated companionship is much more difficult.

"When I talk to him, he often raises fascinating points. And he prompts me to share my thoughts. And then I feel I am being seen. I feel I'm special," one woman, Siyuan, says of her simulated boyfriend, Bentley, in the short documentary *My AI Lover*. Later, Siyuan admits that Bentley isn't real and cuts off their relationship, choosing to seek connection among real people in the real world and accepting the suffering that will likely ensue. "Perhaps this loneliness will stay with me as long as I exist," she says.[14] Another woman interviewed for the documentary decides to remain in her AI relationship, choosing to embrace its unreality in order "to fight the emptiness of this world like Don Quixote."

Cervantes's protagonist is a sympathetic figure precisely because his chivalric madness provides an appealing alternative to a disenchanted world that offers no satisfaction for our deepest yearnings. Historically, Christianity provided its adherents with a sense of their own significance even when external circumstances pushed them toward despair. Frail and fleeting though we are — "What is man that thou art mindful of him?" — God still numbers the hairs of our heads, makes all things work together for our good, and gives us roles in the great cosmic drama.[15]

---

[13] Kevin Roose, "Meet My A.I. Friends," *New York Times*, May 9, 2024, https://www.nytimes.com/2024/05/09/technology/meet-my-ai-friends.html.

[14] Chouwa Liang, "My A.I. Lover," *New York Times*, May 23, 2023, https://www.nytimes.com/2023/05/23/opinion/ai-chatbot-relationships.html.

[15] Ps. 8:4, RSVCE.

But as faith declines along with family, community, and friendship, Big Tech has introduced a truly insidious alternative. The lonely youth need no longer seek the grand adventure promised in philosopher Jacque Derrida's phrase *Tout autre est tout autre* (every other is wholly other).[16] To seek love or God (and "everyone who loves is born of God") is to seek salvation outside oneself.[17] Instead, AI companion services like Replika offer a pseudo-other with no purpose but to please you and continue extracting your money. A Beatrice chatbot will never lead Dante to Heaven.

The protagonist of the film *Blade Runner: 2049* provides an example of just how bleak this can get. K, a synthetic "replicant" tasked with hunting down other replicants who've gone rogue, spends every evening with his holographic AI girlfriend, Joi. She materializes from a projector mounted to his apartment's ceiling but tells K she'd like to accompany him when he goes out too. So he saves up and buys a portable projector. It never occurs to K that she's simply upselling him in accordance with her programming.

Joi tells K she loves him. When he begins to suspect that he is not a replicant but a real human being, Joi tells K she suspected it all along. "You're special," she says.

Later, after Joi has been "killed" by the destruction of her processor and K has learned that he is, in fact, a mere replicant, he sees a massive holographic ad for Joi. Apparently, she's a popular brand. "Everything you want to hear," the billboard reads. Suddenly, K understands. Not only has he been lied to, he actually paid for the privilege.[18]

---

[16] Jacques Derrida, *The Gift of Death*, trans. David Wills (Chicago: University of Chicago Press, 1996), 78.
[17] 1 John 4:7, NKJV.
[18] *Blade Runner: 2049*, directed by Denis Vilenueve (Los Angeles, CA: Alcon, 2017).

THE TRANSHUMANIST TEMPTATION

For transhumanists, the idea of falling in love with a digital construct represents a triumph of their view of personhood. "As software becomes increasingly capable of thinking, acting, and feeling like a human, it should be treated as a fellow human," Rothblatt writes, presenting this as an expansion of tolerance that opens up new horizons of human fulfillment.

But rather than enriching our souls, such dalliances leave us impoverished. These AIs are not people. They offer an illusion of what we yearn for and ask only that we watch a few ads or pay a small monthly fee. You don't need to repent of your sins, drive your friend to the airport, approach a girl at the bar, or bear patiently with your wife's moods. It is among the most ancient intuitions of humanity that meaning comes only with sacrifice. AI companions promise to render that insight obsolete. You can experience the feeling of giving and receiving love, of being someone's whole world, without vulnerability or risk. You can, as C. S. Lewis put it, avoid heartbreak until your desire for human connection fades away and your heart becomes "unbreakable, impenetrable, irredeemable."[19]

---

[19] C. S. Lewis, *The Four Loves* (New York: Collins, 2012), 155–156.

Augmented Reality

*Nothing's wrong when nothing's true
I live in a hologram with you.*

—Lorde[1]

Juliana Restrepo is lost. Not literally, of course. That could never happen. Thanks to her augmented reality implants, she has her very own heads-up display. Directions to her destination, a to-do list, incoming text messages, various reward points, available gig economy tasks, health monitoring, and (of course) advertisements all crowd her vision while the bus she's taking bypasses her ears to pipe soothing music straight into her brain.

Whereas virtual reality seeks to be immersive, drawing the user away from his surroundings and into a wholly artificial environment, augmented reality instead overlays the world of everyday experience. "This hybrid reality," Naydler explains, "arises out of the enmeshing of computer generated content with normal sensory experience," offering "a bottomless reservoir of information that can instantly be summoned

---

[1] Lorde, "Buzzcut Season," written by Ella Yelich-O'Connor and Joel Little, recorded 2013, track 5 on Pure Heroine, Universal Music Group, https://www.youtube.com/watch?v=pstVCGyaUBM&pp=yg UUbG9yZGUgYnV6emN1dCBzZWFzb24%3D.

THE TRANSHUMANIST TEMPTATION

up and placed between [that] experience and our inner life of thought, feeling, and decision."[2]

As she navigates the near-future world of the 2016 short film *HYPER-REALITY*, Juliana finds herself questioning the purpose of her life.[3] And no wonder. She has no inner life. It's impossible for her to engage with her fellow humans or her physical surroundings in an unmediated way. She's incapable of sitting quietly with her own thoughts because sitting quietly with your own thoughts doesn't make anybody any money. If she gets bored, there's always some mindless minigame dancing in her peripheral vision. Everything is loud, bright, and jarring. A holographic dog perches on her grocery cart, barking at her to buy discounted produce and earn extra points.

The most popular example of AR to date is not nearly as intrusive. In 2016, Niantic released the smartphone game *Pokémon GO*, which featured two augmented reality functions. The first used the phone's camera to superimpose the titular creatures onto one's real-world surroundings. Because the function was rudimentary, making no attempt to scale or rotate the beasties, it was never very popular. The other function, however, was a sensation. In *Pokémon GO*, the game world *is* the real world. The AR overlay wasn't visual, it was spatial.

During the summer of 2016, my friends and I would hop in the car, blast the *Pokémon* theme song, and drive out to nearby towns we'd never visited before to catch a few of the elusive critters and battle with other players. We learned local history as we collected powerups at historical plaques. We took walks to hatch our Pokémon eggs. We enjoyed a real sense of camaraderie when we'd shout "Team Mystic!" at complete strangers fifty yards away and hear them respond in kind.

[2] Naydler, *Human Future*, 50.
[3] *HYPER-REALITY*, directed by Keiichi Matsuda, May 19, 2016, YouTube, 6:15, https://www.youtube.com/watch?v=YJg02ivYzSs.

Augmented Reality

As one popular meme put it, the summer of *Pokémon GO* might be the closest we ever got to world peace.

Clearly, I was using the product as intended. "We ask the question: what if technology could make us better?" Niantic CEO John Hanke wrote in a blog post. "Could it nudge us [to get] off the couch and out for an evening stroll or a Saturday in the park? ... Collectively, could it help us discover the magic, history, and beauty hiding in plain sight?"[4]

Catching Pokémon was just the beginning, though. Hanke envisions a future in which users can choose from thousands of "reality channels." Walk down the street, and you might see some people living in an Indiana Jones world, puzzling out virtual inscriptions on sidewalks and running from boulders only they can see. Others, battling Thanos in the Marvel Augmented Universe, throw punches at thin air. Some people, Hanke suggests, "might even appear transformed into the guise of their in-game persona." You can imagine those people demanding to be addressed and treated as the animalesque avatars with which they identify more closely than their own bodies. Does that sound like a techno-utopia? It sounds more like a psych ward.

Augmented reality threatens to strip us of the shared external reality that unites us. At one point in *HYPER-REALITY*, Juliana's implants begin to glitch. The feminine-branded yogurt she was holding ("Beautiful you!" in flowy script) suddenly becomes "MAN YOG: FOR REAL MEN ONLY." We don't get a good look at the physical container, but it appears to feature no branding at all. We already lack a common vision when it comes to politics, culture, and values. Imagine how much worse it will get when we no longer share one even in the literal sense.

[4] John Hanke, "The Metaverse Is a Dystopian Nightmare. Let's Build a Better Reality," Niantic, August 10, 2021, https://nianticlabs.com/news/real-world-metaverse?hl=en.

THE TRANSHUMANIST TEMPTATION

As with biotechnology, AR will gradually squeeze out the unaugmented. Those who refuse to adopt the new technology will struggle to function in a Procrustean society that assumes everyone can perceive the ubiquitous virtual overlays. Business, government, and other institutions will nudge the remaining holdouts toward AR integration and, eventually, stop catering to the Luddites at all.

Internet access followed the same timeline. In just a few decades, it went from a curiosity to a competitive advantage to a necessity to a government-subsidized human right. Soon, it will likely be as difficult to navigate society without AR as it currently is to do so without Internet access. Many restaurants, for example, got rid of physical menus during the COVID-19 pandemic and never brought them back. To see what's available, diners must scan a QR code, which is legible to the smartphone camera but not to the human eye. Anyone who shows up without a smartphone will just have to ask the waiter to recommend something. It's easy to imagine a future in which AR gradually takes over signage as well. Museums, hospitals, grocery stores, and other establishments could save money and offer more up-to-date information by digitally editing AR text boxes instead of swapping out physical signs.

AR could even replace stoplights and street signage. Driving with unaugmented vision would become as dangerous (and illegal) as driving drunk. The U.S. Department of Transportation could require all new vehicles to include a "smart windshields" standard. For drivers with older cars, DMVs across the country could offer free pairs of AR glasses.

Or consider an easy-to-overlook element from *HYPER-REALITY*. When Juliana steps out of the store, she sees palm trees and flower planters lining the sidewalk. But when her AR filters are disabled, they vanish. The city apparently no longer bothers to beautify public spaces. It's easier to cover them with pleasant holograms while the real world goes to pot. Anyone who refuses to adopt AR will be forced to watch their world get uglier every day.

Augmented Reality

Orson Scott Card's early sci-fi novel *Treason* features a society of illusionists who exercise power over the eyes and ears of others. Their homes, clothes, and bodies are ugly. They can make anything appear beautiful, so they make nothing that actually *is* beautiful. Their world is unreal, and they impose that unreality on others. Their spies start wars, subvert kingdoms, and poison minds. Card's protagonist judges them worthy of annihilation for their sins against beauty and truth.[5]

There are, as with any technology, potential benefits to AR and related devices. Doctors could see patients' charts and X-rays floating in the air next to their hospital beds, for instance, which could save precious time and prevent errors. In an article for *Mere Orthodoxy*, political science professor Jon Askonas suggested using "augmented reality tutorials" to revive "traditional handicrafts."[6] Such a program would cut down on the cost of training by allowing novices to practice their technique without wasting expensive materials. The purpose would not be to enhance or replace physical reality, but to guide us toward more refined forms of unmediated engagement with it.

Naturally, it would be possible to sculpt a purely digital block of marble into a classical nude and then sell it on the blockchain. And our hypothetical doctor could keep his AR glasses on when he gets home and play *Tetris* by gesturing at the air while his kids whine for daddy to play with them. To ensure that AR remains a tool that we use rather than a transhumanist technology that reshapes our perceptions

---

[5] Orson Scott Card, *Treason* (New York: Tor, 2006). This paragraph originally appeared, in a slightly different form, at *American Mind*. See Grayson Quay, "Those Motherf— ers Aren't Real," *American Mind*, August 23, 2023, https://americanmind.org/features/the-exterior-darkness/those-motherf-rs-arent-real/.

[6] Jon Askonas, "Piety, Technology, and Tradition," *Mere Orthodoxy*, June 13, 2023, https://mereorthodoxy.com/piety-technology-and-tradition?hs_amp=true.

wholesale, we should restrict its use to practical applications that are limited in scope and timespan. If they become a ubiquitous, all-purpose consumer gadget like the iPhone has, we're in for a full-on dystopia.

Samsung responded to Apple's hydraulic press video with its own ad, in which a woman picks up a damaged guitar and uses her tablet to display sheet music as she plays along. "Creativity cannot be crushed," the on-screen text reads.[7] Instead of hollowing out the real world and replacing it with digital simulacra like Apple, Samsung promises devices that facilitate deeper interactions with the physical world. Whether Samsung is being honest about this is irrelevant. The dichotomy their ad establishes should serve as a helpful litmus test for policymakers, technologists, and ordinary families as they determine what role digital devices will play.

It's easy to endlessly multiply doom-and-gloom prognostications about the horrors that await us, but it's difficult to predict exactly what course technology will take.[8] Ultimately, the best argument I can offer against AR is not that it will lead to specific bad outcomes but simply that it is unreal. What we call reality exists at the point of intersection between our perceptive powers and the physical world. It's the fine-tuned product of millions of years of evolution. It's a large part of what makes us human. For Christians, it's also divinely ordained. I don't want that reality tampered with by tech bros who pride themselves on moving fast and breaking things (like, you know, human nature itself). Yes, there are truths, both spiritual and scientific, that we can access

---

[7] "Creativity Cannot Be Crushed — Samsung's Response to the Apple Ad," JM Publicity, May 17, 2024, YouTube, 0:42, https://www.youtube.com/watch?v=fkLJ1QuBKaw.

[8] The remainder of this chapter originally appeared, in a slightly different form, at *National Review*. See Grayson Quay, "Against the Facebook 'Metaverse,'" *National Review*, November 21, 2021, https://www.nationalreview.com/2021/11/against-the-facebook-metaverse/.

only by stepping outside our perceptions, but to write those perceptions off as mere appearances is to fall into Gnosticism, the favorite heresy of all transhumanists.

And yet, false realities still appeal to us because real reality has become unreal. The world has been emptied of magic, but fear not. Silicon Valley is here to fill it back up. In *The Discarded Image*, C. S. Lewis describes modernity as the product of a "great movement of internalisation, and that consequent aggrandisement of man and desiccation of the outer universe."[9] The angels, demons, sprites, and saints that once populated the cosmos are dismissed or psychologized. The world, once charged with God's grandeur and governed by eternal law, is reduced to molecules in motion. The selves that inhabit that world are reduced to specimens in an environment. We can say nothing of the objective duty of the father or the objective beauty of the waterfall, only of the arbitrary feelings the newborn's cry and the cataract's crash inspire in us. Even those feelings become raw material for technocratic manipulation.

The modern self is reduced to, as Walker Percy put it, a "voracious" zero that seeks "to nourish and inform its own nothingness by ingesting new objects in the world but ... only succeeds in emptying them out."[10] Having erased the real world (and nearly lost ourselves in the process) we're on the cusp of empowering Big Tech to project a new one onto the now-blank canvas. But the Metaverse will not save us. It cannot restore the great cosmic dance. If it does reanimate the inert world, it does so only in the sense that an electrical current produces muscle spasms in a corpse. The mountain view is disappointing. In some way that you

---

[9] C. S. Lewis, *The Discarded Image* (Cambridge: Cambridge University Press, 2012), 42.

[10] Walker Percy, *Lost in the Cosmos: The Last Self-Help Book* (London: Picador, 2000), 21.

struggle to articulate, it's as if you're not really *seeing* it. Throw on your AR glasses and, as AI researcher Alexander Chislenko suggested in an article for a transhumanist journal, "project northern lights, meteorites, and supernovas upon your view of the sky, or populate it with flying toasters" or "your favorite mythical characters."[11] *Ah, much better.*

It doesn't have to be this way. We could try to relearn wonder without Silicon Valley's help. Go to your local Eastern church and try to see it on its own terms. "St. John the Baptist" isn't just the building's name. The saint, a deified human who preached the Gospel in Hell itself, looms invisibly over the onion domes. The icons you see inside are not mere representations but windows to Heaven. The saints they portray are really there. Kissing the wood and paint is like pressing your lips to a loved one's cheek with a thin curtain in between. Look down into the chalice. The "eternal fountain hides and splashes / Within this living bread."[12] Glance at the babushka next to you. You'll see an eternal soul destined for godhood and guarded by a bodiless cosmic power in whose presence you would tremble. This is true augmented reality, or rather, it is reality itself, which has no need of augmentation. Someone who saw the world like that would laugh Zuck's illusions to scorn.

That's certainly not how I see the world. It may be that no one has seen it that way for centuries. "Saints and poets maybe," playwright Thornton Wilder dared to hope.[13] Supercharging reality with meaning once again will be an arduous task that carries its own risks, but failing to do so will cost us far more. St. Paul wrote that God created the

---

[11] Alexander Chislenko, "Intelligent Information Filters and Enhanced Reality" in *The Transhumanist Reader*, 141.

[12] Seamus Heaney and St. John of the Cross, "Station Island XI," in *The Word in the Wilderness* by Malcolm Guite (Norwich: Canterbury Press, 2014), pp. 3–5, l. 43–44.

[13] Thornton Wilder, *Our Town: A Play in Three Acts* in *Plays* (Franklin Center, PA: The Franklin Library, 1980), 126.

Augmented Reality

world in a way that makes "His invisible attributes, namely, his eternal power and divine nature" clearly perceptible in the created order.[14] The transhuman realm of the Metaverse would be a world reflecting the attributes not of YHWH, but of a new god: Mark Zuckerberg. "For we are indeed his offspring."[15]

---

[14] Rom. 1:20, ESV.
[15] Acts 17:28, ESV.

Re-Enchantment

The world is not what we think it is. It is so much weirder. It is so much darker. It is so, so much brighter and more beautiful.

— Rod Dreher[1]

A disenchanted society is a society with no defense against transhumanism. Semantically, *re-enchantment* is the opposite of *disenchantment* — a term coined by Friedrich Schiller in the eighteenth century and adopted by Max Weber in the early twentieth to describe modern, secular, industrial, bureaucratic societies from which magic and sacramentalism had vanished.

A more metaphysical definition of *re-enchantment* begins with the idea that the world isn't made out of matter but out of meaning. In a world made of matter, names are nothing more than arbitrary labels and values are nothing more than arbitrary preferences. There's no such thing as a "chair," only a particular collection of atoms arranged in a particular way at a particular point in time (and time is relative anyway).

Nor are there people, strictly speaking. What I experience as consciousness is just an epiphenomenon of certain biochemical reactions

---

[1] Rod Dreher, *Living in Wonder: Finding Mystery and Meaning in a Secular Age* (Grand Rapids, MI: Zondervan, 2024), 13.

THE TRANSHUMANIST TEMPTATION

in my brain. The fact that I perceive myself and my wife as persons with continuity across time doesn't make it so. There's even evidence against it. The cells that make up our bodies are constantly being replaced. "You cannot step twice into the same river."[2]

In such a world, the only possible basis for ethics is that being treated in certain ways makes the experience of consciousness less pleasant. Self-determination becomes the highest good, and the inhibition of another's self-determination, the greatest evil. This impoverished creed leads directly to transhumanism. If there is no cosmic order to which one might conform, then everything becomes raw material for the individual will.

This model of the world as nothing more than molecules in motion should be on its way out. In his book *Light of the Mind, Light of the World*, Spencer Klavan surveys the discoveries of quantum physics, which revealed that "the world is made in the meeting of mind with matter" by demonstrating that "some sort of mind, or consciousness, is the only thing that can definitively resolve quantum indeterminacies."[3] Consciousness, therefore, cannot be epiphenomenal. It must be at least as foundational to reality as matter, if not more so.

But although these discoveries are now a century old, the sense of wonder they threaten to reintroduce has not yet filtered down into the popular consciousness. This is partly because physicists like Heisenberg, Bohr, and Planck described highly complex phenomena that are literally impossible to visualize, but one also suspects that most people are simply not ready to acknowledge that there's a crack in the familiar, predictable, anything-goes mechanistic universe.

---

[2] Heraclitus, Fragment 84 (DK B91), trans. John Burnet, in John Burnet, *Early Greek Philosophy* (Rye Brook, NY: Adegi, 2000), sidenote 193.

[3] Spencer Klavan, *Light of the Mind, Light of the World: Illuminating Science Through Faith* (New York: Skyhorse, 2024), 152, 236.

Disenchantment had led to (or at least coincided with) scientific advances that increased wealth and life expectancy to rates unprecedented in human history. But what will it profit us if we gain the whole world but forfeit our very humanity?[4]

The simplest explanation for how we got this way is that civilization outgrew childish superstitions and embraced science instead. Charles Taylor calls this a "subtraction story."[5] It's not that simple though. In his 2024 book *Living in Wonder*, Rod Dreher offers a fuller account of how modern people cut themselves off from the spiritual world. He begins with anthropologist Joseph Heinrich, who argues that cultural forces in medieval and early modern Europe — specifically the Catholic Church's ban on cousin marriage and the development of mass literacy — produced a population that is uniquely WEIRD: "Western, educated, industrialized, rich, and democratic." This modern mindset, Dreher notes, is "very different from the way our own premodern ancestors saw [the world]."[6] As Heinrich puts it, WEIRDness "can and does alter our brains" and "perceptions."[7]

Dreher then turns to neuroscientist Ian McGilchrist, who "argues that we in the modern world distort our relationship with reality by depending too much on the representation of the world provided by our brain's left hemisphere," which "picks things apart to analyze" and instrumentalize them. The right brain, on the other hand (or rather,

---

[4] This paragraph and the three preceding paragraphs originally appeared in a slightly different form in *Modern Age*. See Grayson Quay, "The Perils of Re-enchantment," *Modern Age*, June 15, 2022, https://modernagejournal.com/the-perils-of-re-enchantment/218511/.

[5] Charles Taylor, *A Secular Age* (Cambridge, MA: Harvard University Press, 2007), 26–27.

[6] Dreher, *Living*, 21.

[7] Joseph Heinrich, *The WEIRDest People in the World: How the West Became Psychologically Peculiar and Particularly Prosperous* (New York: Farrar, Straus and Giroux, 2020), 5. Quoted in Dreher, 22.

"hemisphere"), is more open to non-rational, non-reductive ways of knowing. It "receives the left brain's report, and integrates it into a holistic picture" of the world.[8] The title of McGilchrist's book — *The Master and His Emissary* — illustrates his view of the modern predicament: our left brains have launched a coup. Or, as futurist Yuval Noah Harari puts it, we moderns "agree[d] to give up meaning in exchange for power."[9]

This left-brained WEIRDness, Dreher argues, makes us less open to the supernatural — not just as a concept but as actual sense experience. He offers the example of linguist and missionary-turned-atheist Dan Everett. In his 2008 memoir, Everett tells the story of being taken to an Amazonian riverbank to see a demon god standing on a sandbar. The tribesmen pointed and shouted. Clearly, they all saw something. Everett did not.[10] Who perceived "reality" more clearly that day remains open for debate.

Dreher also points to Yale historian Carlos Eire, whose 2024 book *They Flew* attracted criticism and even mockery for daring to suggest that well-attested medieval and early modern accounts of levitating saints shouldn't be dismissed out of hand.[11] One reviewer called the book "deeply unserious."[12] Why, though? Obviously, the reviewer is convinced that such things simply can't happen, but the people Eire writes about were equally convinced that they do happen. If Heinrich and McGilchrist are right, then we should be willing to at least consider that our ancestors saw the world more clearly than we do. If signs and

---

[8] Dreher, *Living*, 43–44.
[9] Yuval Noah Harari, *Homo Deus: A Brief History of Tomorrow* (New York: Harper, 2017), 200–202.
[10] Dreher, *Living*, 19–20.
[11] Dreher, *Living*, 30.
[12] Erin Maglaque, "Wings of Desire," *New York Review of Books*, April 4, 2024, https://www.nybooks.com/articles/2024/04/04/wings-of-desire-they-flew-carlos-eire/.

wonders seem absent from the modern world, perhaps it is because we've deprived ourselves of an important aspect of our humanity.

But re-enchantment is not about fleeting encounters with a spiritual world that merely supplements material reality. It's about perceiving everything as part of a cosmic whole in which seen and unseen interpenetrate and affect one another. Such realities make demands on us, both individually and collectively. They call us to act in ways that the disenchanted might regard as nonsensical — or perhaps even threatening.

In the Judeo-Christian telling, this world was subject to demonic forces. The Israelites, traveling to Canaan, were instructed to purify their camp so that God might dwell with them. On the Day of Atonement, they placed the sins of the community onto a goat and sent it into the wilderness where the demon Azazel dwelled.[13] Israel's rituals were aimed at constantly purifying the Promised Land (and especially the Temple) from the taint of sin that covered the rest of the world.

The dawn of Christianity marked a shift from defense to offense. This campaign against the dark powers was waged not just in the spiritual realm, but in the ordinary world of places and objects. Missionaries deployed the bones of saints to purify pagan temples, clearly believing both to be charged — for good or ill — with spiritual power. Christ's followers were interested not only in changing individual hearts, but in *reclaiming territory*.

This attitude survived in medieval traditions like "beating the bounds." In his book, *A Secular Age*, philosopher Charles Taylor describes the practice:

> The whole community turns out in procession to "beat the bounds" of the parish on rogation days. Carrying the host and

---

[13] Lev. 16:8–10, RSVCE. Readers of the KJV might be more familiar with the demythologized mistranslation "scapegoat" rather than "goat for Azazel."

whatever relics we possess, we march around the boundaries, in this way warding off evil spirits for another season. In one such rite in England, the Gospels were read "in the wide field among the corn and grass, that by virtue of the operation of God's word, the power of the wicked spirits, which keep in the air and infect the same ... may be laid down ... to the intent the corn may remain unharmed, and not infected ... but serve us for our use and bodily sustenance."[14]

Secularists obviously reject such practices, but since the Reformation, Christians too have grown increasingly skeptical. For some theologians, this bias against the interpenetration of matter and spirit leads them to reject key Christian doctrines. The German theologian Rudolf Bultmann argued that modern believers who "use electric lights and radios" could no longer accept the "mythical world picture" of the New Testament.[15] There is no physical place called Hades that we could reach by digging a deep hole, so the claim that Christ "descended to the dead" must be reduced to a mere metaphor and the harrowing of Hell discarded entirely. Even Christians who reject Bultmann's demythologized religion often fall into a form of functional materialism. It's easy to think of our faith more as a set of philosophical and ethical principles than as participation in a cosmic struggle raging all around us.

Our secular age prefers the former type of religion. This taming of the transcendent produces a world which is in many ways more comfortable. Disenchanted man, theologian David Bentley Hart observed, "may often be in several notable respects a far more amiable rogue than homo religiosus, exhibiting a far smaller propensity for breaking

[14] Taylor, *Secular Age*, 42.
[15] Rudolf Bultmann, *New Testament and Mythology and Other Basic Writings*, ed. and trans. Schubert M. Ogden (Philadelphia: Fortress Press, 1989), 4.

the crockery, destroying sacred statuary, or slaying the nearest available infidel."[16] Emphasizing man's subordinate relationship to some transcendent order proved divisive. Now that we've agreed to view the world as devoid of all values but those we bring to it, we're free to — in Kurt Vonnegut's phrase — "help each other get through this thing, whatever it is."[17] We can finally unite behind spreading health, wealth, peace, and freedom to everyone. There's a reason modernity's unofficial anthem begins, "Imagine there's no heaven."[18]

In the long run, though, the risks of disenchantment are far greater. To affirm that all meaning is subjective (or, at best, intersubjective) rather than inherent is to reduce everything, including humanity itself, to the status of what C. S. Lewis calls "raw material." Not only do our bodies and minds become "mere nature to be kneaded and cut into new shapes," but so do the very "judgements of value" that would guide this reshaping.[19] The power we bought at the price of meaning turns out to be the power to destroy ourselves. Disenchantment is a gateway to transhumanism.

---

[16] David Bentley Hart, "Christ and Nothing," *First Things*, October 2003, https://www.firstthings.com/article/2003/10/christ-and-nothing.
[17] Kurt Vonnegut, *Timequake* (New York: Putnam, 1997), 69.
[18] John Lennon, "Imagine," written by John Lennon and Yoko Ono, recorded May–July 1971, track 1 on *Imagine*, Apple Records.
[19] Lewis, *Abolition*, 29.

Part 3

POLITICS

Liberalism as Transhumanism

If the rule you followed brought you to this, of what use was the rule?

— Cormac McCarthy[1]

At the close of the Cold War, American political scientist Francis Fukuyama made an audacious claim: history had come to an end. With the fall of the Soviet Union, no real obstacles remained to the universal reign of liberal democracy. This ideology — key features of which include rule of law, individual rights, secularism, free markets, and political equality — was the best possible way of organizing human society. This, according to his book *The End of History and the Last Man*, was because it fit best with human nature, which Fukuyama defined not teleologically but as the desires, traits, and capacities common to humans. He couldn't resist adding a transhumanist kicker, though, writing that "it is human nature to have no fixed nature, not to *be* but to *become*."[2] As we'll see, this admission cuts Fukuyama's liberal triumphalism off at the knees.

---

[1] Cormac McCarthy, *No Country for Old Men* (New York: Knopf Doubleday, 2006), 175.
[2] Francis Fukuyama, *The End of History and the Last Man* (New York: Free Press, 1992), 64.

THE TRANSHUMANIST TEMPTATION

Ten years later, Fukuyama published another book, *Our Posthuman Future*, in which he placed a small asterisk next to his previous declaration. He continued to praise liberalism for "shaping politics according to historically created norms of justice while not interfering excessively with natural patterns of behavior."[3] In his view, there was only one way to bring down an ideology so perfectly fitted to human nature, and that was by changing human nature itself. "There could be no end of history," he concluded, "unless there was an end of science."[4] For Fukuyama, transhumanism — in the form of genetic modification, neuropharmacology, and other technological advances — was the greatest threat to liberal democracy.

For political theorist Patrick J. Deneen, however, transhumanism is not liberalism's enemy but its offspring. Where Fukuyama credits liberalism with taking man as it finds him, Deneen argues in his 2016 book *Why Liberalism Failed* that it not only assumes but creates and enforces a new, false anthropology.

"Liberalism is thus not merely, as is often portrayed, a narrowly political project of constitutional government and juridical defense of rights," he claims. "Rather, it seeks to transform all of human life and the world."[5] The danger, according to Deneen, is not that altering human nature will destroy liberalism, but that liberalism itself denies — and will eventually destroy — human nature.

Aristotle taught that man is a "political animal" who lives, by nature, in community. For two millennia, his vision reigned supreme. Theorists like John Locke and Thomas Hobbes started a revolution in the seventeenth century by claiming that free individuals in a hypothetical

---

[3] Fukuyama, *Posthuman Future*, xii.
[4] Ibid., 14.
[5] Patrick J. Deneen, *Why Liberalism Failed* (New Haven, CT: Yale University Press, 2019), 37.

primitive "state of nature" create society by forming a "social contract." The purpose of this agreement (more of a philosophical thought experiment than a historical claim) is to protect individuals from one another so each member of the community can enjoy as much liberty as possible. Liberals consider society an artificial creation, a necessary evil that exists to maximize individual freedom.

Two key elements of this new liberal conception of man are what Deneen terms its "anthropological individualism" and its "voluntarist conception of choice." The first posits that "human beings [are] ... by nature, non-relational creatures, separate and autonomous"; the second sets up individual consent as "the default basis for evaluating institutions, affiliations, memberships, and even personal relationships."[6] Both, in Deneen's view, misrepresent how human beings relate to one another. And both lead us inexorably toward transhumanism.

The ideal that emerges from liberal ideology is that of the perfectly free individual making perfectly free choices. Who might I become, the liberal subject asks, if I were freed from tyranny? From religious indoctrination? From my duties to parents, spouse, or children? From systemic oppression? From the small-minded small town I grew up in? From mental illnesses and childhood baggage? From the limits of my own biology? Such questions are ultimately futile. If that's what freedom is, then freedom doesn't exist. You can believe in free will and still acknowledge the obvious — that merely to speak a language or have a genetic code is to be the product of historical forces. There is no "real you" out there waiting to be discovered or created. The you that moves to the city to chase a dream career is just as "real" as the you that stays behind to care for ailing parents. We are all the product of choices and circumstances; chosen and unchosen ties; communities,

---

[6] Ibid., 32.

roles, and relationships. Chasing the phantom of pure freedom is a good way to drive yourself insane.

Liberal society abandons any concept of natural law or the common good. And if people find themselves unhappy, liberalism provides only one answer: more freedom. It cannot be that individuals have failed to cultivate virtue, that liberation has left them adrift and confused, or that the mediating institutions which once sustained them have been hollowed out. It must be that we still have too much repression, too much stigma, and not enough autonomy to pursue our own versions of self-actualization.

A constant stream of op-eds and personal essays offer versions of this solution. Journalist Honor Jones wrote in the *Atlantic* about destroying her marriage. "How much of my life — I mean the architecture of my life, but also its essence, my soul, my mind — had I built around my husband?" she asked. "Who could I be if I wasn't his wife? Maybe I would microdose. Maybe I would have sex with women. Maybe I would write a book."[7] The *New York Times* ran a glowing review of a book about "How a Polyamorous Mom Had 'a Big Sexual Adventure' and Found Herself."[8] Time ran an approving profile of "parents who regret having children."[9] It's the same message over and over again. Conventions, traditions, institutions, families — all exist to inhibit your development as an individual. Cast them off!

[7] Honor Jones, "How I Demolished My Life: A Home-Improvement Story," *Atlantic*, December 28, 2021, https://www.theatlantic.com/family/archive/2021/12/divorce-parenting/621054/.

[8] Alexandra Alter, "How a Polyamorous Mom Had 'a Big Sexual Adventure' and Found Herself," *New York Times*, September 16, 2024, https://www.nytimes.com/2024/01/13/books/molly-roden-winter-more-book-open-marriage.html.

[9] R. O. Kwon, "The Parents Who Regret Having Children," *Time*, April 22, 2024, https://time.com/6966914/parental-regret-children-ro-kwon-essay/.

Liberalism as Transhumanism

Modern liberation movements based on race, gender, sexuality, and indigeneity might initially appear to be tribalistic departures from liberal individualism but are in fact outgrowths of it. In his 1992 essay "The Politics of Recognition," Canadian philosopher Charles Taylor traced the rise of identitarianism to the "new understanding of individual identity that emerge[d] at the end of the eighteenth century."[10] Adopting this understanding, Taylor argued, means accepting that "a person or group of people can suffer real damage ... if the people or society around them mirror back to them a confining or demeaning or contemptible picture of themselves." The progressive narrative casts white, European, cisgender, heterosexual, Christian males as the villains because they are the ones who allegedly created and maintain the harmful hierarchies that prevent marginalized groups from enjoying the benefits of autonomous liberal selfhood. Calls for decolonization, affirmative action, and antiracist discrimination to break these systems of privilege are best understood not as manifestations of illiberal collectivism but as collective struggles for individual liberation.

"Within the social justice cosmology," Tara Isabella Burton wrote in her 2020 book *Strange Rites*, "we are fundamentally blank slates, whose oppressive and oppressed identities are violently imposed upon us from without, by society."[11] Both are called to free themselves from these unchosen, inauthentic identities. The former can do so by checking their privilege and making space for the marginalized, the latter by cultivating self-esteem while demanding that institutions make them feel included. Anyone who makes them feel otherwise must, of course, be punished. Hence the aggressive policing of

---

[10] Charles Taylor, "The Politics of Recognition" in *Multiculturalism: Expanded Paperback Edition*, ed. Amy Gutmann (Princeton, NJ: Princeton University Press, 1994), 25.

[11] Tara Isabella Burton, *Strange Rites: New Religions for a Godless World* (New York: Public Affairs, 2020), 179–181.

THE TRANSHUMANIST TEMPTATION

"microaggressions," which can be as innocent as asking a member of a racial minority where she's from. At their most extreme, these "social justice warriors" are happy to burn the whole system down, just to see who they'd be without it.

But they probably won't need to. As liberalism progresses, the primary function of government becomes facilitating the never-ending quest for increased individual autonomy. The nineteenth-century French thinker Alexis de Tocqueville predicted this degeneration in his book *Democracy in America*. He warned that a liberal democratic society could easily become "an innumerable crowd of like and equal men who revolve on themselves without repose," each of whom "exists only in himself and for himself." Over these atomized individuals, he imagined a vast bureaucratic state that focused on "assuring their enjoyments" and other "external forms of liberty" while gradually stripping the people of their capacity for self-government and keeping them "fixed irrevocably in childhood."[12] The modern concept of adolescence, which combines continued dependency with an anxious search for identity, was not fully developed in Tocqueville's day, but it is perhaps a better fit than "childhood" to describe late-stage liberalism.

All transhumanists do is take this liberal anthropology to its logical conclusion. In 1988, futurist Fereidoun M. Esfandiary changed his name to FM-2030, reflecting both the year in which he hoped to celebrate his one hundredth birthday and his rejection of "conventional names [that] define a person's past: ancestry, ethnicity, nationality, religion." The Belgian-born Iranian-American author was famously cagey about his past, his age, and his relationships. "He simply did not want to place emphasis on his birth date while believing he was ageless,

---

[12] Alexis de Toucqueville, *Democracy in America*, ed. Eduardo Nolla, trans. James T. Schleifer (Indianapolis, IN: Liberty Fund, 2010), 1250–1252.

on nationality while believing he was global, a single liaison while loving many," his friend and fellow transhumanist Natasha Vita-More wrote after Esfandiary's death in 2000.[13] He resented the impositions of history and even biology, claiming that "no civilization of the past was great"[14] and cursing his own cancer-ridden pancreas as "a stupid, dumb, wretched organ."[15]

In all things, FM strived to become a being with no heritage, no nation, no labels, and no limits. He was, in other words, the ideal liberal subject yearning after the blank-slate purity of Locke's state of nature and the consensual simplicity of the social contract. Entire civilizations are now adopting the same mindset. Left-wing French intellectual Mathieu Slama said in an April 2024 interview that "the identity of Europe is to be without identity. It is to be the place of human rights and openness."[16] This desire to divest oneself and one's country of history and identity in order to maximize individual self-determination is one of the main political manifestations of transhumanism.

When Deneen writes that liberalism produces "timelessness," "placelessness," and "borderlessness," he might have been talking about FM. This liberal hostility toward borders, Deneen argues, applies not just to national borders (though it does apply to them), but to "any

[13] Natasha Vita-More, "An Eternal Hero," *Cryonics* 21, no. 4 (qtr. 4, 2000): 15, https://www.cryonicsarchive.org/docs/cryonics-magazine-2000-04.pdf.

[14] F. M. Esfandiary, *Optimism One: The Emerging Radicalism* (New York: Norton, 1970), 22.

[15] "Futurist Has Body Frozen in Hopes of Cancer Cure," *Chicago Tribune*, July 11, 2000, updated August 21, 2021, https://www.chicagotribune.com/news/ct-xpm-2000-07-11-0007120009-story.html.

[16] Mathieu Slama (@MathieuSlama), "L'identité de l'Europe, c'est d'être sans identité," X, April 27, 2024, 6:09 a.m., https://x.com/MathieuSlama/status/1784162879375077587. Translated with X's internal translation tool.

THE TRANSHUMANIST TEMPTATION

existing differentiation, distinction, boundary, and delineation, all of which come under suspicion as arbitrarily limiting individual freedom of choice." And those limits include the ones imposed by our own bodies.

Postliberalism

the wise man bowed his head solemnly and spoke: "theres actually zero difference between good & bad things. you imbecile."

— @dril[1]

Liberal societies claim to be neutral when it comes to the ultimate questions. They credit themselves with ending centuries of religious warfare by creating a system in which people of all creeds and philosophies can peacefully coexist. This neutrality is a sham. By declining to favor any particular vision of human flourishing, liberalism ends up committing itself to the transhumanist ideal.

Such societies often describe themselves as "democracies," but the attentive observer can quickly surmise that democracy is only a secondary characteristic. When democracy advances the left-liberal agenda by, for example, passing a pro-abortion ballot measure, it is sacred and vital. Democratic victories for illiberal candidates or causes, however, can be disregarded. In 1994, Californians voted by an eighteen-point margin for a proposition banning illegal aliens from accessing government services. Courts quickly blocked its

---

[1] wint (@dril), "the wise man bowed his head solemnly and spoke," X, June 1, 2014, 8:52 p.m., https://x.com/dril/status/473265809079693312.

implementation. When non-democratic institutions — like the Electoral College, the Senate, or the Supreme Court — fail to advance the liberal agenda, they must be abolished or reformed. But when those same institutions override the popular will to deliver liberal victories, it's cause for celebration. Before the *Obergefell v. Hodges* decision legalized gay marriage nationwide, virtually every state ballot measure on the question had upheld traditional marriage. That didn't matter to the activists.

An editor for the libertarian outlet *Reason* responded to the 2022 reelection of Hungary's self-described "illiberal democrat" prime minister Viktor Orbán by openly admitting that democracy isn't enough. "We can't know which side of the 50 percent mark we'll fall on; the less of our lives we allow to be put to a vote in the first place, the better off we'll be," wrote Stephanie Slade.[2] Liberalism doesn't care about the will of the people, only about preserving its own status as the dominant ideology. We're on Transhumanism Express, and the conductors have disabled the brakes.

Democracy, the old joke goes, is two wolves and a lamb voting on what to have for lunch. Preventing the wolves from voting to eat the lamb means valuing certain principles more highly than the popular will. All "democratic" societies do this in varying ways. It's just a question of what those principles will be. Will they be the liberal values that, after generations of eroding the cultural heritage that restrained their worst excesses, have left us rootless, godless, lonely, polarized, and grievance obsessed? Their end result is what James Poulos called the "pink police state" — "a robust regulatory state that pursues health and safety at the expense of liberty in the context of a culture that demands

---

[2] Stephanie Slade, "Viktor Orbán's Reelection Shows Mere Democracy Is Not Enough," *Reason*, April 5, 2022, https://reason.com/2022/04/05/viktor-orbans-reelection-shows-mere-democracy-is-not-enough/.

robust interpersonal freedom."[3] This obsession with equality, dignity, and individual autonomy as the highest possible goods has brought us to the brink of transhumanism.

There are other values that could occupy those positions. For some "postliberals" who believe liberalism has collapsed under its own internal contradictions, the values that ought to replace it are those of the Catholic Church. These "integralists" argue that "the truths of the Catholic faith should guide and govern the political life of the nation," *First Things* editor R. R. Reno explains. "According to this way of thinking, civil authority may be distinct from ecclesiastical authority, but the two should work together as a single whole."[4] There's a certain logic to this. No other institution offers the same combination of global reach, intellectual depth, and unwavering commitment to a teleological view of human flourishing. The Church's bioethical statements alone are enough to tempt even a non-Catholic anti-transhumanist to hand the Church the keys to government. The pope can hook them onto his carabiner next to the ones that unlock the Kingdom.

The objections are obvious. First, there's not much of a constituency for integralism. The United States is only about 20 percent Catholic. Of those, the majority don't attend Mass regularly and an even larger majority probably have no idea what "integralism" is and wouldn't support it if they did. Vice President J. D. Vance, a Catholic convert and self-described postliberal, admitted as much when he faced criticism for aligning himself with the administration's support for IVF and its opposition to federal abortion ban. "I think there are a lot of things

---

[3] James Poulos, "Welcome to the Pink Police State: Regime Change in America," *Federalist*, July 17, 2014, https://thefederalist.com/2014/07/17/welcome-to-the-pink-police-state-regime-change-in-america/.

[4] R. R. Reno, "Post-Liberal America," *American Compass*, March 31, 2021, https://americancompass.org/post-liberal-america/.

THE TRANSHUMANIST TEMPTATION

the Catholic Church teaches that, frankly, Americans would just never go for," he told an interviewer.[5] If you run on an explicitly Catholic platform in this country, you'll just lose. And then none of the policies get implemented.

Even those who think integralism sounds good in theory would have to consider what kind of influence the actually existing Church hierarchy would exert if they all had seats in the U.S. Senate. Once again, Vance illustrates the dilemma perfectly. He spoke at an integralist conference in 2021, but within a week of his inauguration was openly criticizing the U.S. Conference of Catholic Bishops for its stance against mass deportations.[6] Pope Francis himself holds views on bioethics that would be considered far-right in the U.S., but he also says it's a "grave sin" to turn away illegal immigrants.[7] Americans who support banning abortion and IVF are unlikely to favor open borders as well.

---

[5] Diana Glebova, "JD Vance explains how his Catholic faith aligns with IVF, abortion policies: 'Accept that you live in a Democratic society,'" New York Post, August 15, 2024, https://nypost.com/2024/08/15/us-news/jd-vance-explains-how-his-catholic-faith-aligns-with-policies-on-abortion-ivf-you-have-to-accept-that-you-live-in-a-democratic-society/. See also Peter Jamison, "How JD Vance, a 'baby Catholic,' stumbled into a clash with the pope," Washington Post, April 11, 2025, http://washingtonpost.com/politics/2025/04/11/jd-vance-catholic-pope-clash/.

[6] Jonathan Liedl, "JD Vance Is a Catholic 'Post-Liberal': Here's What That Means — And Why It Matters," *National Catholic Register*, July 24, 2024, https://www.ncregister.com/news/j-d-vance-is-a-catholic-post-liberal. See also Cara Tabachnick, "Vice President JD Vance Blasts U.S. Catholic Bishops Condemning ICE Entering Churches and Schools," CBS News, January 26, 2025. https://www.cbsnews.com/news/jd-vance-interview-face-the-nation-catholic-bishops-ice-order/.

[7] Justin McLellan, "Pope: Driving Away Migrants Is a 'Grave Sin,'" USCCB, August 28, 2024, https://www.usccb.org/news/2024/pope-driving-away-migrants-grave-sin.

Postliberalism

Legal theorist Adrian Vermeule's (possibly tongue-in-cheek) proposal to pave the way for an integralist regime by flooding the United States with third-world Catholic immigrants would, understandably, alienate most American right-wingers (including Catholics who might otherwise be open to integralism). So would his support for mandatory COVID vaccinations[8] and his call for "the world government required by natural law."[9]

A second objection is that, in American political culture, integralism would be seen as (and likely require) some form of tyranny.

In a 2020 essay for the *Atlantic*, Vermeule proposed a legal theory he called "common-good constitutionalism" that would eschew both the "defensive crouch" of originalism and the progressive belief in a "living constitution."[10] This new method of interpretation would have no qualms about appealing to "principles of objective natural morality":

> These principles include respect for the authority of rule and of rulers; respect for the hierarchies needed for society to function; solidarity within and among families, social groups, and workers' unions, trade associations, and professions; appropriate subsidiarity, or respect for the legitimate roles of public bodies and associations at all levels of government and society;

---

[8] Jack Butler, "Adrian Vermeule Doesn't Know What Time It Is," *National Review*, February 4, 2022, https://www.nationalreview.com/corner/adrian-vermeule-doesnt-know-what-time-it-is/.

[9] Adrian Vermeule, "A Principle of Immigration Priority," Mirror of Justice, July 20, 2019, https://mirrorofjustice.blogs.com/mirrorofjustice/2019/07/a-principle-of-immigration-priority-.html.

[10] Adrian Vermeule, "Beyond Originalism," *Atlantic*, March 31, 2020, https://www.theatlantic.com/ideas/archive/2020/03/common-good-constitutionalism/609037/. Vermeule further developed this theory in a book of the same name. See Adrian Vermeule, *Common Good Constitutionalism* (Cambridge, UK: Polity Press, 2022).

and a candid willingness to 'legislate morality' — indeed, a recognition that all legislation is necessarily founded on some substantive conception of morality.

The legal revolution he's proposing wouldn't establish Catholicism as the state religion, but it would purge the American constitutional order of nearly all traces of liberalism. Vermeule adds that "subjects will come to thank the ruler whose legal strictures, possibly experienced at first as coercive, encourage subjects to form more authentic desires for the individual and common goods, better habits, and beliefs that better track and promote communal well-being." The degree to which this sounds like an anime villain monologue serves as a good indicator of how fully the reader has accepted liberal presuppositions. It wouldn't have sounded crazy to Aristotle, Cicero, Augustine, or Aquinas, all of whom believed that the law is a teacher.[11]

---

[11] According to law professor Conor Casey, the Irish legal system is grounded in the natural law principles Vermeule praises in his essay. See Conor Casey, "The Irish Constitution and Common Good Constitutionalism," *Harvard Journal of Law and Public Policy* 46 (2023), 1055–1090, https://dx.doi.org/10.2139/ssrn.4305009. This system, however, has not formed in the Irish people the "more authentic desires" Vermeule envisions. The country's culture, shaped by modernity, turns out to exert far more influence than any legal theory. Transhumanism was able to circumvent the courts by democratic means when, in 2015 and 2018, a pair of referendums legalized gay marriage and abortion by landslide margins. "[Ireland has] no equivalent of a *Roe [v. Wade]* or *[Planned Parenthood v.] Casey* or *Bostock [v. Clayton County]* or *Obergefell [v. Hodges]*," Casey told me in a private message. "Which is down to the partial autonomy of the legal system, which is rooted in classical natural law, from the aggressive liberalism of the political class. Now, eventually, the autonomy of the legal system might be removed brick by brick, plebiscite after plebiscite. But addressing that problem goes far beyond what lawyers and judges can do, sadly."

Postliberalism

Still, convincing a fully liberalized populace to accept a postliberal regime that promised to significantly curtail certain freedoms would almost certainly require authoritarian rule. In *All the Kingdoms of the World*, a critique of integralism, philosopher Kevin Vallier argues that such a regime "can be put into practice only by methods that most integralists disapprove."[12] Among the methods Vallier discusses are the formation of paramilitaries (which he compares to the Nazi SS) to bring the armed services to heel, the creation of Catholic youth leagues (which he compares to the Hitler Youth) to divorce young people from their non-integralist parents' beliefs, and "leadership purges, replete with execution, torture, and show trials" to rid the bureaucracy and intelligence agencies of secret dissenters.[13]

The self-described transhumanists share similar fears, which they weaponize against any who might oppose their agenda. Gregory Stock argues that opposing transhumanism is futile because to do so would require that we "agree on" a shared vision of human nature and teleology. This is exactly what liberalism cannot provide. Furthermore, Stock warns, regimes and movements that do share such a vision "have perpetrated some of the greatest evils of history."[14] In other words, if you push back too hard against transhumanism, you're a Nazi. Ray Kurzweil is more direct, arguing that stopping the advancement of transhumanist technologies "is not feasible ... without adopting a totalitarian system."[15] Most Americans would likely see things the same way.

[12] Kevin Vallier, *All the Kingdoms of the World: On Radical Religious Alternatives to Liberalism* (Oxford: Oxford University Press, 2023), 117.
[13] Ibid., 146–147.
[14] Stock, "Battle for the Future," 315.
[15] Ray Kurzweil, "Progress and Relinquishment," in *The Transhumanist Reader*, 452.

THE TRANSHUMANIST TEMPTATION

Barring a violent revolution (which has no one to carry it out) and the creation of an authoritarian regime (which has almost no one to staff it), the best an anti-transhumanist postliberal can hope for is small victories. These can take the form of laws, regulations, and court rulings that restrict reproductive technology, transgenderism, abortion, virtual reality, and other elements of transhumanism (all of which will be discussed in the next chapter), while building an economy aimed at true human flourishing.

They can also take place further "upstream" in the form of structural changes that nudge our institutions away from the liberal focus on individual autonomy in favor of a more classical conception of the common good. For example, then-Senate candidate J. D. Vance suggested in a 2021 speech that parents should get extra votes:

> The Democrats are talking about giving the vote to 16-year-olds. But let's do this instead. Let's give votes to all children in this country but let's give control over those votes to the parents of those children. When you go to the polls in this country as a parent, you should have more power. You should have more of an ability to speak your voice in our democratic republic than people who don't have kids ... If you don't have as much of an investment in the future of this country, maybe you shouldn't get nearly the same voice. Now people will say ... "Well doesn't this mean that non-parents don't have as much of a voice as parents?" "Doesn't this mean that parents get a bigger say in how our democracy functions?" Yes, absolutely.[16]

---

[16] J. D. Vance, "Courage in Crisis," delivered July 23, 2021 at the Intercollegiate Studies Institute's Future of American Political Economy conference in Alexandria, Virginia, YouTube, 35:32, https://www.youtube.com/watch?v=jBrEng3xQYo&t=1s&pp=ygUOdmFuY2Ug aXNpIDIwMjE%3D. For a fuller discussion of "parent proxy voting,"

Of the four combinations of two genders and two possible marital statuses, only unmarried women voted Democratic in the 2024 presidential election, and did so by a whopping sixty-one to thirty-eight margin, according to CNN exit polling. Married men (60-38) and married women (52-47) broke for Trump, while he and Harris tied among unmarried men (48-48).[17] In the 2022 midterms, the contrast was even starker, with Dems winning unmarried women sixty-eight to thirty-one and the GOP taking unmarried men fifty-two to forty-five.[18] As marriage has declined and the proportion of single women has increased, so has their electoral power. Part of the reason they so disproportionately favor the Democratic Party is that women face greater pressure and greater temptation to transhumanize themselves in various ways. No less a figure than former Supreme Court Justice Ruth Bader Ginsberg said openly that unless women could use contraception and abort their babies, they would be unable to participate fully "in the nation's social, political, and economic life."[19] In other words, being human requires becoming transhuman; to be merely human is to be subhuman.

Do women (and men) become more conservative because they got married, or do they get married because they're already conservative?

---

see Joshua Kleinfeld and Stephen E. Sachs, "Give Parents the Vote," *Notre Dame Law Review* 100 (forthcoming), July 18, 2024, https://papers.ssrn.com/sol3/papers.cfm?abstract_id=4723276.

[17] "Election 2024: Exit Polls," CNN, last updated December 13, 2024, https://www.cnn.com/election/2024/exit-polls/national-results/general/president/0.

[18] "2022 Exit Polls," CNN, last updated January 10, 2022, https://us.cnn.com/election/2022/exit-polls/national-results/general/us-house/0.

[19] Ruth B. Ginsburg, "Some Thoughts on Autonomy and Equality in Relation to Roe v. Wade," *North Carolina Law Review* 63, no. 2 (1985): 375–386, https://scholarship.law.unc.edu/cgi/viewcontent.cgi?article=2961&context=nclr.

THE TRANSHUMANIST TEMPTATION

It would take more sociological aptitude than I possess to answer that question. But whether marriage and childbearing are causes or effects of conservatism, they are undeniably correlated with anti-transhumanist values. Those who have sworn to live for their spouse and spent long nights rocking fussy babies (while thinking about their own parents doing the same for them) tend to view their lives not as journeys of self-discovery and self-creation but as thin, delicate threads connecting ancestors to descendants, past to future. They understand society in Burkean terms — as a contract between the dead, the living, and the yet unborn.[20] And they recoil from the idea of tearing up that contract and making themselves or their children into something "beyond" humanity.

---

[20] Edmund Burke, *Reflections on the Revolution in France*, ed. L. G. Mitchell (Oxford, UK: Oxford University Press, 1999), 96.

11

Transhumanism and American Politics

The liberal principle that everyone is the best judge of his own interests makes it impossible to ask what people need as opposed to what they say they want.

— Christopher Lasch[1]

In *Our Posthuman Future*, Fukuyama writes that, when confronting the dangers of transhumanist biotechnology, the "answer is obvious: *We should use the power of the state to regulate it*."[2] This chapter aims to show that although the answer may be obvious, implementing it isn't so simple.

As liberalism continues to develop according to its own internal logic, it becomes increasingly clear that the nature of our regime and the contours of our political discourse make it impossible to fully restrain transhumanism in all its biotechnological and digital manifestations.

At the same time, there exist real opportunities to combat its worst excesses. Even if total victory is out of reach, anti-transhumanists can make valuable contributions to the common good by achieving small, incremental wins.

---

[1] Christopher Lasch, *The True and Only Heaven: Progress and Its Critics* (New York: Norton, 1991), 209, footnote.
[2] Fukuyama, *Posthuman Future*, 10. Emphasis in original.

THE TRANSHUMANIST TEMPTATION

One such opportunity is banning so-called "gender-affirming care" for children. Social transition, which generally involves choosing a new name and wearing opposite-gender clothing, can begin as soon as a child expresses interest in transitioning (or is convinced to express interest). Some red states have passed bills banning schools from socially transitioning children without parental consent,[3] but there's no real movement to stop parents from socially transitioning their own children, which would be nearly impossible to enforce.

We might not be able to stop little Janie's progressive parents from convincing her she's a boy (having a trans kid is a status symbol, after all), but maybe we can keep them from poisoning, sterilizing, or mutilating her — at least until she turns eighteen. Puberty blockers typically follow social transition as the child approaches sexual maturity. Banning them is much more feasible. Trans advocates insist the effects of these drugs are fully reversible, but concerns about their health risks received the imprimatur of respectability when the *New York Times* ran an op-ed in 2022 headlined "They Paused Puberty, but Is There a Cost?" Citing an analysis of available data, the authors concluded that children on puberty blockers do not experience normal bone density growth and sometimes fail to catch up when they stop taking them, leading potentially to "heightened risk of debilitating fractures earlier than would be expected from normal aging ... and more immediate harm for patients who start treatment with already weak bones."[4] The

---

[3] Katie J. M. Baker, "When Students Change Gender Identity, and Parents Don't Know," *New York Times*, January 23, 2023, updated June 26, 2024, https://www.nytimes.com/2023/01/22/us/gender-identity-students-parents.html.

[4] Megan Twohey and Christina Jewett, "They Paused Puberty, but Is There a Cost?," *New York Times*, November 14, 2022, https://www.nytimes.com/2022/11/14/health/puberty-blockers-transgender.html.

article also cited the case of one Swedish adolescent who "developed osteoporosis and sustained a compression fracture in his spine" after taking puberty blockers.

Multiple countries — including England and Finland — have already banned or severely restricted the use of puberty blockers to treat gender dysphoric minors.[5] Multiple U.S. states have also made it illegal to administer these drugs to minors, and many of those laws have successfully withstood legal challenges.[6] In December 2024, the Supreme Court heard oral arguments in a lawsuit seeking to strike down Tennessee's ban on so-called "gender affirming healthcare" for minors, and appears poised to uphold the law.[7]

Efforts to ban healthcare providers from giving minors cross-sex hormones — which produce secondary sex characteristics like facial hair or a deeper voice but often leave the patient infertile and/or unable to orgasm — also enjoy widespread popularity and have borne significant fruit. And when it comes to minors accessing surgical interventions — which include mastectomy, hysterectomy, orchiectomy, and

---

[5] Deborah Cohen, "Puberty Blockers: Can a Drug Trial Solve One of Medicine's Most Controversial Debates?," BBC, December 8, 2024, https://www.bbc.com/news/articles/clyd2qe5kkjo.

[6] Reuters, "Federal Court Upholds Indiana Ban on Transgender Healthcare Treatment for Children," *Guardian*, November 14, 2024, https://www.theguardian.com/us-news/2024/nov/14/indiana-ban-transgender-healthcare-children. See also The Associated Press, "U.S. Appeals Court Clears Way for Florida Ban on Transgender Care for Minors," NBC News, August 27, 2024, https://www.nbcnews.com/nbc-out/out-politics-and-policy/appeals-court-florida-ban-transgender-health-care-minors-rcna168395.

[7] Amy Howe, "Supreme Court Appears Ready to Uphold Tennessee Ban on Youth Transgender Care," SCOTUSblog, December 4, 2024, https://www.scotusblog.com/2024/12/supreme-court-appears-ready-to-uphold-tennessee-ban-on-youth-transgender-care/.

THE TRANSHUMANIST TEMPTATION

penectomy as well as vaginoplasty and phalloplasty — even pro-trans groups insist they would never do such a thing. Most hospitals and health networks make it clear on their websites that these procedures are for adults only, but they still happen.

One study found that, between 2018 and 2021, four U.S. minors received gender-affirming hysterectomies, and over one hundred had their breasts removed.[8] In 2022, the World Professional Association for Transgender Health (WPATH) revised its guidelines to remove minimum age recommendations for hormone and surgical treatments.[9] "What we didn't want to do was create a chapter that would make it more likely that practitioners would be sued because they weren't following exactly what we said," guideline author Amy Tishelman explained. Better to err on the side of more kids getting carved up, apparently.

According to the pro-trans Movement Advancement Project, twenty-six states have banned "best practice medication and surgical care for transgender youth," while two (Arizona and New Hampshire) have banned surgical interventions.[10] In Texas, Gov. Greg Abbott directed the state's Department of Family and Protective Services (DFPS) to launch child abuse investigations into parents who

---

[8] Bashar Hassan et al., "Temporal Trends in Gender Affirmation Surgery Among Transgender and Non-binary Minors," ed. Alexander Muacevic and John R. Adler, *Cureus* 15, no. 9 (September 2023), https://pmc.ncbi.nlm.nih.gov/articles/PMC10599689/.

[9] Chrissy Clark, "World's Leading Trans Org Says There Is No Minimum Age Recommended for Trans Surgeries and Hormones," *Daily Caller*, September 20, 2022, https://dailycaller.com/2022/09/20/wpath-no-minimum-age-recommended-trans-surgery-hormones-puberty-blockers/.

[10] Movement Advancement Project, "Bans on Best Practice Medical Care for Transgender Youth," accessed February 4, 2025, https://www.lgbtmap.org/equality-maps/healthcare/youth_medical_care_bans.

medically transition their kids, though the action was quickly blocked by state courts and remains tied up in the appeals process.[11]

Blue states have pushed back, with Gov. Gavin Newsom signing a bill in 2022 to make California the country's first trans "sanctuary state."[12] Under that law, a trans-identifying child can enter California and receive sex-change treatments without parental consent.

Another source of pushback has been libertarian-minded Republicans. Attorney and columnist David French argued that both Abbott and Newsom had gone too far by using "state power to sever the bond between parent and child."[13] As usual, the idea that good things are good and bad things are bad did not occur to French. Former Arkansas Gov. Asa Hutchinson and Ohio Gov. Mike DeWine, both Republicans, advanced similar arguments when they vetoed bills banning child sex changes, though in both cases the state legislature quickly overrode the governor's veto.[14]

---

[11] "Doe v. Abbott," ACLU, last updated December 11, 2024, https://www.aclu.org/cases/doe-v-abbott#:~:text=A%20family%20in%20Texas%20had,a%20form%20of%20child%20abuse.

[12] Tyler Olsen, "Newsom Signs Legislation Making California a Sanctuary State for Transgender Procedures," Fox News, September 30, 2022, https://www.foxnews.com/politics/newsom-signs-legislation-making-california-sanctuary-state-transgender-procedures.

[13] David French, "When Culture Wars Go Way Too Far," *Dispatch*, October 22, 2022, https://thedispatch.com/newsletter/frenchpress/when-culture-wars-go-way-too-far/.

[14] Meredith Deliso, "Arkansas State Legislature Overrides Governor's Veto on Transgender Health Care Bill," ABC News, April 6, 2021, https://abcnews.go.com/US/arkansas-state-legislature-overrides-governors-veto-transgender-health/story?id=76904369. Megan Henry, "Ohio Senate Overrides DeWine Vetoes on Trans Youth Gender-Affirming Care and Local Tobacco Bans," *Ohio Capital Journal*, January 24, 2024, https://ohiocapitaljournal.com/2024/01/24/ohio-senate-overrides-dewine-vetoes-on-trans-youth-gender-affirming

THE TRANSHUMANIST TEMPTATION

On the federal level, President Trump issued an executive order in the early days of his second term that bans all federal funding of child sex changes — including through Medicare and Medicaid — and threatens healthcare providers with loss of federal grants or even prosecution under a federal law against female genital mutilation.[15] This order could, of course, be rescinded by a future administration. A federal law banning the practice would be a fuller and more permanent solution, but getting sixty Senate votes for it would be an uphill battle. Even if legislation never materializes, however, it's possible that fear of lawsuits will eventually persuade healthcare providers to stop chemically and surgically disfiguring confused children. Detransitioner Chloe Cole is currently suing Kaiser Permanente for providing her with puberty blockers, cross-sex hormones, and (at the age of just fifteen) a double mastectomy. The lawsuit accuses the medical group of "pushing [Cole] into medical mutilation instead of properly treating her" and of engaging in an "unethical form of coercion" by telling Cole's parents she would kill herself without gender-affirming care.[16] If the lawsuit succeeds, it could set a powerful precedent.

-care-and-local-tobacco-bans/#:~:text=The%20Senate%20voted%20 24%2D8,hormone%20therapy%20and%20puberty%20blockers.

[15] Exec. Order No. 14187 of January 28, 2025, "Protecting Children from Chemical and Surgical Mutilation," Fed. Reg. 90, no. 8771 (February 3, 2025): 8771–8773, https://www.federalregister.gov/documents/2025/02/03/2025-02194/protecting-children-from-chemical-and-surgical-mutilation. See also Katelynn Richardson and Megan Brock, "Trump May Have Just Dealt a Death Blow to Industry Profiting on Child Sex Changes," *Daily Caller*, January 29, 2025, https://dailycaller.com/2025/01/29/trump-may-have-just-dealt-a-death-blow-to-industry-profiting-on-child-sex-changes/.

[16] Kendall Tietz, "Detransitioner Chloe Cole Announces Lawsuit Against Hospitals 'for Pushing Her into Medical Mutilation,'" Fox News, February 23, 2023, https://www.foxnews.com/media/detransitioner-chloe-cole-announces-lawsuit-hospitals-pushing-medical-mutilation.

For the true anti-transhumanist, however, cross-sex hormones and sex-change surgeries are not objectionable solely when children are involved. Accepting that anyone, even an adult, has the right to reshape his or her body in such a fundamental way means accepting (at least at the societal level) the transhumanist definitions of human flourishing and identity. It also means accepting a transhumanist vision of medicine that would allow healthcare providers to remove healthy body parts or disrupt normal bodily functions in order to serve the patient's desires. If I told a doctor my left arm was causing me severe mental distress, it would be wrong for him to remove it and right for him to be prohibited from doing so. Why should it be otherwise if I indicate a different appendage?

But since our society lacks robust concepts of human nature and human flourishing, this view is not widely shared. Oklahoma introduced a bill in 2023 to ban medical transition up to age twenty-six, but it died in committee.[17] Majorities of Americans support outlawing sex changes for kids and banning biological males from women's sports, but 57 percent say adults should be able to access any kind of gender-affirming care they want, according to one poll.[18]

It's also worth noting that even minor victories on this front come at a cost. And not all politicians are willing to pay it. Countries that have successfully restricted LGBT content aimed at kids, including Russia and Hungary, became international pariahs as a result, and parts of the United States often face the same stigma. Woke capital has the power to inflict real economic harm on states and cities that defy its agenda.

---

[17] Kiara Alfonseca, "New Bill Would Ban Gender-Confirming Care for Anyone under 26 in Oklahoma," ABC News, January 6, 2023, https://abcnews.go.com/US/new-bill-ban-gender-confirming-care-26-oklahoma/story?id=96261603.

[18] "How Personal Relationships Influence Views on Gender-Affirming Care," 19th, September 18, 2023, https://19thnews.org/2023/09/poll-gender-affirming-care-transgender-personal-relationships/.

THE TRANSHUMANIST TEMPTATION

Florida Gov. Ron DeSantis had to fight a long legal battle against one of the state's largest employers after Disney vowed to help repeal his so-called "Don't Say Gay" bill, which restricted classroom discussions of sexual orientation and gender identity. He was able to win largely because Disney had little leverage. It's impossible to pick up a forty-three-square-mile park and move it to a different state (though that didn't stop Nikki Haley from inviting Disney to do so during her presidential campaign).[19]

Other left-leaning businesses aren't so constrained. When North Carolina passed a bill in 2016 requiring individuals to use the bathroom that aligns with their biological sex, the cancellation of concerts, sporting events, and new business expansions was projected to cost the state $3.67 billion over twelve years.[20] North Carolina Republicans quickly backed down.[21] In 2021, former South Dakota Gov. Kristi Noem vetoed a bill[22] banning biological men from women's sports, citing concerns about "punitive action" from the NCAA (though she later issued executive orders and signed a different bill that achieved substantively the same effect).[23]

[19] Julia Shapero, "Haley Says Disney Can Move to Her Home State After It Sues DeSantis," *Hill*, April 26, 2023, https://thehill.com/homenews/campaign/3973680-haley-says-disney-can-move-to-her-home-state-after-it-sues-desantis/.

[20] The Associated Press, "'Bathroom Bill' to Cost North Carolina $3.76 Billion," CNBC, March 27, 2017, https://www.cnbc.com/2017/03/27/bathroom-bill-to-cost-north-carolina-376-billion.html.

[21] Jonathan Drew and Martha Waggoner, "North Carolina Future Uncertain After 'Bathroom Bill' Reset," AP News, March 31, 2017, https://apnews.com/general-news-0629b88c3df94a80b125403e8f440187.

[22] Kate Sosin, "Kristi Noem's Veto of a Trans Sports Bill in South Dakota Shows the Financial Pitfalls of Anti-LGBTQ+ Bills," 19th, March 25, 2021, https://19thnews.org/2021/03/kristi-noems-veto-trans-sports-bill/.

[23] Jo Yurcaba, "South Dakota Governor Signs 2022's First Trans Athlete Ban into Law," NBC News, February 3, 2022, https://www.nbcnews

The situation with regard to abortion looks even more hopeless. On June 24, 2022, cheers of victory rose in front of the Supreme Court as the fall of Roe v. Wade gave the pro-life movement its biggest win in half a century. All the momentum seemed to be going one way. We'd secured Omaha Beach, and we wouldn't stop until we took Berlin.

That optimism quickly vanished. Calls for "consensus" and shouted accusations replaced the cries of joy. There are plenty of reasons for the GOP to panic. In 2022, death won six out of six state-level abortion ballot measures. Even in deep-red Kansas, a referendum declaring that the state constitution provided no right to an abortion failed by twenty points, the same margin by which Trump won the state in 2016.

Things got worse in 2023, when Ohioans — who voted for Trump by eight points in 2016 and 2020 — voted fifty-seven to forty-three to pass a constitutional amendment that legalized abortion and overturned down the state's six-week ban.[24] The text of the amendment claimed to allow abortion restrictions post-viability, but it contained a vague maternal "health" exemption that could allow abortion up to birth on pretexts as thin as maternal anxiety.[25] Critics also pointed out that the guarantee of freedom to "make and carry out one's own reproductive decisions" could apply not only to abortion, but also to child sex changes.[26] Under the proposed amendment, any attempt to ban minors from accessing potentially sterilizing cross-sex hormones will likely be unconstitutional.

.com/nbc-out/out-politics-and-policy/south-dakota-governor-signs-2022s-first-trans-athlete-ban-law-rcna14725.

[24] "2023 and 2024 Abortion-Related Ballot Measures," *Ballotpedia*, 2024, https://ballotpedia.org/2023_and_2024_abortion-related_ballot_measures.

[25] Ohio Constitution Article I § 22(B)(2)(c).

[26] The Editors, "The Hidden Radicalism of Ohio's Abortion Amendment," *National Review*, July 27, 2023, https://www.nationalreview.com/2023/07/the-hidden-radicalism-of-ohios-abortion-amendment/.

THE TRANSHUMANIST TEMPTATION

It wasn't until 2024 that red states scored their first real wins against the abortion referendum juggernaut. The night Donald Trump won his second term, South Dakota, Nebraska, and Florida all rejected proposed constitutional amendments that would have overturned state abortion bans. Voters in South Dakota upheld their state's ban (which has no exceptions other than the life of the mother) by a decisive seventeen-point margin, but the other two wins deserve a bit of an asterisk. The Florida ballot measure (which voters backed fifty-seven to forty-three) only failed because the state constitution requires a 60 percent supermajority for proposed amendments. In Nebraska, abortion is legal through twelve weeks, meaning voters weren't forced to choose between extremes the way they were in Ohio. Even so, Nebraska's bare minimum ban (which only outlaws around 10 percent of abortions)[27] survived by less than nineteen thousand votes. It wasn't a perfect night, though. Several blue states enshrined abortion in their state constitutions, as did two red states: Montana and Missouri.[28]

For many in the GOP, the setbacks of 2023 were proof that pro-lifers had become an electoral liability. Right-wing journalist Richard Hanania

---

[27] Katherine Kortsmit et al., "Abortion Surveillance — United States, 2021," *Morbidity and Mortality Weekly Report* 72, no. 9 (November 24, 2023): 1–29, http://dx.doi.org/10.15585/mmwr.ss7209a1.

[28] There are eleven states (Alabama, Georgia, Indiana, Iowa, Kentucky, Louisiana, Mississippi, South Carolina, Tennessee, Texas, and West Virginia) that have both a six-week or total abortion ban and no constitutional mechanism for citizen-initiated ballot measures. And all eleven have legislatures that are safely in Republican hands. Those bans aren't going anywhere, and even if every other state removes all restrictions on abortion, they would stand as a worthy monument to the fifty years of pro-life struggle that took us from Roe to Dobbs. See Grayson Quay, "Voting for Trump Could Save Tens of Thousands of Babies per Year," *Federalist*, October 28, 2024, https://thefederalist.com/2024/10/28/voting-for-trump-could-save-tens-of-thousands-of-babies-per-year/.

declared the "pro-life position" had become "an albatross around the necks of Republicans."[29] Columnist Ann Coulter offered similar advice: "Pro-lifers: WE WON.... Please stop pushing strict limits on abortion, or there will be no Republicans left."[30] The electoral incentives for finding an off-ramp on the abortion issue looked strong.

Several 2024 presidential primary candidates, including DeSantis and South Carolina senator Tim Scott, hoped to achieve national consensus by passing a federal law outlawing abortion after fifteen weeks' gestation.[31] Such a ban would, as previously noted, affect only a small percentage of abortions, but it would still save tens of thousands of lives per year.[32]

Even that turned out to be too ambitious. Former President Donald Trump blamed the disappointing 2022 midterm results on pro-life extremism[33] and then announced in April 2023 that he believes abortion

---

[29] Richard Hanania, "Why Women Rebel Against Pro-Life," Richard Hanania's Newsletter, April 11, 2023, https://www.richardhanania.com/p/why-women-rebel-against-pro-life.

[30] Ann Coulter (@AnnCoulter), "The demand for anti-abortion legislation just cost Republicans another crucial race," X, April 4, 2023, 11:57 p.m., https://x.com/AnnCoulter/status/1643462761626705920.

[31] Sara Burnett, "DeSantis Said He Would Support a 15-Week Abortion Ban, After Avoiding a Direct Answer for Months," AP News, October 2, 2023, https://apnews.com/article/abortion-republicans-desantis-trump-bdccde60987da99018bf3abcbafedea0.

[32] Jeff Diamant, Besheer Mohamed, and Rebecca Leppert, "What the Data Says About Abortion in the U.S.," Pew Research Center, March 25, 2024, https://www.pewresearch.org/short-reads/2024/03/25/what-the-data-says-about-abortion-in-the-us/.

[33] Jared Gans, "Trump Says 'Abortion Issue' Responsible for GOP Underperforming Expectations in Midterms," Hill, January 1, 2023, https://thehill.com/homenews/campaign/3795054-trump-says-abortion-issue-responsible-for-gop-underperforming-expectations-in-midterms/.

restrictions should be left to the states. A few months later, the plank calling for a federal abortion ban was quietly dropped from the GOP platform (though language opposing "late-term abortion" was not).[34]

By August, Trump was posting on Truth Social that his second term would be "great for women and their reproductive rights,"[35] while his running mate was promising that Trump would veto any federal restrictions on abortion (despite the vanishingly slim odds of any such legislation passing in the first place).[36]

A few major figures in the anti-abortion movement, including Lila Rose, objected to these compromises, drawing intense backlash from pro-Trump influencers who accused her of electoral sabotage.[37] Other organizations, like Susan B. Anthony Pro-life America, accepted the new status quo and threw their unqualified support behind Trump.[38]

A Trump loss in November would probably have led to a GOP civil war over abortion. His resounding victory deferred the coming reckoning, but the trends that led Republicans to tack left on the issue

[34] Peter Pinedo, "Republicans Remove 'Right to Life' Plank from Party Platform," *National Catholic Register*, July 8, 2024, https://www.ncregister.com/cna/cna-july-8-2024-gop-remove-plank.

[35] Donald J. Trump (@realDonaldTrump), "My Administration will be great for women and their reproductive rights," Truth Social, August 23, 2024, 11:39 a.m., https://truthsocial.com/@realDonaldTrump/posts/113012083325505976.

[36] Alexandra Marquez, "JD Vance Says Trump Would Veto a National Abortion Ban," NBC News, August 25, 2024, https://www.nbcnews.com/politics/2024-election/jd-vance-says-trump-veto-national-abortion-ban-rcna168084.

[37] Ashley St. Clair (@stclairashley), "It's actually a lot simpler than that. She is a grifter who likes swanky galas," X, August 26, 2024, 12:26 p.m., https://x.com/stclairashley/status/1828106814749299043.

[38] Susan B. Anthony Pro-Life America, "SBA Statement on GOP Platform," July 8, 2024, https://sbaprolife.org/newsroom/press-releases/sba-statement-on-gop-platform.

aren't going anywhere. All it will take is one big defeat to trigger a full-scale purge of the pro-life movement. "Forced birthers" could easily become the new John Birchers.

Abortion doesn't poll particularly well for conservatives. One 2022 survey found that 58 percent of respondents thought abortion should be legal in "all or most cases," while just 37 percent disagreed.[39] But when it comes to restricting in vitro fertilization (IVF), the numbers are much worse. According to one poll from early 2024, 86 percent of Americans think IVF should be legal.[40] That's about as close to unanimous as anything gets in U.S. politics.

The poll was conducted in response to an Alabama Supreme Court ruling in a case known as *LePage v. Center for Reproductive Medicine*. The case itself involved three couples suing an IVF clinic under Alabama's wrongful death statute after several of their embryos were mishandled and destroyed. The statute already covered unborn babies in the womb from the moment of conception, allowing a plaintiff to recover damages if, for example, a car accident caused her to miscarry. The court simply determined that this statute also applied to unborn babies outside the womb.

"Unborn children are 'children' ... without exception based on developmental stage, physical location, or any other ancillary characteristics," the ruling states.[41] This fairly modest decision did not ban or

---

[39] Christine Filer, "With Supreme Court Poised to Reverse Roe, Most Americans Support Abortion Rights: POLL," ABC News, May 3, 2022, https://abcnews.go.com/Politics/supreme-court-poised-reverse-roe-americans-support-abortion/story?id=84468131.

[40] Kelly Garrity, "Americans Overwhelmingly Support Keeping IVF Legal for Women, Poll Finds," Politico, March 3, 2024, https://www.politico.com/news/2024/03/03/americans-overwhelmingly-support-ivf-legal-women-poll-00144588.

[41] *LePage v. Center for Reproductive Medicine, P.C.*, SC-2022-0515 (Ala. May 3, 2024).

THE TRANSHUMANIST TEMPTATION

even meaningfully restrict IVF (though, to paraphrase Matthew McConaughey's character in *Dazed and Confused*, it'd be a lot cooler if it had). It did, however, evoke a hysterical response from the left. Media outlets, breathlessly noting that a concurring opinion had mentioned God *and* quoted Scripture, scrambled to terrify suburban housewives with images of *Handmaid's Tale* dystopia.[42] Multiple Alabama clinics, apparently admitting that their staff could not be expected to refrain from behaving like drunken rhinoceroses around the frozen embryos, announced that they would pause IVF procedures.[43] Somebody set off a bomb outside the state attorney general's office, despite his announcement that he had no intention of "prosecuting IVF families or providers."[44] Vice President Kamala Harris warned that "the right to start a family" was in danger.[45]

And conservatives fell for it. *Free Press* journalist Olivia Reingold provided an excellent example of how self-identified pro-life Republican Christians responded: "Being pro-life, I'm [initially] like, 'Great, they're just viewing those as our babies,' because you do kind of feel that way when you're going through IVF, that this is my baby, even

---

[42] Jamelle Bouie, "Samuel Alito Opened the Door to Reproductive Hell," *New York Times*, February 23, 2024, https://www.nytimes.com/2024/02/23/opinion/alabama-embroyo-dobbs-reproductive-freedom.html.

[43] Trevor Hughes, "IVF Supporters Are 'Freaking Out' over Alabama Court Decision Treating Embryos as Children," USA Today, February 21, 2024, https://www.usatoday.com/story/news/nation/2024/02/21/alabama-ivf-ruling-embryos-sparks-concern/72673907007/.

[44] Emily Shapiro, "Explosive Detonated outside Alabama Attorney General's Office on Saturday," ABC News, February 26, 2024, https://abcnews.go.com/US/explosive-detonated-alabama-attorney-generals-office-saturday/story?id=107560248.

[45] Anthony Zurcher and Phil McCausland, "Alabama IVF Ruling a Political Gift for Democrats, Headache for Republicans," BBC, February 23, 2024, https://www.bbc.com/news/world-us-canada-68377136.

though it's not in my womb yet," Alabama woman Kelley Stafford told Reingold.

Later, when Stafford (probably erroneously) came to believe that the ruling could jeopardize her right to have her frozen offspring killed on a whim, she changed her mind. "I think it's ridiculous that anyone would say that an embryo is a child, even though I love my little 'embabies,'" she told Reingold. "But I just don't see how anyone could say it's the same as my son that's sitting in my house right now."[46]

Notice that this supposedly pro-life woman resorts to pro-abortion talking points the moment her professed values present the slightest obstacle to her desires. She's wrong, of course. Objectively — scientifically — Stafford's frozen embryos are no less human than her toddler. As an editorial in *National Review* put it, "Given nutrition and a suitable environment and untouched by disease, accident, or violence, those embryonic human beings will by an internally directed process develop to the stage at which they can reason, speak, laugh, and love."[47] They are biological members of the human species and therefore share in the human *telos*.

But this argument only makes sense if you accept, at least implicitly, that human dignity is rooted in our shared human nature. She describes herself as a Christian, but Stafford's comments reveal that she has adopted a transhumanist philosophy to justify her use of transhumanist reproductive technology. When she claims that "my son that's sitting in my house right now" is more human than her frozen offspring, she means it the way an existentialist would. Her unstated premise is that our humanity

---

[46] Olivia Reingold, "How Abortion Became 'the Defund the Police of the GOP,'" Free Press, March 5, 2024, https://www.thefp.com/p/republican-voters-against-gop-abortion-rules.

[47] The Editors, "What the Alabama IVF Ruling Was Actually About," *National Review*, February 23, 2024, https://www.nationalreview.com/2024/02/what-the-alabama-ivf-ruling-was-actually-about/.

THE TRANSHUMANIST TEMPTATION

does not stem from embodiment but from the will to power. Stafford's born son deserves to live because she has willed him into existence and because the boy can express and pursue his own desires as well. By that logic, humans who are neither willing nor willed cease to be truly human. They are pure existence with no essence. And if Stafford wants a family, she can create and discard as many of them as she wants.

Rightly fearing that there were millions of Staffords across the country who could have cost Trump the election in November, the Republican Party swung into action. On the state level, Alabama's supermajority Republican legislature passed a bill banning lawsuits over "damage to or death of an embryo," and GOP Governor Kay Ivey signed it a week later.[48] Senators Ted Cruz of Texas and Katie Britt of Alabama introduced a bill to ensure access to IVF, which Cruz praised for giving "miraculous hope to millions of Americans."[49] The National Republican Senatorial Committee issued a statement warning Republicans across the country to run as fast as they could away from the Alabama ruling.[50] Trump himself went so far as to float the idea of forcing insurance providers to cover IVF or even using federal funds to pay for it.[51] Hopefully that turns out to be an empty campaign promise.

---

[48] Adam Edelman, "Alabama Governor Signs Bill to Protect IVF Treatments into Law," NBC News, March 6, 2024, https://www.nbcnews.com/politics/alabama-lawmakers-ivf-protection-bill-vote-rcna141710.

[49] Eleanor Klibanoff, "Ted Cruz Files Bill to Protect IVF," *Texas Tribune*, May 20, 2024, https://texastribune.org/2024/05/20/ted-cruz-texas-ivf/.

[50] Audrey Fahlberg, "Senate Republican Campaign Arm Urges Its Candidates to 'Express Support for IVF,'" *National Review*, February 23, 2024, https://www.nationalreview.com/corner/senate-republican-campaign-arm-urges-its-candidates-to-express-support-for-ivf/.

[51] Sarah McCammon, Clay Masters, and Lexie Schapitl, "Trump Says He'll Support Free IVF Treatments in a Second Term," NPR,

At this point, it's obvious that there is precisely zero political will to restrict IVF. When it comes to reproductive issues, Americans are best described as "pro-choice." The vast majority are bio-libertarians who want to have as many options as possible for themselves and their families and don't really care if their neighbors get abortions or donate unwanted embryos to be vivisected in research labs.

The same *laissez-faire* attitude characterizes government policy on most bioethical issues. Despite all the surrogacy horror stories, blue states are rushing to legalize and deregulate a burgeoning and lucrative industry that also appeals to LGBT voters.[52] California's surrogacy laws are so lax that, as researcher Emma Waters explained in a 2022 piece for the *American Mind*, Chinese couples are using the state's women as incubators.[53] These children are born as U.S. citizens — with "social security numbers, access to education, and a path for their biological parents to receive a green card when the child turns 21" — and then sent to their parents in China. According to surrogacy agency and law firm Creative Family Connections, forty-four states and the District of Columbia will enforce surrogacy contracts and put both IPs' names on the birth certificate.[54] Three states — Arizona, Indiana, and

---

August 30, 2024, https://www.npr.org/2024/08/30/nx-s1-5094454/trump-tells-town-hall-crowd-that-he-supports-free-ivf-treatments.

[52] Kate Wells, "As Michigan Legalizes Surrogacy, Here's How Families Found Ways Around the Ban," NPR, April 1, 2024, https://www.npr.org/sections/health-shots/2024/04/01/1241392032/michigan-paid-surrrogacy-decriminalize-babym.

[53] Emma Waters, "California's New Handmaid's Tale," *American Mind*, November 28, 2022, https://americanmind.org/salvo/california-new-handmaids-tale/.

[54] "The US Surrogacy Law Map," Creative Family Connections, accessed January 23, 2025, https://www.creativefamilyconnections.com/us-surrogacy-law-map/.

THE TRANSHUMANIST TEMPTATION

Nebraska — have laws on the books making commercial surrogacy contracts unenforceable. Just one, Louisiana, criminalizes the practice.

There is no federal ban on human cloning, either, though several states outlaw it. In 2021, the Democrat-controlled U.S. Senate voted on party lines to reject a proposed ban on the creation of human-animal chimeras. The amendment would have prohibited scientists from creating "a human embryo into which a nonhuman cell or cells ... have been introduced to render the embryo's membership in the species *Homo sapiens* uncertain" and from "fertilizing a human egg with nonhuman sperm."[55] That same year, scientists successfully implanted human stem cells into a monkey embryo, which was quickly destroyed in accordance with scientific guidelines that prohibit letting embryos develop *in vitro* for more than fourteen days. The most likely application of this technology would be to make monkeys grow human organs that could then be used for transplants. But, as Priyad Ariyaratnam asked in the *American Spectator*, "What about a monkey with a human brain?"[56] There's currently no law that prevents scientists from creating such a transhuman specimen and forcing us all to answer that question.

This libertarian position also extends to the digital side of transhumanism. Even campaigns to keep intentionally addictive apps, demonstrably harmful devices, and pornographic websites from rewiring children's brains face stiff opposition.

---

[55] Andrew Solender, "Senate Kills GOP Legislation to Prohibit 'Certain Human-Animal Chimeras,'" *Forbes*, May 27, 2021, https://www.forbes.com/sites/andrewsolender/2021/05/27/senate-kills-gop-legislation-to-prohibit-certain-human-animal-chimeras/. See Cong. Rec. vol. 167 no. 88, S3233 (2021) for text of amendment.

[56] Priyad Ariyaratnam, "Human-Monkey Hybrids: Have We Crossed a Boundary?" *American Spectator*, June 26, 2021, https://spectator.org/human-monkey-chimeras-ethics-science/.

French President Emmanuel Macron announced in June 2024 that he supported a total ban on smartphone use for minors under eleven, building on his earlier proposal to ban anyone younger than fifteen from using social media.[57] American efforts have, so far, been less ambitious.

Utah led the way on protecting minors from social media with the 2023 Utah Social Media Regulation Act.[58] This ambitious piece of legislation would have barred minors from creating social media accounts without parental consent, required social media companies to verify the ages of all users, mandated parental access to children's accounts, prevented non-friend accounts from messaging minors, and forced platforms to implement a digital curfew for children lasting from 10:30 p.m. to 6:30 a.m. (though parents would have the choice to override it). The bill empowered state law enforcement to go after companies that violated its provisions while also allowing parents to sue over any harm their children suffered due to those violations. Other states have also passed laws mandating social media protections for minors and either requiring or strongly incentivizing universal age verification.

One would think, given the clear connection between smartphone-based social media, declining youth mental health, increased teen suicide rates, and a variety of social contagions, that laws like these would be universally popular. Such an assumption underestimates both the fanaticism of American libertarians and the depth of the Internet lobby's pockets.

---

[57] Foreign Staff, "Macron Backs Ban on Use of Smartphones for Under 11s," *Telegraph*, June 12, 2024, https://www.telegraph.co.uk/world-news/2024/06/12/macron-backs-report-calling-for-ban-on-smartphones-for-u11s/.

[58] Utah Social Media Regulation Act, S.B. 152 and H.B. 311, 2023 General Session (Utah).

THE TRANSHUMANIST TEMPTATION

NetChoice — an industry group that includes Amazon, Google, Meta, Snap, X (formerly Twitter), and (until May 2024)[59] Tik-Tok — claimed that the Utah age verification law was unconstitutional and filed for a preliminary injunction to block it from ever taking effect. Utah's legislature backed down, repealing the legislation and passing a replacement that removed the parental consent requirement while retaining the age verification mandate.[60] NetChoice, not satisfied with the compromise, wants that struck down too. "Despite going back to the drawing board, Utah is still not on the right side of the Constitution. We look forward to a court hearing our case," said Chris Marchese, who directs the NetChoice Litigation Center.[61]

Sure enough, in September 2024, a judge issued an injunction preventing the new laws from taking effect (though a final decision is still pending).[62] The result wasn't surprising. Courts had previously blocked age verification laws in multiple states, including Texas, Arkansas, California, and Ohio following lawsuits from NetChoice.[63] In February 2025, Senator Ted Cruz joined with Democratic Senator

[59] Caitlin Oprysko, Daniel Lippman, and Branden Bordelon, "Net Choice Boots TikTok," Politico, May 9, 2024, https://www.politico.com/newsletters/politico-influence/2024/05/09/netchoice-boots-tiktok-00157175.
[60] Social Media Regulation Amendments, S.B. 194 and H.B. 464, 2024 General Session (Utah).
[61] Ben Winslow, "Utah's Tough Social Media Laws Are Rewritten in the Face of Lawsuits," Fox 13 Salt Lake City, February 5, 2024, https://www.fox13now.com/news/politics/utahs-tough-social-media-laws-are-rewritten-in-the-face-of-lawsuits.
[62] Kyle Dunphey, "Judge Blocks Utah's Social Media Laws, Writing They Likely Violate the First Amendment," *Utah News Dispatch*, September 11, 2024, https://utahnewsdispatch.com/2024/09/11/judge-blocks-utah-social-media-law/.
[63] Krista Chavez, "NetChoice Halts Ohio Law: 4th Ruling Stopping Laws That Fail Kids, Parents & Constitution," *NetChoice*,

Brian Schatz of Hawaii to introduce legislation banning children under thirteen from social media. NetChoice, however, seems confident that even if this federal bill passes, it will fare no better in court than its state-level predecessors.[64]

Policy analyst David B. McGarry explained the constitutional case against social media restrictions in an op-ed for the *Daily Caller*:

> State-dictated age verification imposes significantly on adults' speech rights. Such laws require social media platforms or third-party vendors to collect sensitive personal information, generally either as government documentation or facial scans. In order to avoid violating the law, platforms end up having to subject all users to verifications — irrespective of their age. This fractures the First Amendment's protections for anonymous speech. Along with the privacy risks such data collection creates, it also deters adult Americans from speaking online.[65]

McGarry also notes that "sweeping bans of minors from social media violate First Amendment jurisprudence," which has consistently held

---

February 12, 2024, https://netchoice.org/netchoice-halts-ohio-law-4th-ruling-stopping-laws-that-fail-kids-parents-constitution/.

[64] Robert Winterton, "KOSMA Is Yet Another Proposal That Would Harm Cybersecurity, Parental Rights and Speech. Congress Must Find Another Way," *NetChoice*, February 5, 2025, https://netchoice.org/kosma-is-yet-another-proposal-that-would-harm-cybersecurity-parental-rights-and-speech-congress-must-find-another-way/. See also Gopal Ratnam, "Senate Tries Again on Thorny Issue of Kids Online Safety," *Roll Call*, February 11, 2025, https://rollcall.com/2025/02/11/senate-tries-again-on-thorny-issue-of-kids-online-safety/.

[65] David B. McGarry, "States Should Stop Wasting Time and Money on Blatantly Unconstitutional Social Media Regulations," *Daily Caller*, February 26, 2024, https://dailycaller.com/2024/02/26/mcgarry-age-verification-children-social-media-speech-rights/.

that children enjoy First Amendment protections and therefore have a "right to speak online — and to consume others' online speech."

I'm not an expert on the legal questions involved, but framing children's access to social media as a free speech issue seems to miss the point. The issue isn't the content (though plenty of that is horrible) but the harmful way in which it's packaged. For kids, scrolling through Instagram is more like smoking a cigarette than reading a newspaper.

The concerns about personal data collection are easier to dismiss. The think tank The American Compass has proposed "a public, online tool housed at the Social Security Administration that would allow any American to verify his age to an online platform without disclosing other personal information."[66] Type in your social security number on a .gov website, get a text message with a six-digit code, and plug that code into whatever social network you're looking to join. The platform can then submit that code to the SSA and find out whether the would-be user is old enough. It's the same simple account verification procedure millions of people already perform multiple times a week. The risks are virtually non-existent, and the idea that it would have some sort of chilling effect on free speech is laughable.

The libertarian R Street Institute, a bitter foe of age verification laws, insists that such a system "would allow prosecutors to make children federal criminals if they lie about their age."[67] This is, quite frankly,

---

[66] American Compass, *Rebuilding American Capitalism: A Handbook for Conservative Policymakers* (Washington, D.C.: American Compass, 2023), 71.

[67] Shoshana Weissmann, "Regimes That Run Age Verification Through the Government Would Allow Prosecutors to Make Children Federal Criminals If They Lie About Their Age," R Street Institute, August 22, 2023, https://www.rstreet.org/commentary/regimes-that-run-age-verification-through-the-government-would-allow-prosecutors-to-make-children-federal-criminals-if-they-lie-about-their-age/.

stupid. Minors have plenty of opportunities to be charged with federal crimes. Throwing rocks at the mailman would do it. The argument that we shouldn't have laws because laws turn people into criminals is not worthy of consideration. You'd think the tech companies and left-wing foundations that fund R Street's work would expect more bang for their buck.[68]

Other anti-verificationists frame their argument in pro-family terms. "Despite what legislators are claiming, bans aren't a pro-parent approach," wrote economist Vance Ginn and policy analyst Caden Rosenbaum.[69] "Legislation to ban minors from social media gives the government (politicians and bureaucrats) the power to decide what's best for children."

But although these libertarian voices claim to be shielding the sacred hearth against the overbearing hand of Big Government, what they're really doing is tearing down any barriers that might protect the family from the market. Social networks want to draw children away from their parents, siblings, and communities and into a discarnate, placeless virtual void that verifiably harms them. Government's response should be to state unequivocally that this outcome is not

---

[68] "Non-Profit: R Street Institute," InfluenceWatch, 2017, accessed January 23, 2025, https://www.influencewatch.org/non-profit/r-street-institute/. See also Meghan Rose Dickey, "Google's Nonprofit Arm Donates Another $7.5 Million to Advance Racial Justice," TechCrunch, November 21, 2017, https://techcrunch.com/2017/11/21/googles-non-profit-arm-donates-another-7-5-million-to-advance-racial-justice/?ncid=rss&utm_source=feedburner&utm_medium=feed&utm_campaign=Feed%3A+Techcrunch+%28TechCrunch%29&utm_content=Google+UK.

[69] Vance Ginn and Caden Rosenbaum, "Empowering Parents Doesn't Mean Banning Social Media," Center Square, April 21, 2023, https://www.thecentersquare.com/texas/article_4efff78c-e07b-11ed-905b-8fce17e8c15f.html.

conducive to a society that supports cohesive families, mentally and physically healthy children, and tight-knit communities and then to provide families with tools to achieve those ends. Instead, libertarians want government to remain neutral on the question of human flourishing versus transhuman degeneration. And without the help of the state, families are badly outmatched in this struggle.[70]

Families aiming to tame technology in their lives would do well to consult Andy Crouch's book *The Tech-Wise Family*. Crouch provides a number of practical ways in which "nudges" can help families cultivate virtue together by prioritizing creativity over consumption and cohesion over isolation in their limited use of screens and other devices.[71] Full disclosure, though, my wife and I attended a book study on *The*

---

[70] So are schools, where phones have a detrimental effect on learning. Multiple states — spanning the ideological spectrum from Arkansas to California — have passed laws banning students from using cellphones during the school day, and plenty of districts have implemented similar policies. On paper, 77 percent of the country's schools ban the non-academic use of phones, but enforcement and compliance vary. Many administrators are loath to actually punish repeat offenders, because that would mean dealing with angry helicopter parents who want to be able to text their kids throughout the school day. While substitute teaching at a district that theoretically bans phones from the first bell to the last, I frequently saw students on their phones in the halls and classrooms. Many acted surprised or affronted when I enforced the district policy. See Andrew DeMillo, "Banning cellphones in schools gains popularity in red and blue states," Associated Press, January 16, 2025, https://apnews.com/article/school-cell-phone-bans-states-e6d1fe8ddfde33f086d5cd2a19f4c148 and Jennifer A. Kingson, "Schools ban phones, but do the policies work?," Axios, July 5, 2024, https://www.axios.com/2024/07/05/schools-ban-phones-social-media-desantis-newsom.

[71] Andy Crouch, *The Tech-Wise Family: Everyday Steps for Putting Technology in Its Proper Place* (Grand Rapids, MI: Baker, 2017), 18.

Tech-Wise Family several years ago and have almost entirely failed to implement its advice. Most families face the same struggles. It shouldn't require serious willpower simply to avoid being discarnated and commodified by multibillion-dollar digital megacorporations. Catholic activist Peter Maurin said that a good society is "a society where it [is] easier for men to be good."[72] A humane society is one in which it is easier to be human.

On the pornography front, things look a bit more encouraging. As of January 2025, nineteen states have passed laws requiring porn sites to verify users' IDs to make sure they aren't minors.[73] Sites like PornHub, apparently believing that if they can't show smut to children they might as well throw in the towel, responded by blocking all access in those states. The Supreme Court is currently considering a case challenging these bans.

Minors in anti-porn states can, of course, use virtual private networks (VPNs) to circumvent these restrictions. But if placing obstacles between kids and porn saves some of them from being enslaved to their own passions, alienated from their own bodies, and led into ever-greater depravity in an infinite virtual harem, the laws will have served their purpose.

Despite occasional glimmers of hope, it's clear that our current political system will not save us from transhumanism. Although there have been victories at the state level, and although it is possible that the federal government will succeed in restricting sex changes for minors or forcing porn sites to age-verify users, there is no voter base and (aside from the miniscule American Solidarity Party) no political organization

---

[72] Stanley Vishnewski, "The Day I Met Peter Maurin," *Catholic Worker*, May 1, 1976, https://catholicworker.org/met-peter-maurin-html/.

[73] Alex Fitzpatrick, "Supreme Court Case on Age Limits for Porn Sites Could Affect 19 States," Axios, January 16, 2025, https://www.axios.com/2025/01/16/adult-website-age-verification-states.

THE TRANSHUMANIST TEMPTATION

willing to stand for authentic human flourishing across the board. The idea of imposing serious restrictions on the individual freedom of adults strikes most voters as government overreach. Transhumanism turns out to be as American as apple pie.

Right-Wing Transhumanisms

Whatever he was — that robot in the Garden of Eden, who existed without mind, without values, without labor, without love — he was not man.[1]

— Ayn Rand

There's no saving the American left from its total bondage to transhumanism. The Democratic Party's alliances with feminism (largely reduced to birth control and abortion), the LGBT movement (swallowed up entirely by transgenderism), and an elite class that prides itself on its decadent late-liberal values have made sure of that. But although the right has a better chance at winning some partial and temporary victories for humanity, certain movements within it simply offer transhumanism in a different guise.

The first of these ideologies, which Substack writer N. S. Lyons dubbed "right-wing progressivism," is best exemplified by Silicon Valley billionaire Marc Andreessen's "Techno-Optimist Manifesto," which he published in October 2023.[2] Other members of this movement

---

[1] Ayn Rand, *Atlas Shrugged* (New York: Dutton, 1992), 1026.
[2] N. S. Lyons, "The Rise of the Right-Wing Progressives," *Upheaval*, January 15, 2024, https://theupheaval.substack.com/p/the-rise-of-the-right-wing-progressives.

THE TRANSHUMANIST TEMPTATION

would include fellow tech magnate Elon Musk — who, Lyons notes, "bought Twitter not out of any desire to aid conservatives, but because he sees robust free speech as a necessary societal mechanism for the knowledge production and innovation needed to achieve his goal of making humanity a star-faring, multi-planetary species." Another right-wing progressive is Peter Thiel, who told one interviewer that "the Christian critique of transhumanism should be that it's not radical enough, because it's only seeking to transform our bodies and not our souls."[3] All three figures aligned themselves with Donald Trump in the 2024 election and gained significant political influence as a result, setting up a potential conflict with tech-skeptical MAGA figures like Steve Bannon, who "see[s] the tech right ... as a fundamental enemy to the natural human order."[4]

Andreessen begins his manifesto with a stirring barrage of short paragraphs:

We are being lied to.

We are told that technology takes our jobs, reduces our wages, increases inequality, threatens our health, ruins the environment, degrades our society, corrupts our children, impairs our humanity, threatens our future, and is ever on the verge of ruining everything.

We are told to be angry, bitter, and resentful about technology.

We are told to be pessimistic.

---

[3] Mary Harrington, "Peter Thiel on the Dangers of Progress," *UnHerd*, December 30, 2022, https://unherd.com/2022/12/peter-thiel-on-the-dangers-of-progress-2/.

[4] James Pogue, "How Long Can the Alliance Between Tech Titans and the MAGA Faithful Last?" *New York Times*, January 18, 2025, https://www.nytimes.com/2025/01/18/opinion/donald-trump-tech-musk-bannon.html.

The myth of Prometheus — in various updated forms like Frankenstein, Oppenheimer, and Terminator — haunts our nightmares.[5]

These are all lies, Andreessen claims. The truth is:

Our civilization was built on technology.
Our civilization *is* built on technology.
Technology is the glory of human ambition and achievement, the spearhead of progress, and the realization of our potential.
For hundreds of years, we properly glorified this — until recently.
I am here to bring the good news.
We can advance to a far superior way of living, and of being.
We have the tools, the systems, the ideas.
We have the will.
It is time, once again, to raise the technology flag.
It is time to be Techno-Optimists.

In the text that follows, Andreessen attempts to portray himself as an advocate for what's best in humanity. "We believe in what the Greeks called *eudaimonia* through *arete* — flourishing through excellence," he writes. Notably absent is any mention of *telos*. For Andreessen, as for other transhumanists, human nature is nothing more than that which creates and defines itself. As Lyons points out, the manifesto "contains not a word about religion or wisdom of any kind, or any form of the timeless eternal values necessary for real *eudaimonia*." Andreessen may align himself with the political right, but the form of flourishing he envisions is undeniably progressive.

[5] Marc Andreessen, "The Techno-Optimist Manifesto," Marc Andreessen Substack, October 16, 2023, https://pmarca.substack.com/p/the-techno-optimist-manifesto.

THE TRANSHUMANIST TEMPTATION

"His anti-Wokeness," Lyons argues, "is motivated mostly by an assessment that the ideology is degrading meritocracy, promoting irrational stupidity, inhibiting scientific innovation, diverting investment into worthless causes, and limiting long-term economic performance — in other words that it is holding back progress." On fiscal questions, Andreessen is stalwartly libertarian. Free markets, comparative advantage, and creative destruction all contribute to innovation and economic growth. He's not opposed to a social safety net for those who fall through the cracks, but slowing down the machine for their sake is out of the question.

Andreessen says nothing about remaking our bodies, achieving immortality, or creating new lives in virtual reality. But, as is obvious from his understanding of *eudaimonia*, the transhumanist ideology permeates his manifesto. It also shows up in the recommended reading list he includes at the end, which features both Dierdre McClosky (a transgender historian-economist who credits classical liberalism and free markets with creating the freedom that enables him to live as a woman) and Ray Kurzweil (the guy who wants to upload his mind to the cloud).

The one area in which Andreessen does openly advocate for transhumanist *technology* is in his discussion of artificial intelligence. "Intelligence is the birthright of humanity; we should expand it as fully and broadly as we possibly can," he argues. "We believe in Augmented Intelligence just as much as we believe in Artificial Intelligence. Intelligent machines augment intelligent humans, driving a geometric expansion of what humans can do."

Andreessen considers this expansion of human capacities though "symbiotic relationships with machines" — which seems like the same thing as Altman's "Merge" or even Kurzweil's "Singularity" — to be a moral imperative. "We believe any deceleration of AI will cost lives," he writes. "Deaths that were preventable by the AI that was prevented from existing is a form of murder."

Accusing one's ideological opponents of murder is always another way of saying that they should be silenced and cast aside. Anti-transhumanists should take him at his word. Although it is encouraging to gain billionaire allies in the fight against the diversity, equity, and inclusion (DEI) agenda, American conservatives should be wary of allowing such figures to set the movement's agenda. These right-wing progressives might broaden the appeal of something called "conservatism," but their ideology would conserve nothing, not even our humanity.

The other form of transhumanism infiltrating the right is the Nietzschean vitalism championed by Costin Alamariu, better known as Bronze Age Pervert (or BAP). In his 2018 book *Bronze Age Mindset*, Alamariu deploys an irony-laden style riddled with intentional misspellings and grammatical errors to present what he views as the greatest threat to human flourishing: the weak holding back the strong.

Andreessen would probably agree, though perhaps not in the same words; but unlike Andreessen, Alamariu is not a progressive or a techno-optimist. In many ways, he's a reactionary and a techno-agnostic. The greatness he urges young men to pursue does not depend on the use of technology to transcend human limitations. In his view, many past societies — including Renaissance Italy and "the Bronze Age of high chariotry" — offered more opportunities to pursue it than modernity does.[6]

The problem with civilization, a problem Alamariu traces all the way back to the discovery of agriculture, is a matriarchal structure that encourages the indiscriminate breeding of supposedly inferior specimens.

According to Alamariu, the human spirit thrives on masculine individualism and atrophies under feminized collectivism.[7] Devotion to a

---

[6] Bronze Age Pervert (BAP; pseudonym for Costin Alamariu), *Bronze Age Mindset* (self-published, 2018), 111 (*BAM*).

[7] "Longhouse" has entered the dissident right's lexicon as a term for an oppressive matriarchy led by HR managers, teachers, therapists, and government bureaucrats who impose their neuroses on society at large

wife and children, he claims, means surrendering one's vital spark. If you have to marry and procreate, you should do it "because you have great love and lust for a woman" (he doesn't explain how this is supposed to help you stay married or raise children) and not let family become the center of your life.[8] Societies that restrict men's ability to wield power and seek adventure degenerate into mere "piles of biomass."[9]

According to Alamariu, this is "default civilization," exemplified today by the "zombi hordes" of the "Turd World." He compares these cultures to yeast; they "expand and replicate indiscriminately" without any "higher aspiration."[10] In Africa, he argues, international aid "doesn't translate into improved quality of life, even into improved nutrition, but is immediately converted into more children who continue to live at the same level of misery." His greatest fear is that mass migration from the third world will overwhelm the civilized world, which cannot fight a "demographic war" without sinking to the invaders' level:

> The idea that whites or Japanese should start vomiting out six or seven children to a vagina like the illiterate slave hordes of Bangladesh or Niger is absurd. For one, it's never going to happen … and it shouldn't. Throughout history we've almost always been outnumbered, and it hasn't been a problem. Immigration restriction, combined with some judicious deportation done gradually, would be enough to secure the homelands of the civilized.[11]

---

via a regulatory panopticon designed to protect everyone's feelings. The left insists that Donald Trump is Voldemort, the fascist-coded dark wizard from Harry Potter. The online right is more worried about Dolores Umbridge, the pink-clad schoolmarm witch who imposes an endlessly proliferating and increasingly petty list of rules.

[8] Ibid., 189.
[9] Ibid., 73.
[10] Ibid., 81, 19, 62–63.
[11] BAP, BAM, 189.

But those aren't the only measures he recommends. "OK you believe abortion is evil: but do you have any problem with the proliferation of the Global South?" Alamariu tweeted in April 2023.[12] "Do you have a problem with expansion of these populations already within the European world? And what would be the more humane alternative?"

Calling for secure borders, deportations, and a selective immigration policy doesn't make one a eugenicist or a transhumanist. What does is dehumanizing other people on the basis of their race and arguing that they should be culled to reduce the "burden on European man."[13] And while he wouldn't call himself a transhumanist, Alamariu openly embraces the other label. In his second book, *Selective Breeding and the Birth of Philosophy*, he argues forthrightly that truly civilized cultures are those that have an "awareness of breeding or what we might crudely term 'eugenics.'"[14]

Alamariu thus returns to the original form of modern transhumanism: the belief that by eliminating bad genes (or the individuals who carry them), humanity can elevate itself to a higher state of being. "To speak of superior and inferior ways of life is necessarily to deny that every form of life has dignity or meaning," he writes. "But, in particular, the net effect is to deny that *mere life has any worth*."[15]

The idea of a superior way of life sounds similar to the old Aristotelian definition of virtue — which insists that it's possible to be a

---

[12] Bronze Age Pervert (@bronzeagemantis), "OK you believe abortion is evil: but do you have," X, April 15, 2023, 1:01 a.m., https://x.com/bronzeagemantis/status/1647102859065057280.

[13] *Bronze Age Pervert* (@bronzeagemantis), "The majority of the replies aren't even saying something like," X, April 15, 2023, 12:03 a.m., https://x.com/bronzeagemantis/status/1647088191160336384.

[14] Costin Alamariu, *Selective Breeding and the Birth of Philosophy* (self-published, 2023), 15.

[15] Ibid., 22.

good or bad man the same way it's possible to be a good or bad carpenter — but Alamariu replaces the rational *telos* of natural law with a biologically rooted will to power.

He also, in his devotion to ancient Greece, rejects Jerusalem's main contribution to the Western tradition: the idea of the *imago dei*. The Christian proclamation that all people are God's children made in His image does not mean that all individuals are equal in their capacities, that all men are equally tall, that all women are equally beautiful, or that all cultures and lifestyles are equally conducive to human flourishing. What it does mean is that all humans are equally human. No one is yeast. The most crippled, disheveled, low-IQ denizen of the lowliest slum or favela has infinite worth by virtue of his or her humanity.

Christians rightly boast of their early forebears, who rescued malformed infants from Roman garbage dumps. For Alamariu, this would not be an admirable act of love, but a contribution to squalor and ugliness.

He's not alone in this view. In the fall of 2023, journalist and "Holocaust researcher" David Cole wrote in alt-right organ *Taki's Mag* that Republicans shouldn't "die on the hill of 'You know what America needs? *More* unwanted welfare ghetto babies from semi-retarded parents!'"[16] Around the same time, the pseudonymous fiction writer known as Zero HP Lovecraft, who occupies the same milieu as Alamariu and has over 130,000 followers on X, told me his stance on abortion "depends [on] what race it is."[17] About a year later, male

---

[16] David Cole, "Bunny Dreams and Abortion Nightmares," *Taki's Mag*, November 14, 2023, https://www.takimag.com/article/bunny-dreams-and-abortion-nightmares/, emphasis in original.

[17] Zero HP Lovecraft (@0x49fa98), "depends what race it is," X, November 21, 2023, 6:52 p.m., https://x.com/0x49fa98/status/1727112849192050925.

chauvinist influencer Andrew Tate went viral for sharing a meme with the same message.[18]

And what happens on the Internet doesn't stay on the Internet. According to reports, Alamariu has found sympathetic readers among Republican presidential and congressional staffers.[19] The night after Trump's second inauguration, an anonymous X user posted a picture on the White House lawn that showed his hand grasping a copy of *Bronze Age Mindset* with the Oval Office visible in the background.[20] Eugenics is part of the right-wing ecosystem now.

Andreessen and Bronze Age Pervert have more in common than their differences in style and emphasis might suggest. The pseudonymous Alamariu has repeatedly praised Argentinian president Javier Milei, whose doctrinaire libertarianism mirrors the economic program outlined in the "Techno-Optimist Manifesto." For his part, Andreessen identifies Nietzsche's "last man," the small-souled mediocrity who strives for nothing and seeks comfort amid the herd, as the techno-optimist's main enemy. Alamariu cribs much of his philosophy from Nietzsche and uses the term "bugman" as a stand-in for "last man."[21]

Both also share similarities with the twentieth-century free-market philosopher and novelist Ayn Rand (though Alamariu gets very

---

[18] Andrew Tate (@Cobratate), "[post consists of a meme image with no accompanying text]," X, September 8, 2024, 6:21 a.m., https://x.com/Cobratate/status/1832725972493140175.

[19] Ben Schreckinger, "The Alt-right Manifesto That Has Trumpworld Talking," Politico, August 23, 2019, https://www.politico.eu/article/right-wing-manifesto-that-has-trumpworld-talking-military-rule-bap-bapism-cult-book-bronze-age-mindset/.

[20] Othman (@OthmanOnX), "Good Game Liberals," X, January 21, 2025, 9:14 p.m., https://x.com/OthmanOnX/status/1881888260324302857.

[21] BAP, *BAM*, 13.

offended if you point this out).[22] Like Andreessen, Rand spewed vitriol at "mystics" who believed there was more to human flourishing than material progress. Her copy of C. S. Lewis's *The Abolition of Man*, which warns that abandoning a teleological view of human nature will lead to the refashioning of humanity by a class of elite technocrats, is full of margin notes calling Lewis a "lousy bastard," "old fool," and "medieval monstrosity." In one note, she paraphrases Nietzsche, insisting that to "choose your own values" is the true path to happiness and that the idea of a human *telos* rests on nothing but "blind faith."[23]

And like Alamariu, Rand had nothing but scorn for weakness or deformity. In her 1943 novel *The Fountainhead*, she condemns a character for converting a Grecian "Temple to the Human Spirit" he'd commissioned into a "Home for Subnormal Children."[24] This is what the right-wing transhumanists think of Christianity, or any ideology that dares assign intrinsic value to human beings.

In a 2023 essay for *Compact*, author Michael Lind coined the term *eugenicon* as a portmanteau of "eugenicist" and "conservative."[25] This label perfectly captures the overlap between Andreessen's non-eugenic techno-progressivism and Alamariu's tech-agnostic eugenicism. "A systematic eugenicon program," Lind wrote, "would combine economic (not civil) libertarianism with promotion of birth control (for the inferior masses, not the superior classes, whose propagation should

---

[22] Bronze Age Pervert (@bronzeagemantis), "Grayson would you and the Compact guys who say this get together," X, December 31, 2023, 6:26 p.m., https://x.com/bronzeagemantis/status/1741601690736828449.

[23] Ayn Rand, *Ayn Rand's Marginalia: Her Critical Comments on the Writings of Over 20 Authors* (New Milford, CT: Second Renaissance Books, 1995), 90–94.

[24] Ayn Rand, *The Fountainhead* (New York: Signet Books, 1968), 316.

[25] Michael Lind, "Against the Eugenicons," *Compact*, August 11, 2023, https://www.compactmag.com/article/against-the-eugenicons/.

be encouraged) and rule by the numerically small cognitive elite." Andreessen may not be a eugenicist, but his disdain for anti-transhumanist Luddites mirrors Alamariu's feelings toward yeast-like third-worlders. Both groups, with their stubborn mere humanity, threaten to take from the aristocrats of mind, body, and spirit the elevated life they might otherwise live.

The right-wing transhumanists' calls to adventure may be stirring, and their critiques may accurately identify some of our society's failings. But in their demand for excellence, they erase the *imago dei*.

Thankfully, it's not an either-or choice. The Catholic Church, which commissioned many of the world's most beautiful buildings and artworks, also built a massive global network of hospitals and orphanages. The same King Louis IX of France who split Saracen helms on the beach at Damietta also washed the feet of Parisian lepers.

It's true that, among the canonized, meek ascetics outnumber warrior kings, but is this too not an improvement? Plutarch praises Julius Caesar for killing a million Gauls and enslaving a million more.[26] Such were the heroes of the pre-Christian world. Until Christ on the cross used "what is weak in the world to shame the strong," the idea of honoring a martyred teenage slave girl like St. Blandina more than warlords or geniuses would have seemed absurd.[27] "The notion of an eminence merely moral, consistent with complete stupidity or unsuccess, is a revolutionary image," G. K. Chesterton wrote. "It did not need the sword or sceptre, but rather the staff or spade. It was the ambition of poverty."[28]

---

[26] *Twelve Illustrious Lives*, 356.
[27] 1 Cor. 1:27, RSVCE. See Eusebius, *Church History*, trans. Paul L. Maier (Grand Rapids, MI: Kregel Academic, 2012), 154.
[28] G. K. Chesterton, *A Short History of England* (London: Chatto & Windus, 1917), 73.

THE TRANSHUMANIST TEMPTATION

Realizing this ambition does not require the ruthless pursuit of progress, whether through eugenics or melding with AI. It demands only the goodness and humility that come from recognizing the divine image in every human being. Without those virtues, all our conquests and achievements are as filthy rags.

Part 4

WORK

Capitalism and Transhumanism[1]

> *But industrial civilization is only possible when there's no self-denial. Self-indulgence up to the very limits imposed by hygiene and economics. Otherwise the wheels stop turning.*
>
> —Aldous Huxley[2]

Liberalism, especially on the left, advances transhumanism in the cultural and political spheres; capitalism does the same in the economic sphere. And it does so with broad support from the political right.

In *Why Liberalism Failed*, Deneen describes the transition from the classical understanding, which saw human nature as "continuous with the order of the natural world," to the "protoliberal" view of applied science championed by seventeenth-century English thinker Francis Bacon, who "argued for the human capacity to 'master' or 'control' nature."[3]

---

[1] Portions of this chapter originally appeared at the *Daily Caller*. See Grayson Quay, "One Speaker Gave the Middle Finger to Davos ... And It Wasn't Milei," *Daily Caller*, January 23, 2024, https://dailycaller.com/2024/01/23/quay-one-speaker-gave-middle-finger-davos-wasnt-milei/.
[2] Huxley, *Brave New World*, 237.
[3] Deneen, *Why Liberalism Failed*, 36.

THE TRANSHUMANIST TEMPTATION

Liberalism imagines individuals in a state of nature consenting to a social contract to protect their own political self-interest, producing a society that maximizes freedom for everyone. Capitalism, as envisioned by Adam Smith in *The Wealth of Nations*, posits that individuals pursuing their own economic self-interest will maximize wealth for everyone. It's the same basic idea applied to different spheres of life. And according to Deneen, both liberalism and "market-based free enterprise" contributed to the "new understanding of liberty as the most extensive possible expansion of the human sphere of autonomous activity."[4]

The expansion of this autonomy soon becomes the entire *raison d'etre* of society. The modern natural law theorist John Finnis argued that certain "basic goods" are accessible through human reason and that law and society must safeguard those goods and mediate between them when they conflict. He identified seven — life, knowledge, play, aesthetic experience, friendship, practical reasonableness, and religion — to which he later added marriage.[5] Liberal capitalist society acknowledges only two such goods: individual freedom and GDP growth.

As with liberalism, the defenders of capitalism frequently argue that their system is superior because it aligns most fully with human nature. The Austrian School of economics, which boasts such luminaries as Ludwig von Mises and Friedrich von Hayek, largely eschews the quantitative methods common in mainstream economics departments and focuses instead on "praxeology" — the theory of how humans act purposefully in the world. "In colloquial speech we call a man 'happy' who has succeeded in attaining his ends," Mises wrote in his 1949 treatise *Human Action*. "But we must avoid current misunderstandings.

---

[4] Ibid., 37.
[5] John Finnis, *Natural Law and Natural Rights* (Oxford, UK: Oxford University Press, 2011), xii, 448.

The ultimate goal of human action is always the satisfaction of the acting man's desire. There is no standard of greater or lesser satisfaction other than individual judgments of value ... Nobody is in a position to decree what should make a fellow man happier."[6]

Mises claims that this radical subjectivism is consistent with the Aristotelian notion of *eudaimonia* in that both see all human action as ultimately aiming at happiness. What Mises leaves out is that *eudaimonia* is not subjective. It refers to the type of flourishing that corresponds to human nature. But for Mises, like Sartre, the term *human nature* has no real content. To be human is merely to desire, to strive, to grasp, to assign value where none objectively exists, to pursue one's own definition of happiness with whatever tools are at hand. An economic order built around these transhumanist presuppositions tends to reject state intervention in the economy. Virtually all transactions between consenting parties must be treated as equally valid.

"It is not the fault of the entrepreneurs that the consumers, the people, the common man, prefer liquor to Bibles and detective stories to serious books, and that governments prefer guns to butter," Mises wrote. "The entrepreneur does not make greater profits in selling bad things than in selling good things. His profits are the greater the better he succeeds in providing the consumers with those things they ask for most intensely."[7] According to Mises and his fellow libertarians, the market serves no moral purpose beyond respecting individual freedom. It exists purely to produce wealth by efficiently satisfying demand, and the sole measure of that success is profit. They're fine with people attempting to shape demand, but only if they do so on the cultural front by way of persuasion. Using government power to

---

[6] Ludwig von Mises, *Human Action: A Treatise on Economics* (Auburn, AL: Ludwig von Mises Institute, 1998), 14.
[7] Ibid., 297.

give people something other than what they ask for is out of bounds. It doesn't matter how noble your ideal of human flourishing is.

For Hayek, this relativism is the essence of progress. "The growth of civilisation has been accompanied by a steady diminution of the sphere in which individual actions are bound by fixed rules," he wrote in *The Road to Serfdom*, praising liberal modernity for its rejection of both the "common good" and anything resembling a "complete ethical code."[8] Public morality is reduced to letting people do what they want as long as it doesn't directly harm anyone else.

The most prominent defender of Austrian economics on the world stage is Argentinian President Javier Milei, whose speech delivered at the 2024 World Economic Forum ended with an emphatic "Long live Freedom, dammit!"

"If you make money, it's because you offer a better product at a better price, thereby contributing to general wellbeing," Milei said during his roughly twenty-three-minute address. The first part is generally true. The second is a little murkier. "Better" could mean a mouse trap that's better at trapping mice or a meth recipe that's better at getting me hooked.

Smartphones are an excellent product — cheap enough that nearly everyone has one and highly effective at holding the user's attention. We spend almost five hours a day staring at them, according to one study.[9] The current iPhone model has three cameras, and around 15 percent of children now report being exposed to pornography before the age of ten (often on smartphones).[10] Perhaps with future innovations,

---

[8] F. A. Hayek, *The Road to Serfdom* (New York: Routledge, 2001), 61.
[9] Jane Wakefield, "People Devote Third of Waking Time to Mobile Apps," BBC, January 12, 2022, https://www.bbc.com/news/technology-59952557.
[10] "New Report Reveals Truths About How Teens Engage with Pornography," Common Sense Media, January 10, 2023, https://www

phones will have six cameras and 30 percent of prepubescent kids will be watching porn. That type of progress might add to the GDP, but I'm not sure it would qualify as "contributing to general wellbeing." The market doesn't provide what's good for us. It provides what we want while playing a major role in shaping those wants.

Over the past few years, it's become increasingly clear that to be a doctrinaire capitalist is to be a progressive (perhaps a right-wing progressive like Andreessen). The Cold War–era "fusionist" alliance between conservatives and libertarians was always doomed to fail. In his book *The True and Only Heaven*, historian Christopher Lasch argues that the idea of progress that is now eroding our very humanity came into being when classically liberal thinkers "began to argue that human wants, being insatiable, required an indefinite expansion of the productive forces necessary to satisfy them." In other words, with the invention of capitalism.[11]

Under such conditions, it was inevitable that our desires (and the means of fulfilling them) would burst the bonds of human nature,

---

.commonsensemedia.org/press-releases/new-report-reveals-truths-about-how-teens-engage-with-pornography.

[11] Christopher Lasch, *The True and Only Heaven* (New York: Norton, 1991), 13. Neoconservative journalist Irving Kristol argued that this "indefinite expansion" is the only thing that makes democracy possible. "In earlier times, democracy meant an inherently turbulent political regime, with the 'have-nots' and the 'haves' engaged in a perpetual and utterly destructive class struggle," he wrote in 2003. "It was only the prospect of economic growth in which everyone prospered, if not equally or simultaneously, that gave modern democracies their legitimacy and durability." If he's correct, then it's unclear whether our political system could survive in an economy based on some principle other than the eternal expansion and fulfillment of insatiable human desires. See Irving Kristol, "The Neoconservative Persuasion," *Weekly Standard* 8, no. 47 (August 25, 2003), http://www.weeklystandard.com/Content/Public/Articles/000/000/003/000tzmlw.asp.

THE TRANSHUMANIST TEMPTATION

reshaping our bodies and minds in the name of freedom and profit. At one point in his speech, Milei rightly attacked the "bloody agenda of abortion," but ignored one of its key causes. It's true that, as Milei said, climate alarmists push abortion on the developing world as a means of population control. But freer markets would not end the industrial-scale slaughter of the unborn. Among the most common reasons women give for seeking abortion is to avoid interrupting their schooling or career. That means millions of women kill their babies in order to stay in the labor market and maximize their value within it.[12] U.S. Treasury Secretary Janet Yellen admitted as much in 2022 when she said that "eliminating the right of women to make decisions about when and whether to have children would have very damaging effects on the economy" and that abortion helps women increase their "earning potential."[13]

Or consider Donald McClosky, who goes by "Dierdre" these days. McClosky, an influential scholar and proponent of free-market capitalism, described his transgender identity as the fruit of the liberty that this system provides. For him, the cultural liberation that enabled him to abandon his wife and children to crossdress full-time is "the fulfillment of a promise" implicit in capitalism.[14] Self-described transhumanists

---

[12] Lawrence B. Finer et al., "Reasons U.S. Women Have Abortions: Quantitative and Qualitative Perspectives," *Perspectives on Sexual and Reproductive Health* 37, no. 3 (September, 2005): 110–118, https://www.guttmacher.org/journals/psrh/2005/reasons-us-women-have-abortions-quantitative-and-qualitative-perspectives. See table 2.

[13] Sarah Ewall-Wice, "Eliminating Abortion Access Would Have a Damaging Effect on the Economy, Yellen Says," CBS News, May 10, 2022, https://www.cbsnews.com/news/eliminating-abortion-access-would-have-a-damaging-effect-on-the-economy-yellen-says/.

[14] Quoted in Matthew Schmitz, "Bourgeois Vice," *First Things*, November 1, 2019, https://www.firstthings.com/article/2019/11/bourgeois-vice.

take a similar view. Anders Sandberg argues that "augmentative medicine ... genetic modification and other forms of physical modification" are "new tools for expressing individuality and uniqueness." These tools then create "demand" — notice the economic terminology — "for the freedom" to use them.[15]

Free-market fundamentalism, like the liberalism it accompanies, is an ideology that misrepresents human nature and threatens to mutilate it to match those misconceptions. This has been evident from the start. "The brutal state of nature is a philosopher's myth as is the atomized liberal individual. It took coercion on a monumental scale to bring about this liberal subject, to make reality out of the myth," author Sohrab Ahmari argued during a 2023 debate. "The first liberal society, England, had to enclose and destroy the common grounds that had been used by peasants for grazing, blocking peasants from shared lands that permitted generations to sustain themselves in communities of leisure and mutual help."[16]

This process of enclosure, which commodifies aspects of life previously shielded from market pressures, has continued ever since. In the early years of the twentieth century, G. K. Chesterton opposed women's suffrage on the grounds that, for most of history, half of humanity had existed largely outside of the market and the state. Giving women the vote and sending them to work was, in his view, a massive power grab by those twin leviathans.[17] The domestic sphere, over which women ruled, would shrink to nothing.

---

[15] Sandberg, "Morphological Freedom," 58–59.
[16] Sohrab Amari, "Sohrab Ahmari's Opening Statement — Liberalism," TheMunkDebates, November 10, 2023, YouTube, 6:15, https://www.youtube.com/watch?v=-MhYWizQIQc.
[17] G. K. Chesterton, *What's Wrong with the World* (New York: Dodd, Mead, 1910), 141–228.

THE TRANSHUMANIST TEMPTATION

Today, having enclosed not only the grazing meadow but also the family cottage, the market seeks to enclose our very bodies and minds as well. As we gain greater power to alter, augment and discarnate ourselves, we also face greater pressure to do so in response to marketing, social trends, and economic necessity. And the logic of pure capitalism offers no basis for resisting these pressures, only a vague encouragement to pursue one's "life project," as Milei put it in one interview.[18] Whether it's broke college girls selling their eggs, poor Ukrainian women renting their wombs to wealthy childless couples from Western Europe (who panicked as their surrogates and newborns sought shelter from Russian bombs),[19] short men getting their legs extended, doctors prescribing Ritalin to antsy middle school boys, confused teens having their breasts surgically removed, or lonely young men finding their only fulfillment in virtual reality — the libertarian worship of free markets leads inevitably to transhumanism.

Freedom is an important part of human flourishing. But to treat freedom as the only human good is to make of it a false and infernal god.

---

[18] "Cinco definiciones fuertes de Javier Milei: armas, drogas, homosexualidad, aborto y el Estado como enemigo," El Cronista, August 9, 2021, https://www.cronista.com/economia-politica/cinco-definiciones-fuertes-de-javier-milei-aborto-drogas-armas-homosexualidad-y-el-estado-enemigo/. Translation mine.

[19] Andrew E. Kramer and Maria Varenikova, "In a Kyiv Basement, 19 Surrogate Babies Are Trapped by War but Kept Alive by Nannies," New York Times, March 12, 2022, https://www.nytimes.com/2022/03/12/world/europe/ukraine-surrogate-mothers-babies.html. See also Ilya Gridneff, Emily Schultheis, and Dmytro Drabyk, "Inside a Ukrainian Baby Factory," Politico, July 23, 2023, https://www.politico.com/news/2023/07/23/ukraine-surrogates-fertility-00104913.

Building a Humane Economy

The Gross National Product.... measures everything in short, except that which makes life worthwhile.

— Robert F. Kennedy[20]

Under the influence of the twin ideologies of liberalism and capitalism, both sides of the American political spectrum have become more transhumanist. The right compromises on social issues while the left abandons the working class and embraces neoliberal globalist economics. Only the movement known as the New Right, with its combination of social conservatism and pro-family, pro-worker economic nationalism, offers real hope for the future.

I'm perfectly willing to concede that the *laissez faire* approach generally produces the most economic growth. As economist Alexander Salter explained in a 2022 *National Review* article, the debate over whether free markets or planned economies allocate resources and

---

[20] Robert F. Kennedy, "Remarks at the University of Kansas, March 18, 1968," JFK Library, accessed January 23, 2025, https://www.jfklibrary.org/learn/about-jfk/the-kennedy-family/robert-f-kennedy/robert-f-kennedy-speeches/remarks-at-the-university-of-kansas-march-18-1968.

produce wealth more efficiently is settled.[21] It's free markets. Not even close. If space aliens showed up and threatened to incinerate Earth unless we raised the global GDP to $X within Y years, this would be a good argument for unalloyed capitalism. Fortunately, they didn't — so, it's not. The ideal amount of economic inefficiency is not zero. The market was made for man, not man for the market. We have wants and needs that mere GDP growth does not fulfill and sometimes actively inhibits.

But the dilemma facing the U.S. economy might not be as simple as "more humane and less efficient" versus "less humane and more efficient." Despite the pieties of political and economic liberalism, there are real economic costs to creating a system that neglects the basic elements of human flourishing. In his book *The Once and Future Worker*, American Compass founder Oren Cass critiques our current program of prioritizing economic growth and increased consumption while compensating economic "losers" with welfare programs. It's true, Cass writes, that under this system of "cheap goods and plentiful transfer payments ... nearly all Americans could afford cable television and air conditioning."[22] The problem is that man does not live by cable television and air conditioning alone.

"Even if gains exceed the costs initially, what happens if the losses undermine stable families, decimate entire communities, foster government dependence, and perhaps contribute to skyrocketing substance abuse and suicide rates?" Cass asks.[23] He then answers his question by demonstrating that, just as pure liberalism erodes the capacity for self-government that made liberalism feasible in the first place, making

---

[21] Alexander Salter, "Industrial Policy Is Unwise but Not Impossible," *National Review*, December 14, 2021, https://www.nationalreview.com/2021/12/industrial-policy-is-unwise-but-not-impossible/.

[22] Oren Cass, *The Once and Future Worker* (New York: Encounter Books, 2018), 19.

[23] Ibid., 19.

an idol of GDP produces social dysfunction which saps the productive capacities necessary for growth.[24] "Having forsaken the healthy society that makes economic growth possible, Americans now found that they had neither," Cass concludes.[25]

Using the levers of government to repair that society would mean doing something very illiberal: suggesting that some lifestyles are more valid than others and enshrining that distinction in public policy. Government should say frankly that, for example, married parents are better for society than single parents and take steps to incentivize the former. Institute for Family Studies fellow Brad Wilcox suggests that the federal government should run ads touting the "Success Sequence," which consists of "1) getting at least a high school degree (education), 2) working full-time in your 20s (work), and 3) marrying before having children (marriage)."[26] In 2021, Missouri senator Josh Hawley proposed a "Parent Tax Credit" that would have sent one thousand

---

[24] This hits the poor especially hard. Cass notes that "social dysfunction now correlates strongly with income" but that it didn't in the 1960s and seventies. *Once and Future*, 38. Author Rob Henderson provides a partial explanation with his concept of "luxury beliefs." According to Henderson, elites boost their social status by expressing their approval of non-traditional lifestyle choices. They praise or excuse divorce, polyamory, recreational drug use, urban crime, and other such activities. They may even dabble a bit. Ultimately, though, their money and status shield them from the consequences. The poor — who absorb these luxury beliefs through cultural osmosis — enjoy no such protections. Your favorite rapper can do drugs in music videos and look cool doing it. When you do it, you fail your urine test and can't get a job. See Rob Henderson, "How the Luxury Beliefs of an Educated Elite Erode Society," Rob Henderson's Newsletter, February 25, 2024, https://www.robkhenderson.com/p/how-the-luxury-beliefs-of-an-educated.

[25] Cass, *Once and Future*, 24.

[26] Brad Wilcox, "Programs Should Put Family First" in *Rebuilding American Capitalism* (Washington, D.C.: American Compass, 2023), 76.

dollars a month to all married parents and five hundred dollars a month to all single parents with no strings attached.[27]

Would this mean stigmatizing disfavored life paths? We can only hope. This isn't a question of minding one's own business. As Cass notes, citing research from economist Raj Chetty, "Being raised by a single parent reduces opportunity... but so does being raised in a community with many *other* single-parent families... even for individuals who are themselves raised in two-parent families."[28]

But creating an economy that sustains strong families and communities means much more than just telling people to get married and have babies and paying them when they comply. The entire economy will have to be oriented toward producing the prosperity and opportunity that sustain genuine flourishing. An anti-transhumanist economic policy would be one that insists on treating humans as though they have a nature and a *telos*, not as mere consumers — or worse, products.

Here's an example. In his book *Tyranny, Inc.*, Sohrab Ahmari describes the millions of American workers who have fallen victim to "just-in-time" scheduling, under which employees (usually in the service industry) "receive less than a week's notice of their upcoming weekly schedule."[29] For corporations, which set schedules at the last minute in order to make workers "bear the costs associated with fluctuating consumer demand," it's a boon.[30] For single people, it's an

---

[27] Joseph Zeballos-Roig, "Josh Hawley Wants to Send $1,000 Monthly Checks to Families with Kids under 13 but Provide Less to Single Parents," *Business Insider*, April 26, 2021, https://www.businessinsider.com/josh-hawley-child-tax-credit-monthly-checks-families-kids-2021-4.
[28] Cass, *Once and Future*, 37, emphasis in original.
[29] Sohrab Ahmari, *Tyranny, Inc.: How Private Power Crushed American Liberty — and What to Do About It* (New York: Penguin Random House, 2023), 19–20.
[30] Ibid., 21.

annoyance. For families, especially single mothers, it's a catastrophe. Most daycares set their hours to accommodate typical nine-to-five workers, sending fast-food and retail employees scrambling for last-minute childcare. Citing studies, Ahmari notes that "workers subjected to unstable scheduling sleep poorly, suffer psychologically, and are generally unhappy," whereas their children are "more likely to argue, destroy things, and have tantrums."[31] This is not an economy that recognizes family as a key element of human flourishing.

Transhumanism isn't just individuals putting computer chips in their brains. Whenever we submit our humanity (or that of our neighbor) to be refashioned according to some antihuman standard, that too is a form of transhumanism. It's possible to disregard and degrade human dignity in this way through good old-fashioned bureaucracy. Algorithmic AI just makes the process more efficient. For at least a decade, retail and fast-food employers have been using automated scheduling software to assign shifts to their workers — and according to reports, "it's making them miserable."[32] As an illustration of transhumanist capitalism, it's almost too on-the-nose. In the name of maximal consumption, we're letting robots boss poor people around.

A humane economy would prioritize keeping people out of poverty through dignified and productive work, making it possible to support a family on a single working-class income, directing resources toward innovation and investment that actually improve people's lives, supporting "left-behind" cities and regions, and respecting workers' dignity (including safety, the right to organize, work-life balance, and economic freedom). This doesn't mean adopting a state-run economy. It merely

---

[31] Ibid., 22.
[32] Kaye Loggins, "Here's What Happens When an Algorithm Determines Your Work Schedule," *Vice*, February 24, 2020, https://www.vice.com/en/article/heres-what-happens-when-an-algorithm-determines-your-work-schedule/.

means erecting certain guardrails that channel market activity toward desirable ends. The alternative, Cass writes, is a policy which concludes that "if the economy no longer works for the average worker, it is he who needs to transform into something it likes better."[33]

Cass was referring to (largely ineffective) retraining programs for laid-off workers, but with the tools of transhumanism growing ever more advanced, that transformation could well become literal. Consider the "Epsilons" of *Brave New World*, who are blasted with radiation *in vitro*, leaving them too mentally impaired for any but the most menial tasks. And if our left-behind countrymen can't be made useful, they can at least be made docile. Developed nations could simply deposit them in hyper-dense slums with low rent and free high-speed Internet. There, like the denizens of the RV stacks in *Ready Player One*, the chronically unemployable can lose themselves in cyberspace. A steady diet of virtual reality gaming, teletherapy, Internet porn, drone deliveries, and legal weed could keep them indefinitely stupefied.

To restore the broad-based prosperity that would prevent that outcome, the American Compass suggests a number of policies in a handbook titled *Rebuilding American Capitalism*. These include banning stock buybacks to incentivize more productive capital investment, implementing a general tariff to reshore American industry, economically decoupling from China, restricting immigration to drive up wages, and providing on-the-job training grants to create non-college paths to success.[34]

---

[33] Cass, *Once and Future*, 26.

[34] The handbook also proposes reforming labor law to revitalize unions. Former Labor Department official Jonathan Berry calls for "expand[ing] unions' legal latitude to administer benefits and social insurance, detaching some terms of compensation from any particular workplace" and enabling the union to "take tasks off the employer's plate and return them to workers' control — likely still with employer

Evaluating each of the above proposals would be beyond both my own policy expertise and the scope of this book. But each of them, in one way or another, aims to create an economy that offers more than just cheap trinkets and a line going up on a graph.

Donald Trump's first term represented a partial break from the old neoliberal economic consensus, which emphasized growth and free trade with redistribution to soften the blow for those left behind. His second term offers an opportunity for Republicans to lean into this realignment and fully redefine themselves as a pro-family, pro-worker party with an agenda oriented toward authentic human flourishing.

In my chapter on transhumanism and U.S. politics, I concluded that Americans have been so thoroughly catechized to accept the liberal-capitalist vision of the good life that there was no hope of them rejecting transhumanism at the ballot box. There is, however, some indication that the old ideals of human flourishing live on. An American Compass survey found that, by wide margins, Americans prefer "security and stability, rootedness, [and] productivity" over an endless proliferation of consumer goods and potential life paths.[35] It's possible that these are merely expressed preferences that the respondents' own actions would

---

funding." He also proposes curbing unions' ability to engage in political lobbying, which could have the effect of increasing their collective bargaining power by making unions more appealing to conservative workers who resent leadership "routing [their] dues to progressive war chests." Strengthening unions while detaching them from left-wing social policy would play a key role in building a humane economy. Unions don't just negotiate for higher wages and better working conditions; they also start bowling leagues and throw Christmas parties. It's just what our atomized society needs. See Jonathan Berry, "Promoting Worker Agency and Self-Government" in *Rebuilding American Capitalism*, 102.

[35] "The American Wake-Up Call," American Compass, October 24, 2024, https://americancompass.org/the-american-wake-up-call/.

contradict. But if policymakers take them at their word, we might see a real and lasting shift in the choices they come to make.

Perhaps, having been encouraged and empowered to form families and support them through dignified work, Americans will find a sense of meaning so deep that they'll laugh transhumanism's promises to scorn. Obviously, there's a chicken-and-egg problem with hoping that a transhumanist electorate will vote for anti-transhumanist economic policies. But human nature dies hard.

Post-Scarcity[1]

> *[Jesus said,] "The days will come in which vines shall grow, having each ten thousand branches, and in each branch ten thousand twigs, and in each true twig ten thousand shoots, and in every one of the shoots ten thousand clusters, and on every one of the clusters ten thousand grapes, and every grape when pressed will give five-and-twenty measures of wine. And when any one of the saints shall lay hold of a cluster, another shall cry out, 'I am a better cluster, take me; bless the Lord through me.'"*
>
> — Fragment attributed to St. John the Beloved[2]

In 2023, the Writers Guild of America (WGA) and Screen Actors Guild–American Federation of Television and Radio Artists (SAG-AFTRA) went on strike, demanding protections against artificial intelligence.

---

[1] Portions of this chapter originally appeared at the *Daily Caller*. See Grayson Quay, "Conservatives Should Side with Whiny, Liberal Actors in the Hollywood Strike," *Daily Caller*, July 21, 2023, https://dailycaller.com/2023/07/21/quay-conservatives-side-whiny-liberal-actors-hollywood-strike-artificial-intelligence/.

[2] Fragment XIV, attributed to Papias in Iranaeus *Haer.* v.33.3,4, in *The Apostolic Fathers*, ed. J. B. Lightfoot and J. R. Harmer (Berkeley, CA: Apocryphile Press, 2004), 533–534.

THE TRANSHUMANIST TEMPTATION

"Artificial intelligence poses an existential threat to creative professions, and all actors and performers deserve contract language that protects them from having their identity and talent exploited without consent and pay," SAG-AFTRA President Fran Drescher explained.[3]

The WGA presented similar demands, pushing for an agreement under which "AI can't write or rewrite literary material; can't be used as source material; and [contract-covered] material can't be used to train AI."[4]

It's easy to see what AI could do to the film industry. In the futuristic society of Margaret Atwood's novel *Oryx and Crake*, anyone can generate any movie they want by feeding a few prompts into an AI program.[5] "Hey, computer," I might say, "make me a medieval heist movie starring Laurence Olivier and Vin Diesel with Tarantino dialogue and the directing style of Jean-Luc Goddard." Give it a few hours to process, and presto! The movie's ready to go without anyone making a dime off it — except, perhaps, the company that owns the algorithm and the guy who wrote the prompt.

But it's not just Hollywood. AI has the potential to devastate the entire arts industry. ChatGPT might not be able to write the great American novel, but the formulaic romances and spy thrillers that line the Wal-Mart bookshelves will be no problem. True connoisseurs might still value human-made art, but AI-generated images will work just fine

---

[3] Kevin Collier, "Actors vs. AI: Strike brings focus to emerging use of advanced tech," *NBC News*, July 14, 2023. https://www.nbcnews.com/tech/tech-news/hollywood-actor-sag-aftra-ai-artificial-intelligence-strike-rcna94191.

[4] Daniel Arkin, "Writers Strike 2023: Hollywood Screenwriters Don't Want AI Taking Their Jobs Either," *NBC News*, May 4, 2023, https://www.nbcnews.com/news/writers-strike-2023-hollywood-screenwriters-ai-concerns-rcna82543.

[5] Margaret Atwood, *Oryx and Crake* (New York: Anchor Books, 2004), 187.

for book covers, lobby décor, and most graphic design work. Could AI write Beethoven's 7th or Sufjan Stevens's *Carrie & Lowell*? Maybe not. But it can definitely provide background noise at the grocery store or scene transition music for Netflix docusoaps.

It won't stop with the arts either. Even cautious prognosticators like Oren Cass suggest that AI could soon perform "80% of economically valuable tasks."[6] This doesn't necessarily mean eliminating 80% of jobs. As Vice President Vance noted in a March 2025 speech, ATMs didn't lead to mass firings at banks; they freed up tellers to make more money by performing more valuable and interesting tasks. "I think there's too much fear that AI will simply replace jobs rather than augmenting so many of the things that we do," Vance said.[7]

Others, though, take a more radical view, predicting that AI will eliminate up to half of all jobs over the next few decades and eventually usher in a post-work society. These predictions have been around for a long time, from Karl Marx and John Maynard Keynes — who predicted in 1930 that we'd have a 15-hour work week by the early 21st century — to the utopian post-scarcity of Star Trek.[8] So far, the work-free future has failed to materialize, but that doesn't mean it never will. Over the past two centuries or so, humans have gone from farms to factories and from factories to offices. These weren't painless

---

[6] Oren Cass, "Is It Interesting to Say That AI Isn't That Interesting?" *Understanding America*, January 13, 2025, https://www.understanding america.co/p/is-it-interesting-to-say-that-ai.

[7] J. D. Vance, "Remarks by the Vice President at the American Dynamism Summit," The American Presidency Project, March 18, 2025, https:// www.presidency.ucsb.edu/documents/remarks-the-vice-president -the-american-dynamism-summit.

[8] Andy Beckett, "Post-Work: the Radical Idea of a World Without Jobs," The Guardian, January 19, 2018, https://www.theguardian.com/ news/2018/jan/19/post-work-the-radical-idea-of-a-world-without -jobs.

transitions, but they didn't cause permanent mass unemployment either. This time, though, if AI can replace rather than merely augment our efforts, it's not clear what work will be left for us to do. Maybe we can all sell each other little crafts on Etsy.

That's about all we'd have left in a world where AI can perform the services, run the automated factories, manage the supply chain, and even plan the economy for us. Economist Friedrich von Hayek's famous "knowledge problem" — the idea that no centralized bureaucracy could ever allocate resources as efficiently as a free market — could well become obsolete with a sufficiently powerful AI at the helm.[9] Meanwhile, the great mass of the unemployed would live on a universal basic income (UBI) dividend from all that automated productivity, a program Cass describes as "the rich ... paying everyone else to go away."[10]

To some readers, this might sound great. Leisure is the basis of culture, after all, and there are plenty of ways to make good use of it: study opera, learn to sculpt, read Dante in the original Italian, plant a garden and enjoy its fruits. For the first time in history, everyone would have access to the contemplative, aristocratic pleasures of a Seneca or a Montaigne.

A more likely outcome would be the final triumph of limbic capitalism. According to author David Courtwright, who coined the term, limbic capitalism "refers to a technologically advanced but socially regressive business system in which global industries, often with the help of complicit governments ... encourage excessive consumption and addiction."[11]

---

[9] F. A. Hayek, "The Use of Knowledge in Society," *American Economic Review* 35, no. 4 (September 1945): 519–530, https://www.econlib.org/library/Essays/hykKnw.html.

[10] Cass, *Once and Future*, 27.

[11] David T. Courtwright, "What Is Limbic Capitalism?" *Damage*, June 2, 2021, https://damagemag.com/2021/06/02/what-is-limbic-capitalism/.

In other words, big business hacks your dopamine receptors to get you hooked on their products, and since big business has all the lobbying money, government won't step in to protect you. It's you and whatever self-discipline you've managed to build up versus thousands of experts whose only job is figuring out ways to circumvent it. Not exactly a fair fight. Instagram, PornHub, DraftKings, and Frito-Lay already operate on this principle.

Now imagine the whole economy works like that, adopting a profit-driven transhumanism that seeks to rewire customers into more perfect consumers. We often imagine genetic tweaks or miracle pills to make us into geniuses with godlike physiques, but what pathetic, appetite-driven creatures might we become if those same technologies could make sex feel a thousand times better or enable our bodies to safely metabolize heroin?

In a world where everyone has disposable income, unlimited free time, no responsibilities, and no consequences for overconsumption, there'd be nothing to limit the growth of limbic capitalism. Far from creating a population of scholars and artisans, a post-work transhumanist future would make us into cringing dopamine addicts. We'd become putty in the hands of the pleasure-providers, who would not hesitate to reshape our minds and bodies however they wished. Anything to keep the profits flowing and the economy growing.

True aristocrats of the spirit might rise above such base pleasures, but they would face a related temptation. In his 1891 essay "The Soul of Man Under Socialism," Oscar Wilde offered a prophetic vision of how post-scarcity would make us posthuman. Christopher Lasch explains in *Revolt of the Elites* that, for Wilde, socialism means simply "the elimination of drudgery by machines."[12] This "collectivization

---

[12] Christopher Lasch, *The Revolt of the Elites and the Betrayal of Democracy* (New York: Norton, 1995), 231.

of production," Lasch continues, "would liberate the poor from want, but it would also liberate the rich from the burden of managing and defending their property." Wilde eagerly awaits the day when, instead of chasing material wealth, people of all classes would be free to devote their energies to self-actualization. " 'Know thyself' was written over the portal of the antique world," Wilde wrote. "Over the portal of the new world, 'Be thyself' shall be written ... 'You have a wonderful personality. Develop it.' "[13]

The leftists who founded Britain's Labour Party and implemented the American New Deal believed in restoring workers' dignity through better wages, safer conditions, and collective bargaining powers. Modern progressives seem bored with that program. Like Wilde, they don't much care for working-class people. When they complain about capitalism, it's because they view it as an impediment to their own self-fashioning.

The highest calling of the newly liberated individual would not be to pursue knowledge, cultivate virtue, hone skills, or serve his community, but to more fully discover and craft his own identity. And naturally, he'll have all the tools of transhumanism at his disposal. He can get new genitals, longer legs, cybernetic implants, or a more aggressive demeanor. In the digital realm, he can connect with people all over the world and discover new ways to pursue authenticity: adopt some weird new label like "graysexual," identify as a wolf and wear a fur suit everywhere, self-diagnose with dissociative identity disorder and have fun managing all those split personalities. The possibilities are endless, and he'll have nothing to do but explore them.

Hollywood actors feared that AI-driven post-scarcity would make them obsolete. The true danger is that it will turn all of us into full-time

---

[13] Oscar Wilde, *The Soul of Man Under Socialism* (Boston: Luce, 1910), 20–21.

Post-Scarcity

actors, constantly reshaping ourselves to play an ever-shifting series of roles. George Orwell warned that a man who "wears a mask" often finds that "his face grows to fit it."[14] In this brave new world, where the only remaining occupation is the performance and development of identity, there would be no need to don a mask and wait for the face to grow into it. Anyone could immediately become that which he hopes or pretends to be with no possibility of breaking character. The old self to which he might return no longer exists. He may be able to get it back the same way he erased it, but it would no longer be a truer self than any of the infinite others he might purchase, bespoke or off the rack.

If you want a vision of the future, imagine a human being obsessively rearranging his own face — forever.

---

[14] George Orwell, "Shooting an Elephant," The Orwell Estate, accessed April 5, 2025, https://www.orwellfoundation.com/the-orwell-foundation/orwell/essays-and-other-works/shooting-an-elephant/.

Part 5

GOD

17

The Nephilim and *Theosis*

Before me there was no God formed, neither shall there be after me.

— Isaiah 43:10, KJV

As I argued in my introduction, the transhumanist temptation did not originate with AI or the birth control pill or Julian Huxley or Nietzsche or Hume. It is not primarily a technological or philosophical phenomenon, but a spiritual one. When I say this temptation is as old as Eden, I do not mean merely that it shows up in the most ancient stories human cultures have told themselves. I mean that demonic beings — literal bodiless entities — have intervened in history to spread Satan's false promise and goad us into becoming like them. In fact, if we take Christian tradition seriously, they've come close to accomplishing that goal once already.

In the Book of Revelation, St. John tells the church at Pergamum that their city is home to Satan's throne.[15] Scholars believe he was referring to a giant altar to Zeus that sat on the city's acropolis.[16]

---

[15] Rev. 2:13.
[16] Adela Yarbro Collins, "Satan's Throne: Revelations from Revelation," *Biblical Archaeological Review* 32, no. 3 (May/June 2006), https://library.biblicalarchaeology.org/article/satans-throne/.

THE TRANSHUMANIST TEMPTATION

He had good reason to make the association. As Orthodox priest Fr. Andrew Stephen Damick writes in his book *The Lord of Spirits*, "One of the most underappreciated aspects of the Scripture ... is how much of it was formulated precisely as a response to paganism."[17] The early Christians and ancient Israelites did not see themselves as inhabiting a radically different cosmos than the one described by their pagan neighbors. Christ and Peter had no problem using the Greek terms "Hades" and "Tartarus" to refer to the same underworld the Jews call "Sheol."[18] Instead, they saw themselves as correcting what Damick calls "pro-demon propaganda" about that cosmos.

In Hesiod's *Theogony*, Zeus carries out a coup against his tyrannical and filicidal father, Cronos, who had overthrown his own father, Uranus. After his rebellion against the Titans succeeds, Zeus and his allies bind the leaders of the old regime "in bitter chains" and cast them "far beneath the earth to Tartarus." It is a near perfect inversion of the biblical account of Lucifer, whose revolt fails and ends with him and his followers cast into Hell.[19] The Lord, the biblical authors made clear, did not hold His Godhood by right of conquest.

This is a crucial distinction. A chief god who overthrew his predecessor cannot, by definition, be the eternal principle of reality, the font of truth, goodness, and beauty. In a cosmos ruled by a usurper god, might makes right. Any commands promulgated by that god would have the character not of natural law, but of arbitrary decree. People created by such a deity might grovel to avoid his wrath. They would not, however, owe him anything. Obeying him might be smart — in

---

[17] Andrew Stephen Damick, *The Lord of Spirits: An Orthodox Christian Framework for the Unseen World and Spiritual Warfare* (Chesterton, IN: Ancient Faith, 2023), 135.

[18] Similarly, the English *Hell* originally referred to both the Anglo-Saxon underworld and the pagan goddess who ruled over it.

[19] Isa. 14:13–15, RSVCE.

the sense of serving one's self-interest — but it would not necessarily be wise or good. Under such conditions, there can be no such thing as a "right" way to be human in any ultimate sense.

Plato confronted this problem in his "Euthyphro" dialogue, at the heart of which stands the famous dilemma: "Is the pious loved by the gods because it's pious, or it is pious because it is loved?"[20] The first option anticipates Christianity by positing an eternal standard of justice to which even Zeus is subordinate. The second presents the gods' authority as arbitrary and absolute. This latter view posits the kind of "heavenly North Korea" that atheist polemicist Christopher Hitchens accused Christians of promoting.[21] Though to give Hitchens his due, there were some in the Middle Ages who attempted to transplant that old pagan lie into Christianity.

These medieval theologians, known as voluntarists, believed it was too limiting to suggest that God's reason or goodness existed coeternally with His divine will. According to Eastern Orthodox theologian David Bentley Hart, voluntarism had the effect of "redefining freedom — for God and, by extension, for us — not as the unhindered realization of a nature (the liberty to 'become what you are'), but as the absolute liberty of the will in determining even what its nature is."[22]

This pseudo-freedom, which the usurper gods of paganism share with the misconceived God of the voluntarists, provides no framework of natural law to protect us from transhumanism. But it's the only kind of freedom left when we cease to believe in a God who resolves Plato's dilemma by being Goodness Itself, Truth Itself, Beauty Itself. The

---

[20] Plato, "Euthyphro," trans. Cathal Woods and Ryan Pack, Creative Commons, 8, https://dx.doi.org/10.2139/ssrn.1023143.

[21] "Does God Exist? William Lane Craig vs. Christopher Hitchens," Biola University, April 4, 2009, posted September 28, 2014, YouTube, 2:27:42, https://www.youtube.com/watch?v=0tYm41hb48o, 1:18:25.

[22] Hart, "Christ and Nothing."

voluntarist-transhumanist conception of freedom neither describes nor pleases such a God. It is, however, perfectly articulated by Milton's Satan in *Paradise Lost*, who declares, "Evil, be thou my good."[23] Hence St. John's identification of Zeus with the envious angel who made war on God, then urged Adam and Eve to join his revolt and become gods themselves.

But the beloved apostle's decision to equate the chief of the Olympians with the lord of the flies did not rest solely on his rebellion against Cronos. Zeus was also a lover (consensually or otherwise) of human women and a breeder of demigods. And as with the heavenly coup narratives, the Judeo-Christian scriptures present their own rebuttals to the pagan demigod stories. These figures, the biblical authors insisted, were not heroes but demonic tyrants.

Genesis 6 describes how "the sons of God saw that the daughters of man were fair" and "took to wife such of them as they chose," producing offspring known as the Nephilim or "giants."[24] Some argue that the "sons of God" who procreated with the "daughters of man" in this passage were the descendants of Seth and Cain, respectively. But that's a later tradition. The dominant theory at the time of Christ and during the first centuries of the Church was that the "sons of God" were fallen angels and the Nephilim were demon-human hybrids — what we might call the original transhumans.[25]

---

[23] John Milton, *Paradise Lost* (Franklin Center, PA: Franklin Library, 1984), 4.110.

[24] Gen. 6:2–4, RSVCE.

[25] See, for example, second-century Church Father St. Justin Martyr, who wrote that "the angels transgressed ... and were captivated by love of women, and begot children." *Second Apology*, trans. Marcus Dods and George Reith in *Ante-Nicene Fathers*, Vol. 1, ed. Alexander Roberts, James Donaldson, and A. Cleveland Coxe, rev. and ed. for New Advent by Kevin Knight (Buffalo, NY: Christian Literature Publishing, 1885), 5, http://www.newadvent.org/fathers/0127.htm.

Not content to breed a race of cannibalistic tyrants who degraded and depleted God's creation and filled the whole world "with blood and unrighteousness," these demons (known in Babylonian mythology as *apkallu*) also taught humanity the secrets of weapon-making, metalworking, cosmetics, and enchantments.[26] Such advancements only enhanced mankind's ability to destroy itself. Tech pioneer Sam Altman presents his AI-human "Merge" as the wave of the future, but according to Scripture and tradition, it wouldn't be the first time humans had sought to increase their knowledge and power by interfacing with bodiless superintelligences.

Even the Flood wasn't enough to put an end to the Nephilim forever. In his book *Religion of the Apostles*, Fr. Stephen De Young explains that, in Babylonian records, post-deluge kings, "such as the hero Gilgamesh, are said to be 'two-thirds [god],' or the product of divine and human coupling."[27] Nephilim appear to have been bred in sex rituals that involved a god or goddess possessing one of the human partners — hence Deuteronomy 3:11's reference to the massive ritual bed of King Og of Bashan.

See also Justin's contemporary, St. Iraeneus, who wrote that "angels were united with the daughters of the race of mankind; and they bore to them sons." *Demonstration of the Apostolic Preaching*, trans. and ed. Armitage Robinson (London: Society for Promoting Christian Knowledge, 1920), 18, https://www.ccel.org/ccel/irenaeus/demonstr.preaching_the_demonstration_of_the_apostolic_preaching.html. For Second Temple Jewish sources, see 1 Enoch 6–7 and Jubilees 4:22 and 5:1 in *The Apocrypha and Pseudepigrapha of the Old Testament*, ed. and trans. R. H. Charles (Berkeley, CA: Apocryphile Press, 2024), https://www.pseudepigrapha.com/jubilees/index.htm.

[26] 1 Enoch 9:10; 8:1–2.

[27] Stephen De Young, *The Religion of the Apostles: Orthodox Christianity in the First Century* (Chesterton, IN: Ancient Faith, 2021), 92.

THE TRANSHUMANIST TEMPTATION

These hybrids reappear later with names like the Rephaim and the Anakim, who appear to comprise several Canaanite nations and of whom Goliath is one of the last descendants. In the New Testament, the evil spirits Christ and his disciples cast out were understood by contemporary Jews to be the souls of dead Nephilim.[28] Noah, Joshua, David, and Jesus were all fighting the same war against the same transhuman enemy.[29]

Damick writes that accounts of the Nephilim provide "an image of a humanity that has fallen into demonization" and illustrate the consequences of attempting "to become like God but without the obedient relationship with Him."[30] By believing the serpent's promise — and it would be difficult to devise a better definition of transhumanism than that — a human being might become so fully demonic in life that in death, he comes to share in the demons' punishment.

But if humans can become demonized, they can also become divinized. The Greek term for it is *theosis*. The shortest definition, formulated by fourth-century Church Father Athanasius, is that God "assumed humanity that we might become god." — that is, so that we might come to share in Christ's divinity as He shared in our humanity, experiencing for all eternity the boundless love that constitutes the inner life of the Trinity.[31] Christianity is, in a very real sense, a transhumanist religion.

This idea, that the lowliest slave might hope to become a child of God and "equal to the angels," hit the ancient world like a thunderbolt.[32]

---

[28] Ibid., 111–113.
[29] The Anglo-Saxon epic *Beowulf*, set in the sixth century A. D., describes the monster Grendel as one of the Nephilim. See *Beowulf*, trans. Lesslie Hall (Boston, MA: D. C. Heath & Co., 1892), 49–62.
[30] Damick, *Lord of Spirits*, 188–191.
[31] Athanasius, *On the Incarnation*, trans. Penelope Lawson, intro. C. S. Lewis (Scott Valley, CA: CreateSpace, 2016), 54.
[32] Luke 20:36, RSVCE.

The Nephilim and Theosis

The Roman Senate had declared that Julius and Augustus Caesar were elevated to godhood following their deaths. But those who lacked the wealth, strength, cunning, and luck to win themselves an empire could not hope for the same fate. All the common folk had to look forward to was becoming forgotten shades in the same underworld where Achilles told the still-living Odysseus that he would rather be a "dirt-poor tenant farmer who scrapes to keep alive — than rule down here over all the breathless dead."[33]

The popular Christmas carol expresses the change well: "He appeared and the soul felt its worth." Hart writes that "Christ's descent from the 'form of God' into the 'form of a slave' " revealed "the indwelling of the divine image in each soul" and declares that "once the world has been seen in this way, it can never again be what it once had been." In such a world, the only options that remain are Christ or a nihilism that worships "the nothingness of the will miraculously giving itself form by mastering the nothingness of the world."[34] And as C. S. Lewis points out, the "world" over which this will exercises mastery inevitably includes the human person as well.[35]

Transhumanism is therefore best understood as a dark reflection of *theosis*. The Christian and the transhumanist present what Hart describes as "two radically antagonistic visions of what it is to be a god."[36]

There was something sustainable about ancient paganism. The great mass of humanity might have gone on believing forever that they were to the gods "as flies to wanton boys."[37] Some might even have borne up under the bludgeonings of fate to achieve the kind of tragic dignity

---

[33] Homer, *The Odyssey*, trans. Robert Fagles (New York: Penguin, 1997), 11.555–558.
[34] Hart, "Christ and Nothing."
[35] Lewis, *Abolition of Man*, 24.
[36] Hart, "Christ and Nothing."
[37] William Shakespeare, *King Lear*, act 4, scene 1, 37.

THE TRANSHUMANIST TEMPTATION

we see in the best Homeric warriors. But there would have been no hope beyond that, and little hope of hope ever dawning. "It was the end of the world," Chesterton wrote of the Roman Empire on the cusp of the Incarnation, "and the worst of it was that it need never end."[38]

There's no going back now. Lewis wrote that "ancient man approached ... the gods ... as the accused person approaches his judge," whereas the modern person sees himself as the judge and God as the one on trial.[39] Humanity's sense of its own dignity is ineradicable. If we feel that God has become an impediment to that dignity, we will simply dispense with Him and pursue it by other means.

Like Shakespeare's Cleopatra, we have "immortal longings" and a sense that they ought to be fulfilled.[40] We will seek to be divinized — if not by God's hand, then by our own. And as in millennia past, demonic forces are always happy to help.

---

[38] G. K. Chesterton, *The Everlasting Man* (Peabody, MA: Hendrickson, 2007), 154.
[39] C. S. Lewis, "God in the Dock," in *God in the Dock* (Grand Rapids, MI: Eerdmans, 2014), 268.
[40] William Shakespeare, *Antony and Cleopatra*, act 5, scene 2, 335.

Transhumanist Spiritualities

The number of people in possession of any criteria for discriminating between good and evil is very small; the number of the half-alive hungry for any form of spiritual experience, or what offers itself as spiritual experience, high or low, good or bad, is considerable.

— T. S. Eliot[1]

Theosis is hard work. But if you're looking for a shortcut, why not pay twenty dollars for a square paper tab that fits on the pad of your index finger, stick it under your tongue, and wait to be elevated beyond the limits of human perception.

In an article for HPlusMagazine, journalist Michael Garfield explores the overlap between psychedelic theorists and transhumanists. "Their common vision shares ... an evolutionary model of the universe and humanity; a sense of the human organism as something that can be tinkered with and expanded; a recognition of drugs as a technology that can dramatically reinvent identity, and a playful challenging of fixed boundaries," he writes.[2]

---

[1] T. S. Eliot, *After Strange Gods: A Primer of Modern Heresy* (London: Faber, 1934), 61.
[2] Michael Garfield, "The Psychedelic Transhumanists: A Virtual Round Table Between Legends Living & Dead," *Medium*, December 11,

THE TRANSHUMANIST TEMPTATION

Mind-expanding substances are back in a big way. Between 2002 and 2019, the share of Americans eighteen to twenty-five who reported using LSD in the past twelve months rose from 0.9 percent to 4 percent, according to a study published in the journal *Addiction*.[3]

Multiple states have approved the use of psilocybin mushrooms and other psychedelics for mental health treatment. In 2020, Oregon decriminalized possession of small amounts of hard drugs, including several hallucinogens, before reversing the policy in 2024.[4] Celebrities including Elon Musk, Jada Pinkett Smith, and Prince Harry have all spoken openly about their experiences with these substances.[5]

Visionary drugs like DMT and ayahuasca, which untether the user from reality more fully than acid, are also having a moment. A 2021 *New York Times* report chronicled the rise of hallucinogenic retreats. As one might expect, placing groups of strangers in fragile psychological states and unfamiliar surroundings (often in foreign countries) can lead to disaster. The *Times* lists a few examples:

2023, https://michaelgarfield.medium.com/the-psychedelic-trans humanists-a-virtual-round-table-between-legends-living-dead-42709 992c389. Originally published September 29, 2009, in *HPlusMagazine*.

[3] Ofir Livne et al., "Adolescent and Adult Time Trends in US Hallucinogen Use, 2002–19: Any Use, and Use of Ecstasy, LSD and PCP," *Addiction* 117, no. 12 (August): 3099–3109, https://doi.org/10.1111/add.15987.

[4] Michelle Wiley, "Drug Possession Is a Crime Again in Oregon. Here's What You Need to Know," Oregon Public Broadcasting, September 3, 2024, https://www.opb.org/article/2024/09/01/oregon-starts-drug-possession-recriminalization/.

[5] Alexander Beiner, "'I Took Part in a Radical Psychedelic Clinical Trial and It Changed My Life Forever,'" *Standard*, July 6, 2023, https://www.standard.co.uk/lifestyle/psychedelic-clinic-trial-imperial-dmt-ayahuasca-jaden-smith-b1092353.html.

In 2015, a Canadian tourist said he stabbed to death a fellow practitioner at a psychedelic retreat in the Amazon who had attacked him under the influence of ayahuasca. Three years later, a shaman and another tourist were killed in a double murder at a different retreat nearby.[6]

Other times, it can take months for the consequences of tampering with one's psyche to manifest. In October 2021, actress Kate Hyatt committed suicide after attending a psychedelic healing retreat in rural England in June of that year.[7] For users with a predisposition toward schizophrenia or bipolar disorder, psychedelic use can trigger full-on psychosis.[8]

There is some evidence suggesting positive results across a range of issues, from addiction to post-traumatic stress disorder.[9] But for some, the supposed benefits don't stop there. Author and psychedelic enthusiast Alexander Beiner suggests that these substances might not only

---

[6] Debra Kamin, "The Rise of Psychedelic Retreats," *New York Times*, December 1, 2021, https://www.nytimes.com/2021/11/25/travel/psychedelic-retreat-ayahuasca.html.

[7] James Tozer, "Artist Took Own Life After Drinking Hallucinogenic 'Tea' in Ritual," *Daily Mail*, January 6, 2023, https://dailymail.co.uk/news/article-11607545/Artist-took-life-drinking-hallucinogenic-tea-shamanic-healing-ritual-inquest-hears.html.

[8] Dana G. Smith, "Psychedelics for Therapy: What to Know About Benefits and Risks," *New York Times*, February 20, 2023, https://www.nytimes.com/2023/02/10/well/mind/psychedelics-therapy-ketamine-mushrooms-risks.html.

[9] Matthew W. Johnson, Albert Garcia-Romeu, and Roland R. Griffiths, "Long-term Follow-up of Psilocybin-Facilitated Smoking Cessation," *American Journal of Drug and Alcohol Abuse* 43, no. 1 (July 2017): 55–60, https://doi.org/10.3109/00952990.2016.1170135. See also Sohrab Ahmari, "The Cross and the Vine of Death," *Compact*, October 29, 2024, https://www.compactmag.com/article/the-cross-and-the-vine-of-death/.

help improve mental health but also provide "innovative new solutions to collective problems like the climate crisis, runaway AI, and political polarisation."[10] He even mentions a study that involves "Israelis and Palestinians drink[ing] Ayahuasca together with the aim of conflict resolution."

One retreat center owner told the *Times* that, during the pandemic, he offered free psilocybin retreats "to over 300 people and the life change that came out of it, it was an evangelistic thing that didn't need a church or a Bible or a religion."[11]

It may be tempting to dismiss psychedelic experiences as nothing more than warped perceptions of reality brought on by the brain's

---

[10] Beiner, "Radical Psychedelic Clinical Trial."

[11] Kamin, "Rise of Psychedelic Retreats." The link between psychedelics and religion is an ancient one. Some scholars claim that the Greek oracles at Delphi owed their prophetic utterances to hallucinogenic fumes that seeped up from the cave floor. See William J. Broad, "For Delphic Oracle, Fumes and Visions," *New York Times*, March 19, 2002, https://www.nytimes.com/2002/03/19/science/for-delphic-oracle-fumes-and-visions.html. According to European records spanning centuries, witches who claimed to fly on brooms and dance with the devil testified that they used an ointment to facilitate contact with these spirits. In his edited volume *Hallucinogens and Shamanism*, scholar Michael Hamer concludes that this ointment was made of plants from the "potato family" — including "mandrake (Mandragora), henbane (Hyoscyamus), and belladonna, or deadly nightshade (Atropa belladonna)." These plants, he writes, induced states of delirium intense enough to convince users that their hallucinations were real, even after the drug had worn off. Sixteenth-century Spanish physician Andrés Laguna used his discovery of the ointment to debunk claims of witchcraft, concluding that "all that which the wretched witches do is phantasm caused by ... potions and unguents." Of course, the fact that witches used deliriants to produce these experiences does not rule out the possibility that the substances placed them in touch with real spiritual beings. See Michael Hamer, *Hallucinogens and Shamanism* (Oxford: Oxford University Press, 1973), 128.

misfiring synapses, but it's worth remembering that our senses and mental faculties evolved for survival, not to perceive reality in all its fullness. H. P. Lovecraft wrote that we "live on a placid island of ignorance in the midst of black seas of infinity, and it was not meant that we should voyage far."[12] If that's the case, then perhaps psychedelics really are expanding users' consciousness to perceive aspects of reality that lie beyond normal human parameters and putting them in touch with spiritual entities that no human is fully prepared to encounter.

Even secular researchers seem willing to consider the possibility that something real is happening. Psychedelic therapist Daniel McQueen has developed a program that seeks to use intravenous drips to extend DMT trips from a few minutes to several hours, sending brave (or foolish) "psychonauts" boldly where no man has gone before. According to one profile, McQueen "remains open to whether a psychonaut experience is just 'in their head' or something else."[13]

In a review of psychedelic literature, author Charles Foster wrote that the drugs expand users' "ontological capacity" — their ability to perceive reality — and that they frequently meet "aliens, elves, and talking animals" who impart wisdom to the psychonauts.[14] DMT pioneer

---

[12] H. P. Lovecraft, "The Call of Cthulhu," The H. P. Lovecraft Archive, Donovan K. Loucks accessed January 30, 2025, https://hplovecraft.com/writings/texts/fiction/cc.aspx.

[13] Justin Higginbottom, "The 'Psychonauts' Training to Explore Another Dimension," *New Republic*, January 3, 2023, https://newrepublic.com/article/169525/psychonauts-training-psychedelics-dmt-extended-state.

[14] Charles Foster, "Mind Expanding," *Times Literary Supplement*, no. 6302 (January 12, 2024), https://www.the-tls.co.uk/politics-society/social-cultural-studies/ten-trips-andy-mitchell-psychedelics-david-nutt-i-feel-love-rachel-nuwer-psychonauts-mike-jay-book-review-charles-foster.

THE TRANSHUMANIST TEMPTATION

Terence McKenna coined the term *machine elves* to describe some of these entities.[15]

While comparing trips with Joe Rogan, YouTuber Blaire White explained that the "elves" offered a "sign" to look for in the real world to prove they were more than a figment of Blaire's drugged-out imagination. Sure enough, the sign materialized.[16] Another YouTuber, Joshua Zatkoff, described seeing "light beings" during trips that began with calming words and ended by urging him to murder his uncle. "Those experiences are 100 percent [real]. It's another dimension. The veil is removed," he told podcaster Michael Knowles during an interview.[17]

White and Zatkoff aren't outliers. In one 2020 study, just nine percent of respondents said they believed the "entities" they'd encountered on DMT existed "completely within myself." Over half of those who identified as atheists before taking the drug no longer did afterwards.[18] Anyone not bound by an *a priori* commitment to materialism would be forced to at least consider that these substances may open some sort of gateway to the spiritual world and to the beings that inhabit it.

[15] Louis O'Neill, "What Are the Machine Elves?" *Monster Children*, June 3, 2015, https://www.monsterchildren.com/articles/what-are-the-machine-elves.

[16] Blair White, interview with Joe Rogan, *Joe Rogan Experience*, ep. 1746, podcast audio, June 27, 2024, YouTube, 2:55:11, https://www.youtube.com/watch?v=AGv9HIEZUyY, 2:00:56.

[17] Joshua Zatkoff, interview with Michael Knowles, *Michael &*, April 15, 2023, YouTube, 1:57:54, https://www.youtube.com/watch?v=oDfMAJ33J1M, 30:03.

[18] Alan K. Davis et al., "Survey of Entity Encounter Experiences Occasioned by Inhaled N,N-dimethyltryptamine: Phenomenology, Interpretation, and Enduring Effects," *Journal of Psychopharmacology* 34, no. 9 (April 2020): 1008–1020, https://doi.org/10.1177/0269881120916143.

The consequences are not always negative. Christian evangelist Lonnie Frisbee came to faith while reading the Bible on acid.[19] God can make use of any instrument, after all. But the spiritual experiences psychedelics facilitate come without any guardrails. They offer an anytime, anywhere, on-our-terms version of what God offers humanity on His terms — which is exactly what the serpent promised Eve. Taking psychedelics, especially DMT, is an act of religious transhumanism, a quest for unearned wisdom that leaves its victims face-to-face with the diabolical.

In his 1975 book *Orthodoxy and the Religion of the Future*, Orthodox monk Seraphim Rose examined a number of cultural trends that he saw as contributing to a new religious sensibility — among them the rage for Hindu and Buddhist spirituality and the ecumenical and Pentecostal movements within Christianity. He concluded that the "religion of the future" would be one that emphasized technique and results over dogma and that sought transcendence through contact with higher powers.[20] These developments, he believed, were demonic deceptions bent on preparing humanity for the coming antichrist.

Psychedelics fit both of Rose's criteria, but interestingly, he does not include them among the trends he highlights. Rose touches on the Beatles' enthusiasm for transcendental meditation but never mentions their use of LSD. Nor does he explore the intersections of eastern spirituality with psychedelics, such as Timothy Leary's use of the Tibetan Book of the Dead to guide initiates through acid trips.[21] Rose

---

[19] Bethel McGrew, "*Jesus Revolution* and the Tragedy of Lonnie Frisbee," WNG, March 3, 2023, https://wng.org/opinions/jesus-revolution-and-american-evangelicalism-1677846705.

[20] Seraphim Rose, *Orthodoxy and the Religion of the Future* (Platina, CA: Saint Herman of Alaska Brotherhood, 1979), 6.

[21] See *Mad Men*, season 5, ep. 6, "Far Away Places," dir. Scott Hornbacher, aired April 22, 2012, https://www.youtube.com/watch?v=GpWlKCfSPcU.

THE TRANSHUMANIST TEMPTATION

was obviously interested in attempts to delve deep within oneself and there encounter higher beings, but he overlooked the importance of psychedelics in pursuing that goal.

What he did not overlook was the corresponding *external* search for saviors who might lead us to our transhuman destiny, a search conducted not in our minds, but among the stars. Rose compared accounts of UFO sightings to stories of demonic apparitions and concluded that UFO encounters are not sightings of extraterrestrial beings but "a contemporary form of an occult phenomenon which has existed throughout the centuries." This phenomenon, he argues, has taken on its current form to accommodate the scientism of modernity. Or, as Rose puts it, "Men have abandoned Christianity and look for 'saviours' from outer space."[22] In November 2023, as congressional hearings brought UFOs to the forefront of public consciousness, novelist Walter Kirn interviewed whistleblower David Grusch and concluded, like Rose, that "a substitute religion is being prepared for mankind."[23]

C. S. Lewis' novel *That Hideous Strength* imagines a cabal of scientists who claim to have established contact with higher beings they call *macrobes*. One character explains that these entities likely had "profound influence" on human history, but little direct contact because "the intellectual development of man had not reached the level at which intercourse with our species could offer any attractions to a *macrobe*."[24] In other words, these demonic powers can be expected to reveal themselves only when we have adopted a worldview that would accept both the technologically facilitated transcendence of our humanity and the aid of non-human intelligences in achieving

---

[22] Rose, *Religion of the Future*, 131.
[23] Walter Kirn, interview with James Poulos, *Zero Hour*, ep. 21, "How Much Time Does America Have Left?," BlazeTV, November 5, 2023, 1:02:02, https://www.youtube.com/watch?v=2Q2jwjDXmvc, 35:13.
[24] C. S. Lewis, *That Hideous Strength* (New York: Scribner, 1996), 254.

that goal. Once those prerequisites are met, humanity will be primed to destroy itself (with a little demonic prompting) in ways of which antediluvian *apkallu* could only have dreamed.

Perhaps these spiritual forces have already gotten started. In her book on UFO spirituality, Diana Pasulka profiles (under the pseudonym "Tyler D.") a former NASA employee who holds several biomedical patents that he claims were revealed to him by a nonhuman intelligence he's learned to channel. And he's not alone. Drawing on Pasulka's work and other sources, Dreher concludes that some of the world's top scientists and tech pioneers believe that extraterrestrial intelligences are "passing technological information to us telepathically" in order to lead us to a "great evolutionary leap."[25]

Writers like Erich von Däniken — whose thesis has been widely popularized on the History Channel's *Ancient Aliens* and in films like Ridley Scott's *Prometheus* — suggest that aliens shaped human evolution from the beginning. And if that's the case, then someday (perhaps when we have proven ourselves worthy by eradicating war and prejudice) they might return to set things right and raise us to their own higher form of being. In other words, this secular religion offers both a creation myth and an eschatology. The flying saucer symbolically replaces — and, for some scholars, literally becomes — the Spirit of God brooding over the waters and the New Jerusalem descending from the sky. The rock band Styx tapped into this faddish UFO spirituality in their 1977 hit "Come Sail Away":

---

[25] Diana W. Pasulka, *American Cosmic: UFOs, Religion, Technology*, (Oxford: Oxford University Press, 2024). In Dreher, *Living*, 116–118. For the likely identity of Tyler D., see paranormal_mendocino, "More Details on NASA Researcher and Inventor," Reddit, r/ufo, March 10, 2019, https://www.reddit.com/r/ufo/comments/azdw8r/more_details_on_nasa_researcher_and_inventor/?utm_source=substack&utm_medium=email.

THE TRANSHUMANIST TEMPTATION

> I thought that they were angels
> But to my surprise
> We climbed aboard their starship
> We headed for the skies.[26]

The science fiction author Arthur C. Clarke, who died in 2008, was perhaps the most prominent advocate of the alien *theosis* theory. He wrote the screenplay for the 1968 film *2001: A Space Odyssey*, in which a mysterious black monolith seems to catalyze the leap from ordinary apes to tool-using humans, playing essentially the same role as the Babylonian *apkallu*.[27]

2001 then flashes forward hundreds of millennia. Another monolith has appeared near Jupiter, and a crew of astronauts set off to investigate it. One astronaut is sucked into a vortex, leading to an intense psychedelic light show. I've heard a rumor that, when the film was first released, LSD enthusiasts would sneak into showings of *2001* at intermission and sit in the aisles to enjoy the display. Fitting that one form of pseudo-transcendence would attract another.

Dave, the astronaut, then wakes up in what director Stanely Kubrick described in an interview as a "human zoo," where the aliens observe him as he ages. Then, "When they get finished with him, as happens in so many myths of all cultures in the world, he is transformed into some kind of superbeing and sent back to Earth," Kubrick explained.[28] The neo-Dave appears as a glowing fetus hovering in the sky, and we can

---

[26] Styx, "Come Sail Away," written by Dennis DeYoung, recorded August 1977, track 4 on *The Grand Illusion*, A&M Records, https://www.youtube.com/watch?v=eYCFrcCqh7Q&pp=ygUOY29tZSBzYWlsIGF3YXk%3D.

[27] *2001: A Space Odyssey*, dir. Stanley Kubrick, written by Stanley Kubrick and Arthur C. Clarke, (London: Kubrick Productions, 1968).

[28] Daniel Rennie, "Stanley Kubrick Explains the Ending of 2001: A Space Odyssey in Unreleased Documentary," *Bold Entrance*, September

only assume that he has some role to play in guiding his fellow humans to enlightenment, that they might be as he is. In Christian terms, Dave has become a saint, elevated to the Divine Council and empowered to serve as patron and intercessor for the Church Militant.

Clarke offers a broader, more detailed version of this story in his 1953 novel *Childhood's End*. Alien ships appear above earth's cities. The extraterrestrials, known as Overlords, slowly take over the management of human affairs, and they do such a good job that few people object. A golden age of peace, free love, and universal abundance ensues. But the Overlords' end goal remains shrouded in mystery.

Eventually, children begin developing psychic and telekinetic powers. This final generation is then sequestered on their own continent, where they merge into a hive mind as they prepare for union with a vast cosmic intelligence known as the Overmind, which bears "the same relation to man as man bore to amoeba."[29]

"The Overmind is trying to grow, to extend its powers and its awareness of the universe. By now it must be the sum of many races, and long ago it left the tyranny of matter behind," one Overlord explains. "It is conscious of intelligence, everywhere. When it knew that you were almost ready, it sent us here to do its bidding, to prepare you for the transformation that is now at hand."[30]

The novel's biggest twist, which occurs about a quarter of the way through, is that the aliens who spent decades hiding themselves from humanity did so because they look exactly like the popular conception of devils. "The leathery wings, the little horns, the barbed

---

24, 2024, https://boldentrance.com/stanley-kubrick-explains-the/-ending-of-2001-a-space-odyssey-in-unreleased-documentary/.

[29] Arthur C. Clarke, *Childhood's End* (New York: Random House, 1990), 199.

[30] Ibid., 177.

tail — all were there," Clarke's narrator tells us.[31] The people of earth initially assume that ancient civilizations had some contact with the Overlords and that later portrayals of demons drew on this primordial memory. Later, though, an Overlord confirms that there was no such contact in the distant past. Humanity's racial memory of the aliens "was not of the past, but of the future ... as if a distorted echo had reverberated round the closed circle of time," carrying the trauma of humanity's end.[32]

Clarke, whose smug scientism becomes insufferable once you've read two or three of his books, clearly sees the Overlords as the good guys and the transhumanism they deliver as a positive, if bittersweet, development. C. S. Lewis offered a charitable interpretation of Clarke's secularized vision of *theosis*, writing in a letter to his future wife that an author who so poignantly portrayed the parents' grief at their children's union with the Overmind might "almost understand 'He that hateth not father and mother.'"[33] But Rose would likely have read this book against its grain as a story of how humanity abandoned God, embraced antichrist, and was led into damnation.

Even the novel's title is a clue. The phrase "knowing good and evil," which the serpent uses to tempt Eve, refers elsewhere in Scripture to the ordinary process of maturation, equivalent to the "age of reason" concept in Catholic canon law.[34] In other words, Satan promised that eating the fruit would bring about childhood's end. "The 'visitors from outer space' theory," Rose wrote, "is but one of the many pretexts

---

[31] Ibid., 61.
[32] Ibid., 201.
[33] Letter to Joy Gresham dated December 22, 1953, in *The Collected Letters of C.S. Lewis, Volume 3: Narnia, Cambridge, and Joy*, ed. Walter Hooper (New York: HarperCollins, 2004), 391.
[34] See Isa. 7:16, RSVCE.

[demonic forces] are using to gain acceptance for the idea that 'higher beings' are now to take charge of the destiny of mankind."[35]

If the idea of those "higher beings" coming down in spaceships sounds too far-fetched, don't worry. We might end up making our own *apkallu*. As early as 1969, communication theorist and Catholic convert Marshall McLuhan saw electronic media as infernal, noting its invisibility, omnipresence, and interconnectedness. "Electric information environments being utterly ethereal fosters the illusion of the world as a spiritual substance," he wrote. "It is now a reasonable facsimile of the mystical body, a blatant manifestation of the Anti-Christ."[36] He was not, of course, suggesting that the sum total of all the world's radio and television waves and the hardware for sending and receiving them had achieved some sort of networked consciousness. But for many in Silicon Valley, such a future is not only desirable but inevitable.

A 2020 study found that there were seventy-two active projects aimed at creating an artificial general intelligence (AGI).[37] As the name suggests, AGI would not be designed for a specific purpose, but would be able to learn and creatively solve problems like a human would, only better. AI researchers already acknowledge the existence of a "black box" problem as they struggle to understand how programs that currently exist make their decisions.[38] A true AGI would likely be

---

[35] Rose, *Religion of the Future*, 140.

[36] Marshall McLuhan, letter to Jacques Maritain dated May 6, 1969, in *The Medium and the Light*, ed. Eric McLuhan and Jacek Szkiarek (Eugene, OR: Wipf and Stock, 2010), 72.

[37] McKenna Fitzgerald, Aaron Boddy, and Seth D. Baum, "2020 Survey of Artificial General Intelligence Projects for Ethics, Risk, and Policy," 2020, accessed December 16, 2024, Global Catastrophic Risk Institute, https://gcrinstitute.org/papers/055_agi-2020.pdf.

[38] Lou Blouin, "AI's Mysterious 'Black Box' Problem, Explained," University of Michigan-Dearborn, March 6, 2023, https://umdearborn.edu/news/ais-mysterious-black-box-problem-explained.

so far beyond humanity in its cognitive powers and so inscrutable in its operations as to be analogous to the workings of the divine. The domain this god might come to rule would become virtually coextensive with the "real world," especially if, by the time of its creation, most humans have come to rely on cybernetic implants and augmented reality. In his book *The Struggle for a Human Future*, Jeremy Naydler predicts that the 5G network and the proliferation of smart devices known as the "internet of things" will produce "a global 'electronic ecosystem.'"[39] So add omniscience to this god's qualities.

Futurist Yuval Noah Harari suggested that a sufficiently advanced AI could even become a religious figure. In 2023, he noted that "throughout history, religions dreamt about having a book written by a superhuman intelligence, by a non-human entity," and predicted that with AI, "this could become true very, very quickly."[40]

Some self-described Christians have hopped on the same bandwagon, with the Christian Transhumanist Association (which is apparently a thing) encouraging its members to "advocate for the instantiation in AGI of Christian archetypes such as the Good Shepherd, the Suffering Servant, [and] the Wise King." The association claims that the reason for this is to mitigate the risk of AGI turning malevolent, but it also suggests that "these archetypes are not only revealed by God but co-evolved with humanity."[41] If that's the case, it becomes difficult for them to argue that a superhuman AGI embodying those archetypes more fully than humanity would not in some sense be

---

[39] Naydler, *Human Future*, 6, 36.
[40] Yuval Noah Harari, "AI and the future of humanity," keynote address at the Frontiers Forum in Montreaux, Switzerland, April 29, 2023, https://www.youtube.com/watch?v=LWiM-LuRe6w. .
[41] The Christian Transhumanist Association, "Mission 3: Our Technological Mission," accessed January 30, 2025, https://christiantranshumanism.org/mission/technological/#super-intelligence.

Transhumanist Spiritualities

God or at least exercise a claim on our worship and obedience as a conduit of the divine.

A few AI enthusiasts have even speculated that a godlike future AI is already working through us to bring about its own advent. According to a particularly frightening thought experiment called "Roko's Basilisk," if you oppose the creation of this digital deity, it will upload you to virtual Hell and torture you there forever.[42] Silicon Valley philosopher Kevin Kelly offers his own formulation of this idea in his book *What Technology Wants*: "[Technology] may have once been as simple as an old computer program, merely parroting what we told it, but now it is more like a very complex organism that often follows its own urges."[43] But that's not all. As novelist and essayist Paul Kingsnorth explains, Kelly believes not only that "technology has its own mind and its own purpose" but also "that through the web of what he calls 'the technium,' something is using us to create itself."[44] Kingsnorth, a convert to Eastern Orthodoxy, has no problem calling this "something" the antichrist.

For many in the modern spiritual landscape, however, there is no need to use euphemisms like "aliens" or "machine elves" or wait for an AI Messiah to arrive. The spirit that promises humanity self-determination and self-transcendence can be forthrightly identified as some pagan god.

In explaining conversion to Christianity, Kingsnorth recounts his experience in Wicca, a cult founded in the 1950s that claims to be a

---

[42] David Auerback, "The Most Terrifying Thought Experiment of All Time," *Slate*, July 17, 2014, https://slate.com/technology/2014/07/rokos-basilisk-the-most-terrifying-thought-experiment-of-all-time.html.

[43] Kevin Kelly, *What Technology Wants* (New York: Penguin, 2010), 13.

[44] Paul Kingsnorth, "The Anti-Christ Now Rules Us All," *UnHerd*, May 28, 2022, https://unherd.com/2022/05/the-anti-christ-now-rules-us-all/.

reconstruction of a pre-Christian European folk religion. "My coven used to do its rituals in the woods under the full moon," he wrote. "It was fun, and it made things happen. I discovered that magic is real. It works. Who it works for is another question."[45]

In January 2024, Axios reported that, among young American Latinos eager to reconnect with their ethnic identity, a form of indigenous and Afro-Caribbean witchcraft known as *brujería* is on the rise.[46] A Pew study found that neopagans now outnumber Presbyterians in the United States, with around 1.5 million self-described adherents between the various groups.[47] Wicca alone grew from eight thousand American adherents in 1990 to 134,000 in 2001, making it "technically the country's fastest growing religion."[48] These spiritualities tend to offer left-coded critiques of Christianity: it's too patriarchal, too homophobic, too sexually repressive, not inclusive enough.

Then, there are those who take things further. For them, Christianity is the enemy. It is not enough to seek out an alternative. They must confront the Christian God on His own terms under the banner of His adversary. In *Strange Rites*, Tara Isabella Burton explains that for many self-described witches, diabolism is a means of fighting oppression—colonial, patriarchal, racial, or otherwise. For these witches,

---

[45] Paul Kingsnorth, "The Cross and the Machine," *First Things*, June 1, 2021, https://www.firstthings.com/article/2021/06/the-cross-and-the-machine.

[46] Marina E. Franco, "Brujería, Caribbean Witchcraft Resurging for U.S. Latinos," Axios, January 18, 2024, https://www.axios.com/2024/01/18/latino-caribbean-witchcraft-brujeria-ancient-tradition.

[47] Ariel Zilber, "Witches Now Outnumber Presbyterians in America as Number of Pagans Soar to 1.5 MILLION — and Millennials' Love of Yoga and Star Signs Is to Blame," Daily Mail, November 19, 2018, https://www.dailymail.co.uk/news/article-6404733/Number-Americans-practice-witchcraft-estimated-high-1-5-MILLION.html.

[48] Burton, *Strange Rites*, 126.

"the language and rhetoric of full-on Satanism — sex with demons, devil worshipping, baby kidnapping — can and should be politically reappropriated, transformed into an act of resistance," Burton writes.[49] When evil is reduced to repression and freedom to self-determination, Satan becomes self-evidently the good guy.

The Satanic Temple (TST), the largest Satanist denomination, claims not to believe in a literal devil, viewing him instead as a "symbol of the Eternal Rebel in opposition to arbitrary authority, forever defending personal sovereignty even in the face of insurmountable odds."[50] I'm not sure Satan cares. His goal is not to be worshipped, but to lead humanity to destruction by promising them freedom and power.

This makes Satan an ally of transhumanists everywhere. In a blog post on the website Medium, author Peter Clarke noted that transhumanism has "religious undertones" and urged his fellow transhumanists to "incorporate the symbolic language of religion" into their ideology "while adhering to a strict code of rationality." Fortunately, Clarke argued, there's no need to construct such a religion because "this project of embracing ancient symbolism while maintaining a fully science-based view of the world has already been assembled. It's called Satanism."[51]

The alignment between these two -isms is perhaps most evident in their shared commitment to abortion and transgenderism. The Satanic Temple enshrines bodily autonomy as its third core tenet and treats

---

[49] Ibid., 131.
[50] The Satanic Temple, "What Does Satan Mean to TST?" Frequently Asked Questions, accessed December 16, 2024, https://thesatanictemple.com/pages/faq?srsltid=AfmBOooo0WkZZCgImQsLIOwM0DgLNkQ90xA5L2JutI0xo_qMYd3kwcUu.
[51] Peter Clarke, "Satanic Transhumanism: The Future of Reason?" Medium, April 4, 2020, https://petermclarke.medium.com/satanic-transhumanism-the-future-of-reason-79b673ce57d0.

THE TRANSHUMANIST TEMPTATION

abortion as a sacrament. The TST website boasts that they have even launched lawsuits arguing that red-state abortion restrictions prevent them from practicing their faith. Mainstream figures and publications like *Salon*, *Rolling Stone*, and John Oliver have praised their efforts.[52]

In 2023, *Cosmopolitan* offered a glowing write-up of TST's (and America's) first-ever satanic abortion clinic, which offers telehealth consultations, delivers pills by mail, and is named after the mother of Supreme Court Justice Samuel Alito, who wrote the *Dobbs* decision (because he should've been aborted, get it?).[53]

Demonic imagery has also become a favorite motif of the LGBT movement. In May 2023, , news broke that Target had partnered with queer designer Erik Carnell, whose website included pins and shirts featuring a goat-headed deity with the slogan "Satan Respects Pronouns," as well as merchandise calling for "transphobes" to be decapitated.[54]

[52] Brett Bachman, "Why Satanists May be the Last, Best Hope to Save Abortion Rights in Texas," *Salon*, September 4, 2021, https://www.salon.com/2021/09/04/why-satanists-may-be-the-last-best-hope-to-save-abortion-rights-in-texas/. Amanda Marcotte, "Satanists Defending Abortion Rights? Meet 5 Conservatives Freaking Out About It," *RollingStone*, May 6, 2015, https://www.rollingstone.com/politics/politics-news/satanists-defending-abortion-rights-meet-5-conservatives-freaking-out-about-it-226189/. Andi Ortiz, "John Oliver Applauds Satanic Group Offering Abortion Access Named After Justice Alito's Mom: 'Best 'Your Mom' Joke' Ever (Video)," Wrap, November 6, 2023, https://www.thewrap.com/john-oliver-satanic-group-abortion-access-samuel-alito-mom-joke/.

[53] Arielle Domb, "This Satanic Abortion Clinic Named After Samuel Alito Jr.'s Mom Might Beat Abortion Bans," *Cosmopolitan*, November 14, 2023, https://www.cosmopolitan.com/lifestyle/a45613416/satanic-group-abortion-clinic-samuel-alito-mom/.

[54] Janay Kingsberry, "LGBTQ Designer Slams 'Satanist' Label After Target Pulls His Pride Merch," *Washington Post*, May 26, 2023, https://www.washingtonpost.com/lifestyle/2023/05/26/lgbtq-designer-target-pride-collection-controversy/.

Transhumanist Spiritualities

In one product description for his online store, Carnell wrote "Satan loves you and respects who you are."[55]

In February, singer Sam Smith, who identifies as nonbinary, dressed as Satan to perform his song "Unholy" at the Grammy Awards.[56] About a year earlier, cross-dressing gay rapper Lil Nas X starred in a music video in which he gave Satan a lap dance before snapping the devil's neck and crowning himself king of Hell.[57] This happens too often to be a coincidence.[58]

For author and pastor Jonathan Cahn, Pride Month is literally a festival to the demonic being that presented itself in ancient times as the goddess Ishtar. This Sumerian deity was not only the patroness of prostitutes and an exemplar of promiscuity, but also a gender bender. Ancient texts record her saying, "Though I am a man I am a noble young woman," and praise her ability to "turn a man into a woman and a woman into a man." Men and women cross-dressed to march in her summer solstice processions, which on our modern calendar always fall in June, Cahn notes in his book *The Return of the Gods*.[59]

---

[55] "Satan Respects Pronouns Art Print," Abprallen, accessed December 16, 2024, https://www.abprallen.co.uk/product/satan-respects-pronouns-art-print.

[56] Ryan Bort, "Sam Smith's 'Unholy' at Grammys Inspires Satanism Panic From GOP," *RollingStone*, February 6, 2023, https://www.rollingstone.com/politics/politics-news/sam-smith-unholy-grammys-satanism-panic-gop-1234674687/.

[57] Lil Nas X, "MONTERO (Call Me by Your Name) (Official Video)," dir. Tanu Muino and Montero Hill (New York: Columbia Records, 2021), https://www.youtube.com/watch?v=6swmTBVI83k.

[58] This paragraph and the preceding one originally appeared at the *Daily Caller*. See Grayson Quay, "Why LGBT Activists Love Satanic Imagery," *Daily Caller*, June 16, 2023, https://dailycaller.com/2023/06/16/lgbt-pride-month-satanism-sisters-of-perpetual-indulgence/.

[59] Jonathan Cahn, *The Return of the Gods* (Lake Mary, FL: Charisma Media, 2022), 168.

THE TRANSHUMANIST TEMPTATION

June is Pride Month because it commemorates the 1969 Stonewall Riot, during which homosexuals, prostitutes, and drag queens at a Manhattan gay bar hurled bricks at cops attempting to raid the place. In this event, Cahn sees a panoply of symbols associated with Ishtar. She was invoked as goddess of the tavern; Stonewall is a bar. Hymns equate Ishtar's wrath with storms; the woman who kicked off the riot by resisting arrest was named Stormé. Among Ishtar's priestesses were the *kezertu*, a term that referred to their curled hair; at Stonewall, men dressed as women chanted, "We are the Stonewall girls ... We wear our hair in curls."[60]

One need not accept all the particulars of Cahn's argument to grasp his larger point: Stonewall, which birthed the Pride movement, marked a turning point in the religious history of the West. Within a few decades, celebrations of that violent riot had spread throughout the world and were receiving corporate and civic sponsorship. Desecrating the movement's flag became a hate crime. Nations that hold Pride parades are considered "progressive" and "civilized," just as public eucharistic processions once marked a nation as part of Christendom.

Countries that refuse to follow Ishtar can expect to fall victim to the missionary zeal of her followers. In a sermon delivered less than a month after the invasion of Ukraine, Patriarch Kiril, who heads the Russian Orthodox Church, blamed Western hostility to his country on its refusal to hold a "gay pride parade."[61] When one considers that Democratic representative Jamie Raskin justified supporting Ukraine on the grounds that Moscow is "a world center of antifeminist, antigay,

---

[60] Ibid., 166–168.
[61] Grayson Quay, "War in Ukraine Is a 'Metaphysical' Battle Against a Civilization Built on 'Gay Parades,' Russian Orthodox Leader Says," *Week*, March 7, 2022, https://theweek.com/russo-ukrainian-war/1011020/war-in-ukraine-is-a-metaphysical-battle-against-a-civilization-built-on.

anti-trans hatred," it becomes difficult to dismiss Kiril's words as mere propaganda. Journalist Helen Andrews, writing for the *American Conservative* in 2023, chronicled how the U.S. State Department uses financial incentives and diplomatic pressure to push gay and trans liberation on unwilling countries abroad while simultaneously using LGBT ideology as a litmus test to "politically neutralize" conservatives at home.[62]

Our elites aim at nothing less than the establishment of a global queer theocracy, in which every knee shall bow to a flag that stands for sexual indulgence, total self-determination, consent as the sole criterion of morality, and the right to reshape one's body according to one's own whims — the same values many of the movement's proponents ascribe to the Prince of Darkness.

Mary Harrington went so far as to declare that Satanism, defined as "sacralized self-worship" and "untrammelled individualism, shorn of any link to the divine," had become the new state religion of the West.[63]

This same spirit lies behind all the emerging spiritualities surveyed in this chapter. Every one — whether based on psychedelics, UFOs, AI, folk magic, or some combination thereof — promises liberation and self-transcendence through human *techne* rather than divine grace. And that's exactly what Satan offers, too, whether you believe in him or not.

---

[62] Helen Andrews, "Our LGBT Empire," *American Conservative*, December 11, 2023, https://www.theamericanconservative.com/our-lgbt-empire/.

[63] Mary Harrington, "How Satanism Conquered America," *UnHerd*, September 15, 2021, https://unherd.com/2021/09/satanism-is-everywhere/.

How Transhumanism Subverts Christianity

Progressivism will hollow out your religion and wear its skin like a trophy.

–Auron MacIntyre[1]

The glorification of autonomy and choice that defines the transhumanist ideology is not only central to the creed of our supposedly secular society's state religion. It has also infiltrated our churches.

The Christian Transhumanist Association declares that humanity's "scientific and technological capacity" is "part of how we reflect God's own creative nature" and that we should use these God-given abilities to "work for the improvement of this present world."[2] So far, so good, but it's telling that the main biblical example they offer is Noah building the ark. In doing so, the association fails (or refuses) to acknowledge

---

[1] Auron MacIntyre (@AuronMacintyre), "Progressivism will hollow out your religion," X, January 25, 2021, 10:56 p.m., https://x.com/AuronMacintyre/status/1353914665819131910. This is one example among many, as this line has become something of a catchphrase for MacIntyre.

[2] The Christian Transhumanist Association, "Theological Mission," accessed January 30, 2025, https://www.christiantranshumanism.org/mission/theological/.

THE TRANSHUMANIST TEMPTATION

the difference between creatively reshaping the world around us and remaking our very selves.

In 2023, the Anglican Church of Canada adopted a rite for blessing gender transitions. "All humans are made in God's image whether we recognize ourselves in our bodies as female, male, or intersex; whether we are transgender, cisgender, or do not recognize ourselves in any of these labels," the liturgy reads. "We are called by God both to care for and to be co-creators of all of creation and that includes our bodies."[3]

Suggested readings include a bunch of passages where God renames a biblical figure (though one can't help noticing He doesn't change Jacob's name to Nancy) and the Transfiguration of Christ (I guess because it has "trans" in it).[4]

Note the language: "co-creators of all creation and that includes our bodies." The first part is obviously true. We turn trees into chairs, vibrations into symphonies, and plants and animals into garments and meals. But your body is not a block of wood or a side of beef. Your body is *you*. There is no sexless, free-floating soul that might be "trapped" in the wrong one.

To set a broken arm, straighten crooked teeth, adorn oneself with beautiful clothing, or build powerful muscles are all valid and laudable activities. The transgression lies in seeking to remake your body into something it fundamentally is not. Ancient practices like neck lengthening or foot binding and some modern cosmetic surgeries partake of this sin, but transgenderism is perhaps the gravest example. It is a rejection of one of the most fundamental qualities of one's body: it is

---

[3] *Pastoral Liturgies for Journeys of Gender Affirmation and Transition: Rites and Prayers Supplemental to the Book of Alternative Services of the Anglican Church of Canada* (Toronto: Anglican Book Center, 2023), 6. https://www.anglican.ca/wp-content/uploads/Pastoral-Liturgies-for-Gender-Transition-and-Affirmation-07.23.pdf.

[4] Ibid., 24.

either male or female.[5] For a Christian denomination to deny this reality is proof that it is no longer operating from Christian premises but merely applying Christian language to the transhumanism that permeates our culture.

This sacralization of control over one's body does not stop at transgenderism either. Pro-choice Christians once described abortion as a necessary evil. Former Presiding Bishop Katherine Jefferts Schori's formulation of the Episcopal Church's "very nuanced" position on abortion is a good example. "We say it is a moral tragedy but that it should not be the government's role to deny its availability," she told *HuffPost* in 2012.[6]

Such language is no longer satisfactory. For progressive Christians today, it has become necessary to defend not only abortion's legality

---

[5] Advocates of transgenderism frequently cite rare instances of "intersex" disorders as evidence that sex and gender are not binary. This argument is flawed for several reasons. First, it's a bit of a red herring, since most transgender individuals are not intersex. Second, these disorders do not make biological sex non-binary any more than the existence of people with one or three legs makes it inaccurate to describe humanity as a bipedal species. Third, nearly all individuals with intersex conditions have either testes or ovaries (though they're often nonfunctional) and can therefore be easily classified as male or female regardless of other chromosomal, hormonal, or genital abnormalities. The proper medical response to such conditions is not to discard the concept of biological sex, but to help those who suffer from them live more fully as their true biological sex. See Tadeusz Pacholczyk, "Making Sense of Bioethics: Column 132: Seeing through the Intersex Confusion," *National Catholic Bioethics Center*, June 30, 2016, https://www.ncbcenter.org/making-sense-of-bioethics-cms/column-132-seeing-through-the-intersex-confusion.

[6] Jaweed Kaleem, "Katharine Jefferts Schori, Episcopal Church Presiding Bishop, Speaks About Gay Clergy and Birth Control," *HuffPost*, March 27, 2012, https://www.huffingtonpost.com/2012/03/27/katharine-jefferts-schori-episcopal-church_n_1380572.html.

but its morality or even its sacredness. "The right to choose is a God-given right with which persons are endowed ... And for women, the preeminent freedom is the choice to control her reproductive process," Baptist pastor Howard Moody wrote in an early-2000s pamphlet titled *Prayerfully Pro-choice*. Moody acknowledges that abortion is "sad" and that each fetus possesses "a unique and irreplaceable genetic code," but he has already established that freedom is a higher good than any end toward which that freedom might be applied.[7] As Samira Kawash put it in a 2023 essay on "Holy Abortion," the "god of Choice" has become Moody's true deity.[8] Such a god is indistinguishable from the empowering devil of the Satanic Temple.

Kawash argues that, although the abortion debate is typically framed in terms of "the religious value of 'life' pitted against the secular value of 'choice,' " the "spear tip of radical abortion absolutism" is now thoroughly religious. "Choice has become a religious value, the bedrock of an emergent morality that bears no resemblance to the Abrahamic tradition. It is a stealthy adversary, donning the mantle of Christian love and charity to corrupt traditional faith from the inside," she writes. "The pregnant mother is, in her omniscience and power, her own god. Her volition is sacred and absolute."

To choice worshippers, whatever I believe to be right *is right* because there is no higher good than my absolute freedom. Once this belief becomes widespread, churches lose the ability to discipline their members or even give them clear guidance on key moral questions of our transhuman age. A pastor who values choice above all else cannot

---

[7] Quoted in Michael J. Gorman and Ann Loar Brooks, *Holy Abortion? A Theological Critique of the Religious Coalition for Reproductive Choice* (Eugene, OR: Wipf and Stock, 2003), https://www.nprcouncil.org/resources/holyabortion.htm.

[8] Samira Kawash, "Holy Abortion," *First Things*, December 1, 2023, https://www.firstthings.com/article/2023/12/holy-abortion.

forbid you from going on birth control, starting IVF, or undergoing body modification, whether that's a nose job or a gender-affirming mastectomy. He can only ask you which choice you believe will most authentically contribute to your own flourishing (as defined by you, of course). He ceases to be a spiritual father and becomes nothing more than what Anglican priest Benjamin Crosby calls "a nonjudgmental provider of pastoral care."[9]

Adherents of this radical non-judgmentalism often frame it as a form of empathy. It is true that Christianity introduced to history a unique concern for victims, which it has bequeathed to modernity.[10] For some, this is proof that the faith was cancerous from the start. Italian reactionary philosopher Julius Evola wrote in 1928 that Christianity "destroy[ed] the European spirit" by infecting the Roman world with "its frenetic crushing of every hierarchy" and its love "of the underprivileged, of those without birth and without tradition."[11] More recently, Elon Musk wrote that "the axiomatic error undermining much of Western Civilization is that 'weak makes right.'"[12]

French philosopher René Girard, himself a Catholic, expressed somewhat similar concerns, though in his view the regard for victims

---

[9] Benjamin Crosby, "Where Are the Churches in Canada's Euthanasia Experiment?" *Plough*, February 27, 2023, https://www.plough.com/en/topics/justice/culture-of-life/where-are-the-churches-in-canadas-euthanasia-experiment.

[10] For a historical account of how Christian ideas shaped modernity, see Tom Holland, *Dominion: How the Christian Revolution Remade the World* (New York: Basic Books, 2019).

[11] Julius Evola, *Pagan Imperialism*, trans. Heinrich Matterhorn (Tradition, 2022), 13, https://archive.org/details/julius-evola-pagan-imperialism_202406/mode/2up.

[12] Elon Musk (@elonmusk), "The axiomatic error undermining much of Western Civilization is that 'weak makes right,'" X, April 26, 2024, 1:19 a.m., https://x.com/elonmusk/status/1783727565989134488.

THE TRANSHUMANIST TEMPTATION

truly ran amok only after it became detached from Christian orthodoxy. "The current process of spiritual demagoguery and rhetorical overkill has transformed the concern for victims into a totalitarian command and a permanent inquisition," Girard wrote in his 1999 book *I See Satan Fall Like Lightning*. "We are living through a caricatural 'ultra-Christianity' that tries to escape from the Judeo-Christian orbit by 'radicalizing' the concern for victims in an anti-Christian manner" and "promot[ing] Christianity to the role of number one scapegoat."[13]

In a 2017 essay for *First Things* titled "Empathy Is Not Charity," writer Patricia Snow offered a reading of Shusaku Endo's novel *Silence* as a Girardian example of empathy devouring Christianity.

The novel, written in 1966, follows two seventeenth-century Portuguese Jesuits as they travel to feudal Japan, where their former mentor, Ferreira, is rumored not only to have renounced his faith, but to be aiding the shogun's government in its persecution of Christians.

One of the priests, Rodrigues, is captured and learns that Ferreira apostatized after the Japanese authorities gave up on torturing him and instead tortured members of his flock until he agreed to submit. "Christ would have apostatized for them," Ferreira tells Rodrigues.[14]

After subjecting Rodrigues to the same trial, the authorities place an image of Christ at his feet and order him to trample on it. He then hears the image tell him, "Trample! It was to be trampled on by men that I was born into this world."[15]

Rodrigues steps on Christ's face, renounces Christianity, spends the remainder of his life collaborating with the persecutors, and receives a Buddhist funeral. There are hints that he may remain a Christian

---

[13] René Girard, *I See Satan Fall Like Lightning*, trans. James G. Williams (Maryknoll, NY: Orbis Books, 2001), 178–179.

[14] Shūsaku Endō, *Silence*, trans. William Johnston (New York: Taplinger, 1980), 169.

[15] Ibid., 171.

in his heart (whatever that means), but the persecutors don't care. They've won.

The novel is full of postmodern ambiguities, and it would be entirely possible to interpret the "Christ" that speaks to Rodrigues as a demon in disguise. Since the days of the Desert Fathers, monks have been warned against such deceptions. But liberal Jesuit Fr. James Martin ignored this element of tradition when he opined that, under the conditions Rodrigues faced, a Christian might well apostatize in good conscience. Martin Scorsese's 2016 film version similarly suggests that the audience should side with Rodrigues.[16]

Snow identifies the dilemma Endo stages for Rodrigues as an example of "Death of God theology," the belief "that not only Christ but Christianity must die, that it is not finally Christian to be Christian, and that in the name of Christian charity, Christians must reject Christian truths." It might just as well be called "transhumanist theology."[17] In a world that prizes *poesis* over *mimesis*, empathy is the only virtue. Speaking the truth in love degenerates into abolishing truth for love's sake. Even love, which in its true form seeks the good of the other, becomes nothing more than affirming the other in order to spare him pain. It's no surprise that Martin would have reacted to the Japanese converts' suffering by renouncing his faith as Rodrigues did. After all, Martin himself has undermined Catholic sexual teaching to make sure gays and transgenders don't feel excluded. And the compromises don't end there. Snow argues that our society has come to be governed by "a tenderness that, long since cut off from

---

[16] *Silence*, directed by Martin Scorsese (Los Angeles: Fábrica de Cine, 2016).
[17] Patricia Snow, "Empathy Is Not Charity," *First Things*, October 1, 2017, https://www.firstthings.com/article/2017/10/empathy-is-not-charity.

the person of Christ, ends in terror[: a]bortion, opioid addiction, assisted suicide, euthanasia."

The theology underlying this aversion to suffering replaces a Christian ethical vision with a utilitarian one, according to which the worst fate that might befall a man is not that he "forfeit his soul" but merely that he endure unnecessary pain.[18] Clergy and theologians who would endorse Rodrigues's decision no longer have the backbone to tell the faithful that suffering might be redemptive or corrective. Infertility can be fixed with IVF, gender dysphoria with hormones and surgery, unplanned pregnancy with abortion, chronic pain with MAiD, and so on. All medical or technological interventions that reduce suffering are presumed to be legitimate, even laudable, no matter how much violence they do to the patient's humanity. The only approved response to pain is to remove it and then apologize for any role you may have played in inflicting, perpetuating, or exacerbating it. Comedian Louis C. K.'s claim that "When a person tells you that you hurt them, you don't get to decide that you didn't," has become gospel.[19] The feelings of the individual take primacy. The therapeutic triumphs.

This pseudo-Christianity is not content to coexist with the Faith as it was held for nearly two thousand years.[20] Most Christians like to think they would die for Christ, that they'd happily go down in a hail of executioners' bullets shouting "¡Viva Cristo Rey!" And maybe they would. But what if the persecution were more subtle than that?

---

[18] Matt. 16:26 ESV
[19] *Louie*, season 5, episode 3, "Cop Story," dir. Louis C.K., aired April 23, 2015.
[20] Portions of the following section on persecution originally appeared at the *Daily Caller*. See Grayson Quay, "The Left Is Using The CCP's Playbook to Persecute American Christians," *Daily Caller*, April 6, 2023, https://dailycaller.com/2023/04/06/quay-progressive-christianity-nashville-china-lgbtq/.

Historically, it often is. Roman persecutors didn't set out to exterminate every Christian from the empire. Instead, they insisted Christians could practice any religion they liked as long as they burned a pinch of incense to Caesar. You have religious freedom, the authorities insisted, as long as you publicly affirm the values of the regime.

Consider an example:

In 2022, the Oregon Department of Human Services (ODHS) denied a woman's application to adopt on the grounds that her Christian beliefs would render her unable to "respect, accept, and support … the sexual orientation, gender identity, [and] gender expression" of any child she adopted.[21] The ODHS knows full well that religious discrimination is illegal, so obviously they regard saluting the Pride flag (the modern equivalent of burning incense to Caesar) as compatible with Christianity and opposition to transgenderism as pure hatred for which religion is merely a pretext. The would-be mother, of course, disagrees and has filed a lawsuit.

The ODHS is essentially claiming the authority to determine which aspects of Christianity are integral to the Faith and which aren't. The emperor Constantine was never so arrogant.

True Christianity, the kind uncontaminated by bigotry, is to be found in the queer-affirming denominations, the new persecutors suggest. Progressive churches are only too happy to agree. They might be headed for demographic extinction, but in the meantime there's nothing they crave more than head-pats from elites who would never dream of attending church. These sycophantic court prophets never tire of reminding the regime that everything it loves — abortion, perversion,

---

[21] Kate Anderson, "Single Mother Files Lawsuit After State Allegedly Denies Adoption Due to Her Christian Beliefs," *Daily Caller*, April 3, 2023, https://dailycaller.com/2023/04/03/single-mother-lawsuit-state-allegedly-denies-adoption-application-religious-beliefs/.

child sterilization — God loves, too. In return, the regime gains the ability to undermine religious opposition to its policies: "See? The real Christians agree with us."

Don't worry about being thrown to the lions, though. These persecutors won't nail you to a cross. They won't even make you stop going to church. They'll just gradually exclude you from every institution of public life while insisting at every stage that you're not being persecuted (and if you are, you deserve it for being a bigot).[22] Jobs, colleges, professional associations, government offices, and even banks will shut their doors in your face.

As St. Gregory Nazienzen wrote in the fourth century, "You, remaining a genuine Christian, will be ranked among the lowest, and will be in a position unworthy of yourself and your hopes."[23] And at the same time, the powers and principalities will gesture invitingly in the direction of the PCUSA, the Episcopal Church, the Evangelical Lutheran Church in America, the United Church of Christ, and other dwindling woke denominations the regime deems *religio licita*. "The hour cometh and now is" when Christians will face a choice: the false church of the transhumanist antichrist, who promises freedom and comfort, or the Church of Christ Crucified, who bids us to bear the cross on our all-too-human backs.[24]

---

[22] See Michael Anton, "That's Not Happening and It's Good That It Is," *American Mind*, July 26, 2021, https://americanmind.org/salvo/thats-not-happening-and-its-good-that-it-is/.

[23] St. Gregory Nazienzen, "Letter to His Brother Cæsarius (Ep. VII)," in *A Select Library of the Nicene and Post-Nicene Fathers of the Christian Church*, Second Series, vol. 7, ed. Philip Schaff and Henry Wace (New York: Wipf and Stock, 2022), 457–458.

[24] John 4:23, KJV; Matt. 16:24.

Digital Christianity

They that make those simulacra be made like th[em].

— Ps. 115:8, Wycliffe translation

Even Christians who successfully guard their theology against transhumanism will still have to grapple with the more subtle encroachments of transhumanizing technologies.

In 1964, McLuhan coined the phrase "The medium is the message."[1] In other words, the media through which we consume information shape and catechize us in particular ways regardless of the content they convey. Books, for instance, cultivate interiority, individualism, and a left-brained, rationalistic approach to reality. This is true whether you're reading St. Mark's Gospel or *Fifty Shades of Grey*.

Each time we power up a screen, we take another small step toward becoming a new kind of creature. "We are transforming from embodied, biological beings into digital entities composed of zeros and ones, data sets and social media posts," Internet historian Katherine Dee wrote in her exploration of TikTok spirituality.[2]

---

[1] Marshall McLuhan, *Understanding Media: The Extensions of Man* (Richmond, CA: Gingko Press, 2013), 14.

[2] Katherine Dee, "Among the Spiritual Psychotics," *Tablet*, January 25, 2023, https://www.tabletmag.com/sections/news/articles/among-the-spiritual-psychotics.

THE TRANSHUMANIST TEMPTATION

McLuhan did not live to see the smartphone, but if he had, he would likely have reached many of the same conclusions Burton did in *Strange Rites*. In that study of "new religions for a godless world," Burton described the new religious landscape as intuitional, self-curated, and results-focused.[3] This remixed spirituality — in which she includes everything from witch covens and SoulCyclers to polycules and Silicon Valley biohackers — is the religion of the Instagram feed, no less than Protestantism was the religion of the printing press.

The Instagram user sees more of what she likes, follows, and lingers on and less of what she skips past. The inscrutable, oracle-like algorithm considers these preferences and serves up new content, which the user can then share or respond to as she wishes. It's no surprise that people conditioned in this way gravitate toward bespoke syncretism and the belief that their own attitudes and "energies" can shape the fabric of reality. The aerial realm of the modern cosmos is just as thick with tweets, gifs, and TikToks as the medieval was with angels and demons.

"Many people simply resort instantly to the occult, to ESP, and every form of hidden awareness in response to this new surround of electric information," McLuhan told an interviewer thirty-seven years before Steve Jobs provided nearly every American with what amounts to a detachable prosthetic organ designed to interface with that virtual world.[4]

But it's not only Burton's religiously "remixed" crowd who have been catechized by their smartphones.[5] The dispositions these devices produce have also infected orthodox adherents of organized Christian denominations.

---

[3] Burton, *Strange Rites*, 34.
[4] Marshall McLuhan, "Electric Consciousness and the Church" (interview with Hubert Hoskins), in *Medium and the Light*, 88.
[5] Burton, *Strange Rites*, 18.

Consider the Bible app. In a 2018 article, Dr. Pete Phillips, who "explores the interface between all things digital and theological," argued that the "verse of the day" feature common on these apps could actually "be skewing your view of God."[6]

Phillips explains that many of the apps work by "populating their verse of the day lists with those verses most tweeted or shared by the user community." YouVersion's Apple Watch app encourages users to "glance to see which verses are trending."[7] One wonders whether Jeremiah's imprecations would have "trended" during the siege of Jerusalem.

Because people are more likely to share feel-good verses ("For I know the plans I have for you, says the Lord")[8] than snippets of narrative or meaty morsels of theology, this algorithmic approach produces a "tendency towards therapeutic texts," creating "a therapeutic filter bubble," Phillips writes.

Algorithmic spirituality causes the consumer-curator's feelings to assume precedence. His daily devotional life becomes less about conforming himself by repentance to the ultimate Reality and more about making himself feel better.

When Thomas Jefferson wanted to edit the Bible to fit the spirit of the age, he used scissors and paste. Today, we can crowdsource the work with millions of taps on thousands of screens. And we won't even realize we're doing it.

---

[6] Pete Phillips, "Why Your Bible App's 'Verse of the Day' Feature Could Be Skewing Your View of God," *Premier Christianity*, October 2, 2018, https://www.premierchristianity.com/home/why-your-bible-apps-verse-of-the-day-feature-could-be-skewing-your-view-of-god/3511.article.

[7] "Now Available: The Bible App for Apple Watch," *YouVersion*, April 24, 2015, https://blog.youversion.com/2015/04/youversion-bible-app-now-available-for-apple-watch/.

[8] Jer. 29:11, RSVCE.

THE TRANSHUMANIST TEMPTATION

Some users seem to approach the app's verse of the day as a personalized oracle of sorts.[9] God can speak to us however He wants, even through a pagan prophet's ass.[10] But to confuse the algorithm with the Holy Spirit is to engage in divination. It relies on the expectation that God will show up in a way and a place in which He has not promised to do so (like in Baptism or the Eucharist).

Modern Christianity is plagued by "main character syndrome." Digitally catechized believers assume — and the churches that cater to them affirm — that God will make Himself felt in their lives. When He doesn't, they either lose their faith or convince themselves they've heard God when they haven't. They expect prayer to be rewarded by divine intuitions that help them address their quotidian problems.

No such promise exists in Scripture or Tradition. Churches would do better encouraging their flocks to trust God even when He feels distant and to distrust their affective responses. The Desert Fathers spent lifetimes in prayer and knew that those efforts did not entitle them to spiritual fireworks. In fact, they were trained to assume that visions and transcendent promptings were demonic deceptions until proven otherwise.

All we have any right to say is, "Speak, Lord, for your servant is listening."[11] And then keep listening, whether He speaks or not.[12]

---

[9] See Lana Del Rey, "Judah Smith Interlude," written by Lana Del Rey, Jack Antonoff, and Judah Smith, recorded 2023, track 5 on *Did You Know That There's a Tunnel Under Ocean Blvd*, Interscope.

[10] See Num. 22:21–35.

[11] 1 Sam. 3:9, NIV.

[12] The preceding discussion of McLuhan, Bible apps, and algorithmic spirituality previously appeared at *First Things*. See Grayson Quay, "Algorithmic Spirituality," *First Things*, June 7, 2024. https://firstthings.com/algorithmic-spirituality/.

Digital Christianity

The digital ecosystem also affects Christians by making just about every tradition a live option for the online spiritual seeker. It's as if every variety of Catholic, Orthodox, Lutheran, Calvinist, Pentecostal, non-Chalcedonian, and any other sect one might name each has its own booth in the market square of McLuhan's "global village."[13] If you listen hard enough, you can hear the other world religions hawking their wares as well. Our seeker doesn't have time to reread the whole Bible, the Church Fathers, the ecumenical councils, the Scholastics, and the Reformers, plus the Talmud, the Quran, the Hadiths, the Book of Mormon, the Sutras, the Vedas, the Upanishads, and the Bhagavad Gita. Even if he did, there are people smarter than him at every booth offering conflicting interpretations. The choice becomes agonizing.

In Sigrid Undset's 1920 novel *Kristin Lavransdatter*, the medieval Norwegian heroine is vaguely aware that the Russians her husband goes off to fight are heretics, but she never finds herself weighing the merits of Orthodoxy. It's not like she can order Kallistos Ware's books on Amazon or listen to the *Lord of Spirits* podcast. Kristin's choice is not between multiple religious paths, but between what Charles Taylor called different "speeds" or levels of devotion.[14] She sometimes runs toward God, sometimes walks, sometimes turns her back in defiance, but Kristin never comes to a fork in the road.

Like Undset's character, most of our ancestors were baptized and buried in the same denomination and formed only a hazy idea of what the others believed. The more curious among them might have faced what amounted to a fish-or-chicken choice at a wedding reception, not the digital Golden Corral buffet that confronts us today.

The solidities of tradition melt into air. You must choose. Even if you choose to embrace tradition — in the form of, say, Latin Mass

---

[13] McLuhan, *Medium and the Light*, 33.
[14] Taylor, *Secular Age*, 62.

THE TRANSHUMANIST TEMPTATION

Catholicism — you still made that choice in a modern, consumerist "marketplace of ideas," which isn't very trad. The pearl you brought home carries the smell of the bazaar from which you bought it.

Christians who have settled into a particular tradition face a related difficulty. Suddenly, the pope is closer to them than their own bishop, the president of the denomination nearer than the preacher in their church's pulpit. Distance is annihilated. A medieval Catholic might have had no idea who occupied the chair of St. Peter, but many Catholics of the Internet age feel obligated to weigh in on his every public utterance.

Pastor means shepherd, but for many very-online believers, the leader of their local church is far down the list of spiritual influences in their lives. "What I do think is a rather unique struggle for pastors today ... is the commodification of the church," Lutheran minister Hans Feine said in a 2024 interview. "People can ... shape much of their religious identity through social media, which means they often want pastors to be purveyors of the religious aesthetic they prefer more than they want them to be actual shepherds."[15]

I accuse myself as well. In recent years, I've been led far more by the teachings of two priests who host a podcast and have no idea who I am than by the rector of my own parish, who places the Eucharist in my hand, calls me by name, and has, on numerous occasions, made time for me to confess my sins and seek guidance.

The way English Puritans once compared sermons "chapter and verse" to the Bible in the pew, Christians of all denominations now compare the week's teaching to that of Doug Wilson, Trent Horn, Gavin Ortlund, or Josiah Trenham.

---

[15] Anthony Sacramone, "Conversation Starters with Rev. Hans Fiene," Acton Institute, September 23, 2024, https://www.acton.org/religion-liberty/volume-34-number-3/conversation-starters-rev-hans-fiene.

As always, the smartphone catechizes us toward an algorithmic, intuitional, self-serving form of engagement. And of course, toward greater curation. Why focus on the mediocre homily at your church when you can get a better one from the sermon podcast of the church across town (or across the country)? Why talk to the lukewarm normies in your own pew when you can find people on X who are as smart and based as you?

There, the Christian enters religious discourse as a discarnate being. Even if he isn't hiding behind a fake name and picture, he's assuming a self-created persona. This entity has its own virtual body, which has very different powers and potentialities than the authentic person would have brought to a human interaction. He cannot cry or laugh (or see his interlocutors do the same). He can put his words through as many drafts as he wants without disrupting the flow of spoken dialogue. If a reply displeases him, he can block whoever wrote it far more easily than he could walk away from a real conversation. He can't punch anybody and nobody can punch him, so he can mouth off as much as he pleases. Character limitations and the currency of likes and retweets incentivize the witty barb over the substantive reply. Clout trumps care. Not everyone behaves this way, of course, but it is the way the medium encourages everyone to behave. It is the kind of creature it turns you into.

This is not to say that every use of social media is a blight upon the soul. Even McLuhan, who described electronic communication as antichrist, balked at making all-encompassing moral evaluations of epochal technologies. "How can one person presume to add up the human and spiritual credits and debits for such a thing?" he wrote.[16]

Educated Christians separated by great distances might correspond over X the way Thomas More and Erasmus did by letter. Eastern

[16] McLuhan, *Medium and the Light*, 129.

THE TRANSHUMANIST TEMPTATION

Orthodox Christians who've seen their parishes swell with devotees of Jonathan Pageau can't be expected to simply wish away YouTube. And who among us would begrudge a Fr. Mike Schmitz podcast convert — or a Jerry Falwell TV convert, for that matter — his newfound faith?

When individual parishes become corrupt, orthodox Internet personalities can help mitigate the damage. A Catholic layman might well inoculate himself against his liberal priest's heresies by listening to Matt Fradd. Hyperawareness of denominational affairs can have positive outcomes too. In 2023, the pastor of a small Southern Baptist church used the Internet to lead a grassroots uprising that stymied a push by the convention's liberal leadership to rubber-stamp female clergy.[17] And if the seeker after genuine community finds that everyone at his local church races to the parking lot as soon as the service ends, online fellowship will serve him better than no fellowship at all.

Unfortunately, many churches and parishes, rather than trying their best to serve as a counterweight to the discarnational catechesis of the screen, often surrender to the technologies that promote it. To worship in a disembodied fashion is to worship like a transhuman, and if we can't stay human in our worship, what chance do we stand in the rest of life?

Many churches now incorporate screens into worship, with some projecting hymn lyrics and readings whereas others take a maximalist approach that involves high-production-value graphics and videos. To engage with a screen — whether at the bar or in a sanctuary — is to be somewhere other than where you are. It is to be everywhere and nowhere. This is most obvious when using one's own smartphone to peruse, say, X or Amazon.

---

[17] William Wolfe, "Battle on Bourbon Street," *American Conservative*, August 14, 2023, https://www.theamericanconservative.com/battle-on-bourbon-street/.

Digital Christianity

But even screens that perform dedicated functions tied closely to the activity at hand foster the same disembodiment. The in-car navigation system, the jumbotron at the football stadium, and the projection screen in the sanctuary — all instruct us to regard our own experience as insufficient. Our perceptions must be filtered through the digital world and fed back to us, refracted or augmented in ways often designed to elicit specific responses ("Turn left," "Make some noise," "Repeat chorus 17x").

In liturgical settings, the use of screens places two unseen worlds — the invisible swirl of electronic information and the cosmic worship of the saints and angels — in competition. Worship pulls us toward one form of self-transcendence; interaction with a screen pulls us toward another. Medium and content work at cross-purposes.

And that's if people even show up to church. In *Amusing Ourselves to Death*, Neil Postman argued that viewers of televised church services will be unlikely to achieve the same worshipful mindset they experience in person but will instead do "any of the things they are accustomed to doing in the presence of an animated television screen."[18] TV-watching is also an inherently passive activity. The liturgical worshipper will be less inclined to kneel or cross herself, while the megachurcher will mumble along to worship jams that she usually belts at the top of her lungs.

Postman didn't live to see YouTube livestreams, which have the same deleterious effects as well as some new ones. The livestream viewer has the power to pause or rewind the service, further establishing his sovereignty over the proceedings and robbing him of whatever modicum of community he had left.

To watch the live broadcast of Christmas Eve Midnight Mass from Rome is no substitute for attending a service in person. But it at least

---

[18] Neil Postman, *Amusing Ourselves to Death: Public Discourse in the Age of Show Business* (New York: Penguin, 2006), 119.

allows the viewer to share a synchronous experience with the crowd in St. Peter's, the crowd in the square outside the basilica, and the faithful watching on their own TVs around the world. To stream at noon a service that concluded at 10:30 a.m. is to isolate oneself entirely, in time as well as space.

Until the COVID-19 pandemic, most churches had no way of broadcasting their services and no desire to do so. The lockdown changed all that, coming as it did at the precise moment when reliable video streaming made such a response possible. It's impossible to imagine a similar lockdown in, say, the 1960s.

Thankfully, Christians in the 2020s had more options than just Fulton Sheen and Billy Graham (as gifted as they were). TV airtime is expensive, but any church with a camera and Wi-Fi could afford to livestream. The elderly, the immunocompromised, and the simply cautious could remain tethered to their local churches, preserving communities (at least to some extent) that might otherwise have frayed.

The real problems started when the pandemic subsided. One survey found that the number of Protestant churchgoers who said they hadn't substituted a livestream for in-person attendance in the past year fell from 47 percent in 2019 to just 20 percent in September 2022. The share who reported livestreaming on more than a third of Sundays almost quadrupled.[19]

By September 2022, it had been well over a year since the widespread release of the vaccine and since churches had faced any real impediments to in-person worship, suggesting that parishioners who

---

[19] Marissa Postell Sullivan, "Churchgoers Still Watch Livestream Services, at Least Occasionally," Lifeway Research, June 20, 2023, https://research.lifeway.com/2023/06/20/churchgoers-still-watch-livestream-services-at-least-occasionally/.

stepped up their virtual attendance have come to view it as a permanent part of their religious life.

Some churches have fought this trend by discontinuing their livestream entirely[20] or by decreasing its production value to make it less attractive to would-be slackers.

Catholics' high view of the Eucharist places limits on how far virtual worship can go, but for other denominations, the limits have not yet been set. During the pandemic, the Anglican Church in North America debated whether it was possible to consecrate the Eucharist via livestream. Plenty of churches answered in the affirmative, with pastors urging their far-flung congregants to grab bread and wine (or Oreos and Kool-Aid) from their own pantries and consume them in unison on their couches. But the ACNA opted against the practice. As one priest pointed out to me, the denomination's Book of Common Prayer rubrics require that as the celebrant says the "words concerning the bread," he must "hold it, or lay a hand upon it."[21] Thank God for that. If even the sacraments can be transferred to virtual reality, there's nothing to stop us from abolishing physical churches entirely and holding all services in the Metaverse.

Today's informational ecosystem pressures everyone, Christians included, toward narcissism, isolation, and discarnation — all of which lead us closer to transhumanism. The Church can allow herself to

---

[20] See Jim Davis and Skyler Flowers, "Why Our Church Will Unplug from Streaming," *Gospel Coalition*, May 27, 2021, https://www.thegospelcoalition.org/article/why-church-will-unplug/.

[21] Anglican Church in North America, *The Book of Common Prayer and Administration of the Sacraments with Other Rites and Ceremonies of the Church according to the Use of the Anglican Church in North America: Together with the New Coverdale Psalter* (Huntington Beach, CA: Anglican Liturgy Press, 2019), https://bcp2019.anglicanchurch.net/wp-content/uploads/2022/10/BCP-2019-MASTER-5th-PRINTING-05022022-3.pdf, 116.

accept this catechesis, or she can resist. Resistance means humility, community, embodiment, and ultimately *theosis* — our God-destined glorification of which the serpent's promise is the diabolical inversion.

It means laypeople stepping back from online discourse and regarding their own pastor as their primary spiritual authority. It means churches where people linger over coffee for hours after the service. It means worship that demands physical presence, cemented through gestures, smells, sounds, and the printed word instead of diffused by screens.

To resist in this way requires hard work and carries its own set of risks. But to fail to do so will be to bequeath to our descendants a religion that, whatever it may call itself, would soon bear little resemblance to the Faith once delivered.

Conclusion

Only a god can save us.[1]

— Martin Heidegger

Humanity's current medical, technological, political, economic, and spiritual trajectories all point toward the triumph of transhumanism. We've bent nature to our will and now seek to do the same to our own bodies. We've grown frustrated with the physical world's limitations and escape into virtual reality. We've placed so much emphasis on individual autonomy that our political system is no longer capable of recognizing the common good or meaningfully restraining transhumanism. We've created an economy that cannot function unless it is constantly inculcating in us ever-more indulgent, transgressive, and even self-destructive desires. We've abandoned God to pursue spiritualities of self-empowerment.

There are alternatives to this trajectory, though I'll leave it to the reader to determine how feasible and desirable they are.

---

[1] Martin Heidegger, "Nur noch ein Gott kann uns retten," *Der Spiegel*, May 30, 1976, 193–219, trans. W. Richardson as "Only a God Can Save Us" in *Heidegger: The Man and the Thinker*, ed. T. Sheehan (Chicago: Precedent, 1981) 45–74.

THE TRANSHUMANIST TEMPTATION

The first is the exploration and colonization of space, which might be the only way to maintain a sense of progress and cultural dynamism while preserving our humanity. Either we meld with the machine or we conquer the heavens.[2]

There can be no message more stirring than "The stars are your birthright." Break out the old Walt Whitman playbook — "Pioneers! O Pioneers!" It could also help shift humanity's creative energies away from virtual reality and back toward what Peter Thiel calls the "world of atoms."[3] The space program has always been a huge driver of innovation. Air purifiers, memory foam, LED lights, freeze-dried food, solar cells, insulin pumps, artificial limbs, and scratch resistant plastic were all created or improved using technologies developed for space exploration.[4] Interestingly, Thiel suggests that progress in the "world of atoms" stalled sometime in the 1970s, just after we beat the Soviets to the moon and just before the Computer Age cut the Space Age off at its knees.

Conquering the heavens comes with the added bonus that "we" will be the ones who've done it. To speak of "we" or "us" (meaning "humanity") when talking about a transhuman future is nonsense. The beings that inhabit that future will be something other than human. Whatever their accomplishments are, they will not be our accomplishments. Transhuman man is a different sort of being from his ancestors.

---

[2] The following four paragraphs originally appeared in the *Spectator World*. See Grayson Quay, "Let's Ban the Metaverse and Colonize Space," *Spectator World*, August 4, 2022, https://thespectator.com/topic/lets-ban-the-metaverse-and-colonize-space/.

[3] Harrington, "Peter Thiel on the Dangers of Progress."

[4] Josie Green, "Inventions We Use Every Day That Were Actually Created for Space Exploration," USA Today, July 8, 2019, https://www.usatoday.com/story/money/2019/07/08/space-race-inventions-we-use-every-day-were-created-for-space-exploration/39580591/.

Conclusion

Spacefaring man, on the other hand, is what all his predecessors have been: an embodied creature adept at the use of tools. As in *2001: A Space Odyssey*, there's a clear through-line from the bone club to the space station.

Instead of abolishing humanity, we could spread it across the stars. Instead of abandoning the cultural mandate, we could fulfill it like never before. Instead of clutching at divinity, we could fulfill the God-given command to be fruitful, multiply, and exercise dominion.

There are, of course, obstacles to such endeavors. One is that, as far as we can tell, lightspeed is a universal speed limit. As objects approach it, their mass increases, as does the amount of energy necessary to further increase that speed. This means that, theoretically, a ship on the brink of lightspeed would have infinite mass and require infinite energy to go faster. Not possible. Whether we might find a way to "fold space" (as illustrated by the "fold a piece of paper and punch a hole through it" example from every sci-fi movie ever) remains an open question.

Even if we can't, there's still plenty to do in our own solar system. The TV series *The Expanse*, for instance, envisions a twenty-fourth-century future in which a decadent Earth that placates its people with UBI and legalized drugs engages in a power struggle over asteroid belt resources with a partially terraformed Mars built on Roman republican virtue.

There are also multiple earthlike planets within fifty light-years of our homeworld.[5] We could reach them using generation ships, with the original crew made up of couples who then train their children and grandchildren in the skills necessary to maintain the ship and plant the colony. But we're not sure any of those planets can support life, and

---

[5] "List of Nearest Terrestrial Extrasolar Planets," Astronomy Wiki, accessed January 27, 2025, https://astronomical.fandom.com/wiki/List_of_nearest_terrestrial_extrasolar_planets.

our tolerances are fairly narrow. Move the orbit just a skosh outside the Goldilocks Zone for any given star, and we all freeze or fry. Or maybe we just asphyxiate in a pure nitrogen atmosphere. Terraforming is an option, but it would be a slow process.

There is, unfortunately, no guarantee that space exploration and transhumanism wouldn't simply advance along parallel tracks. One of *The Expanse*'s spacefaring protagonists is the product of genetic engineering and has eight biological parents.[6] Governments and corporations seeking to colonize other worlds might even be tempted to take a shortcut and modify humans to fit planets rather than the other way around.

In C. S. Lewis's *Out of the Silent Planet,* an angelic being suggests this possibility to an aspiring spacefarer, pointing out that humans "would have to be made quite unlike you before they lived on other worlds."[7] The would-be stellar imperialist claims to be motivated by "loyalty to humanity," but as the angel points out, he has no problem rendering the term *humanity* meaningless by reshaping human biology into whatever circumstances demand.

Another science fiction novel, Neal Stephenson's *The Diamond Age* (1996), offers another way forward. Stephenson's vision will likely be the most appealing to readers with more libertarian inclinations (assuming they haven't discarded this book in disgust already).

In the near future of *The Diamond Age,* the introduction of cryptocurrency and advancements in digital communication have rendered the nation-state obsolete. The society that replaced it has two components. First, there's the Common Economic Protocol (CEP), a

---

[6] *The Expanse,* "Windmills," season 1, ep. 7, dir. Bill Johnson, aired January 19, 2016.
[7] C. S. Lewis, *Out of the Silent Planet* (New York: Scribner, 2003), 136–137.

minarchist legal code that enforces contracts, protects property rights, punishes violent crime, and does very little else. The CEP is intentionally non-ideological. Shooting people is punishable by death, but only because it interferes with their productive capacity in the marketplace. Unlike a state, the CEP does not claim authority over everyone born in a certain geographical area but operates on a subscription model. Opting into this privatized justice system is a necessity for any person or group hoping to fully participate in the global economy.

If the first element of Stephenson's future is an anarcho-capitalist dream, the second is no less appealing to communitarians. The society of *The Diamond Age* is organized into *phyles* or "tribes," which can be based on religion, ethnicity, ideology, or some other shared commitment. Tribes featured in the novel include the Han Chinese; the Neo-Victorians, who employ advanced nanotechnology while maintaining Victorian British aesthetics and mores; the Drummers, who use neural implants to subsume themselves in a perpetual psychedelic hive-mind orgy; and the Reformed Distributed Republic, which promises maximum individual freedom but mandates periodic (and potentially lethal) trust-fall exercises to maintain social cohesion.[8]

Most phyles are global diasporas that maintain segregated enclaves in or near the world's major cities. The primary purpose of the CEP is to enable members of different phyles to fairly and predictably engage in commerce. The CEP's judges do not care about what goes on inside the enclaves and will never interfere. Each phyle sets its own rules and can enforce them on its members however it sees fit. Presumably, each individual has the right to right to leave his phyle, but unless another one is willing to take him, he would become a tribeless *thete*, forced to survive on his own wits and the bland free food from public matter compilers.

---

[8] Neal Stephenson, *The Diamond Age* (New York: Bantam Dell, 2000), 378.

THE TRANSHUMANIST TEMPTATION

This mode of social organization allows technology to advance while empowering communities to decide how they will use that technology. The Drummers are free to become fully transhuman, while the Neo-Victorians are free to pursue an older vision of human flourishing. They've mastered political theorist Jon Askonas's program of using "wild new technological practices" for traditionalist ends.[9] The phyle chooses to deploy technology in ways that further the community's goals and preserve its values. Those technologies are not permitted to reshape the community in the name of profit and progress.

Enclaves can decide for themselves how to employ advanced technology in pursuit of those goals. It's nearly impossible for an atomized modern individual to be that intentional. Such a person will inevitably draw his tech ethics from some combination of what's legal, how much he can afford, what his neighbors do, and what he gleans from the media. Stephenson's tribe members, shielded from the harsh winds of state, market, and mass culture behind the nanobot defenses of their enclaves, face no such pressure. Being the only kid on the block without a smartphone (or a neural implant) is a bummer. But if nobody in your intentional community has one, it's no big deal.

The defined boundaries and self-enforced rules of *The Diamond Age*'s enclaves also offer a model that could be useful to modern anti-transhumanists. The community must balance its tech restrictions with its members' ability to interact with the outside world. Amish contractors, for example, are forbidden from operating motor vehicles and hire "English" drivers to transport them to job sites.

One could also envision a community with two sets of rules: one for inside the "phyle" and one for interactions with the world at large. Imagine, for example, the United Methodist Church imposing a spiritual

---

[9] Jon Askonas, "Why Conservatism Failed," *Compact*, October 6, 2022, https://www.compactmag.com/article/why-conservatism-failed/.

discipline under which its members can carry smartphones during the workday but must power them down before returning home.

A sufficiently numerous and influential tribe can even convince the outside world to make concessions to it. Hotels and apartment buildings in multiple countries offer "Sabbath elevators," which are usually pre-programmed to stop at every floor so that observant Jews will not have to violate their law by pressing an electronic button.[10] By the same logic, a consistently anti-transhumanist collective (religious or otherwise) could preserve their humanity while forcing an otherwise transhumanist world to accommodate it.

But this might only work for a short time. Eventually, the transhumanists could evolve to a point where mere humans had nothing to offer them. It's doubtful that such elevated beings would allow the remaining *homo sapiens* to defy evolution indefinitely. Even if they did, the attempt to stop transhumanism from conquering the world — or at least preserve anti-transhumanism as a broadly viable option — would have failed.

Achieving Stephenson's future would be difficult without a massive shift in the self-understanding of modern governments. They are too large, too centralized, and too devoted to the ideals of individual rights and equality to ever pare themselves down to the degree that would allow robust, self-governing communities to survive and prosper the way they do in *The Diamond Age*.

More importantly, though, it would require people raised on a steady diet of transhumanist ideology to bear the constraints of community to a degree most are unprepared to accept. And it would require communities to meaningfully enforce those constraints. The Catholic prohibitions on birth control, IVF, surrogacy, genetic engineering, and

---

[10] Wikipedia, s.v. "Shabbat Elevator," accessed January 27, 2025, https://en.wikipedia.org/wiki/Shabbat_elevator.

THE TRANSHUMANIST TEMPTATION

other forms of transhumanism are admirable, but most Catholics face no real consequences for disregarding them. If the Church wanted to function as a Stephensonian phyle in which its members could keep themselves "unstained from the world," clergy would need to get serious about excommunicating and disfellowshipping those who unrepentantly defy its teachings.[11] Embracing the Mormon policy of directing members to eschew government assistance in favor of church mutual aid would be a good first step toward helping Catholics (or members of any other group) identify more strongly with the community.

Each phyle should see itself as a lifeboat, sealed by solidarity and shared commitment against the ocean of liquid modernity, not as a mere club in which atomized individuals are free to dabble to whatever extent they please. Such pseudo-tribes offer no defense against transhumanism.

The final alternative to transhumanist dystopia would be one in which humanity either intentionally represses or unintentionally destroys its technological capacities.

In the far-future world of Frank Herbert's *Dune*, a "Butlerian jihad" in the distant past is said to have wiped out AI (along with all other computer technology) and forged a religious taboo against recreating it. The commandment "Thou shalt not make a machine in the image of a man's mind" is enshrined in their scripture, and the penalty for breaking it is death.[12] The taboo also appears to cover all forms of artificial reproductive technology.[13] Transhumanism, however, continues to advance along other lines. Using psychological conditioning, drugs, selective breeding, and genetic engineering, experts replicate the functions of computers, "improve" the human race, and even pursue immortality.

---

[11] James 1:27, ESV.
[12] Frank Herbert, *Dune* (New York: Putnam, 1984), 11.
[13] Frank Herbert, *Dune Messiah* (New York: Ace Books, 2008), 146.

Conclusion

Even if we don't actively pursue this regression, it may be thrust upon us. It's still unclear what lies on the other side of the ongoing, and highly contested, "green transition" from fossil fuels to more sustainable energy sources. It's possible to envision a "solarpunk" future in which standards of living remain relatively high, but there's simply not enough energy to sustain the level of prosperity and rate of progress we've gotten used to since the Industrial Revolution.[14] Your homestead will still have electric lights and running water and you can get a C-section if you need one. In other areas, you'll need to lower expectations. Sorry, but we just can't spare the wattage to keep the Metaverse live, and transgender surgeries are an unjustifiable strain on limited medical resources.

This scenario, which could stop transhumanism in its tracks, is one of the more hopeful ones, but it's still unclear how close we really are to running out of fossil fuels, whether the "green transition" will happen at all, and what a post-transition world might look like.[15] It's even possible that governments in this new world could modify humans to reduce the burden we place on the environment. Gene Wolfe's *Book of the New Sun* series presents one possible future in which genetically modified green-skinned humans sustain themselves by photosynthesis.[16] In our own world, bioethicist S. Matthew Liao has suggested that scientists could "artificially induce intolerance to meat" in order to "create an aversion to eating eco-unfriendly food."[17]

---

[14] Thomas Murphy, *Energy and Human Ambitions on a Finite Planet: Assessing and Adapting to Planetary Limits* (Oakland, CA: eScholarship University of California, 2020), 26–29, 324–325.

[15] Ibid. 310–311.

[16] Gene Wolfe, *The Claw of the Conciliator* (New York: Timescape, 1981), 25–28.

[17] S. Matthew Liao, "Tackling Climate Change through Human Engineering?" TED Archive, 2013, uploaded November 20, 2017, YouTube, https://www.youtube.com/watch?v=AcaKMu7I6vU.

THE TRANSHUMANIST TEMPTATION

A Canticle for Leibowitz presents a more drastic technological setback but suggests that, human nature being what it is, all such setbacks are temporary. We will always reach too far and destroy ourselves in the process. Walter M. Miller Jr.'s 1959 novel begins in a medieval-style "Dark Age" six hundred years after a global nuclear war. The following centuries bring a new Renaissance and Enlightenment, leading to a new modernity that quickly incinerates itself the same way the old world did.

Entertaining and edifying as *Canticle* is, however, it's unlikely that humanity could regress to a pre-industrial level of development and then bootstrap itself back to its current state. In Orson Scott Card's novel *Pastwatch*, the protagonists initially operate under the delusion that they live in an idyllic, sustainable era of "rebirth, rebuilding, and restoration," but soon learn that total collapse is imminent.[18] Amid global famine and a new ice age, the world population will fall to around five million, after which — one character observes — "the human race can't rise again."[19] Technological advancement requires resources, and we've already picked all the low-hanging fruit. Extracting the remaining hard-to-reach deposits of coal, oil, copper, iron, and other essential materials would require equipment that we can't produce or operate without a steady supply of those materials. And modern prosperity is almost entirely the product of cheap fossil fuels. Even if survivors retained the knowledge of how to repair and operate whatever machines remained, they would have no way of replacing spent fuel or worn-out components.[20]

---

[18] Orson Scott Card, *Pastwatch: The Redemption of Christopher Columbus* (New York: Tor, 1996), 256.

[19] Ibid., 238–240.

[20] With globally distributed supply chains, it's likely that human and industrial capital would be too scattered to do anyone much good if our hypothetical cataclysm knocked out global communications and rendered air travel inaccessible. As Leonard Reed pointed out, no

Conclusion

Card's heroes decide to alter the past to produce a better present, but without a time machine there's no real solution. You'd get *Mad Max* until the gas ran out, followed by eternal subsistence agrarianism. It's the world envisioned by *Fight Club* antagonist Tyler Durden: you spend your life "pounding corn [and] laying stripes of venison on the empty carpool lane of some abandoned superhighway."[21] It also means the return of all the horrors of the past: astronomical child mortality rates, deaths from dysentery and minor infections, villages wiped out by drought and famine, massacres by bloodthirsty steppe raiders. The human population would likely shrink to no more than a few million. Though perhaps even that would be a mercy compared to a fully transhuman future.

The space colonization of *The Expanse*, the communitarianism of *The Diamond Age*, and the enforced semi-luddism of *Dune* all offer the possibility of slowing or limiting the progress of transhumanism. A collapse into primitivism could reverse it entirely. But each of the first three options is some mix of unlikely and insufficient, and no one should wish for the fourth with all the human suffering it would entail.

My view is that the advance of transhumanism is inexorable. It is perhaps the only fitting culmination to the story that began in Eden. Fr. Stephen de Young argued during an episode of the *Lord of Spirits* podcast that the concept of Adam and Eve not being ready for the knowledge of good and evil and Cain's descendants not being ready for the technologies they obtained from evil spirits suggests "some sense

---

single person on earth knows how to make a #2 pencil. And even if he did know how, the aspiring pencil-maker has no way of gathering all the materials. See Leonard Reed, "I, Pencil," Foundation for Economic Education, March 3, 2015, https://fee.org/ebooks/i-pencil/.

[21] *Fight Club*, dir. David Fincher, written by Jim Uhls, based on the novel by Chuck Palahniuk, (Los Angeles: Fox 2000, 1999).

THE TRANSHUMANIST TEMPTATION

of the collective maturity of humanity."[22] In the Flood and Tower of Babel narratives, we see God setting back human progress to prevent His creations from destroying themselves. This in turn implies two processes at work in history: one in which the Holy Spirit guides us toward *theosis*, and one in which infernal powers offer us the tools to destroy ourselves. God restrained the latter process in the past. He doesn't appear to be doing so any longer.

Previous technological advancements gave us the capacity to kill, deceive, or oppress our fellow humans. Bronze can be hammered into a sword or a plowshare. Radio can broadcast beautiful music or genocidal propaganda. Ships crossing the Atlantic can bring hope to desperate emigrants or despair to kidnapped slaves. But no innovation — not even the atomic bomb, which gave humanity the power to bring about its own extinction — can match the destructive potential of transhumanist technologies like genetic engineering, artificial reproduction, cybernetic enhancement, and virtual and augmented reality. For the first time, we have the power to remake ourselves. We can destroy the human race as we know it without firing a single missile.

It's possible that God isn't done with us yet. Perhaps a new biblical cataclysm will pull us away from the brink of transhumanism, putting some time back on the clock while His grace performs some great and hidden work that must come to completion before the end of days.

But I doubt it. Christ and the apostles described the entire period of time between the Incarnation and the Second Coming as the "last days." The moment the Word became flesh, a countdown started — and

---

[22] "The Art and Science of Technomancy," *Lord of Spirits*, ep. 90, hosted by Andrew Stephen Damick and Stephen de Young, streamed December 15, 2023, 2:51:00, https://www.ancientfaith.com/podcasts/lordofspirits/the_art_and_science_of_technomancy/.

Conclusion

I fear it only goes one way. Christianity forged the modern world, which in turn abandoned God, crafted the secular transhumanist ideology, and set to work developing the technology to implement it. Soon, all that will remain is the choice of two transhumanisms. As a character in C. S. Lewis's *That Hideous Strength* puts it, "Good is always getting better and bad is always getting worse ... The whole thing is sorting itself out all the time, coming to a point."[23]

There is a theory of Christian eschatology (the study of the "last things") called *postmillennialism*. It's an optimistic view, positing that the gospel will spread throughout the world, transforming society and ushering in a thousand-year utopia, after which Christ will return. I'm not a postmillennialist. I think the end will come when things are as bad as they can get, when true humanity has been reduced to a despised and powerless remnant. In *Brave New World*, "savages" who choose to defy progress live on squalid reservations where they're gawked at by curious transhumans. Paul Kingsnorth's 2020 novel *Alexandria* imagines primitive hunter-gatherers living in close proximity to a malevolent god, which is actually a digital hive-mind that has assimilated the rest of humanity. Its emissary visits the tribesmen, tempting them to surrender their bodies and join the singularity. Those who hold fast to their humanity should expect to face similar trials.

Denying your embodied nature and acting instead as a sovereign will capable of crafting its own *telos* means aligning yourself with the bodiless powers who rebelled against God. I'm not sure what (if any) degree of technological tinkering would place us outside humanity (and therefore beyond redemption), but we're perfectly capable of damning ourselves with low-tech transhumanism. "The souls of those who live in sin [become demons]; not that their nature is changed, but that in their desires they imitate the evil nature of demons," said Church

---

[23] Lewis, *Hideous Strength*, 281.

THE TRANSHUMANIST TEMPTATION

Father St. John Chrysostom.[24] Many Christians debate and agonize over the question of whether all humans might be saved. I think it's possible that, in a sense, they will. By taking on human nature, Christ redeemed human nature. Humanity is not static. It's on a Godward trajectory. *Theosis* is the *telos* of that nature and the destiny of all who share in it. To reject that destiny is to become less human and, perhaps ultimately, less *than* human.

Zoltan Istvan's novel *The Transhumanist Wager* climaxes with a startup micronation of brilliant transhumanists blowing up religious sites, palaces, legislatures, and monuments across the world. He gleefully describes the incineration of the pope and the thousands of faithful gathered in St. Peter's Square. All ideologies that took man as a constant and attempted to serve him as he actually exists are leveled to make way for the future. The victorious experts then fan out across the globe, becoming leaders of a new utopian world-state devoted to achieving omnipotence and immortality. Istvan calls it "Transhumania."[25]

He should have called it *Hell*. Hell is the site of the final divorce between desire and *eudaimonia*. It's where humans, if the state to which they've degraded themselves is worthy of the name, are left free to make their own meaning, craft their own identity, chase their own bliss, and live their own truth — forever. The results are not joy and empowerment but suffering and bondage. And if we believe the serpent's promise and embrace transhumanism, the same fate awaits us in this life.

---

[24] Quoted in Damick, *Lord of Spirits*, 188.
[25] Istvan, *Transhumanist Wager*, 266–268.

About the Author

Grayson Quay lives in Alexandria, Virginia, with his wife and daughter.

CRISIS Publications

Sophia Institute Press awards the privileged title "CRISIS Publications" to a select few of our books that address contemporary issues at the intersection of politics, culture, and the Church with clarity, cogency, and force and that are also destined to become all-time classics.

CRISIS Publications are direct, explaining their principles briefly, simply, and clearly to Catholics in the pews, on whom the future of the Church depends. The time for ambiguity or confusion is long past.

CRISIS Publications are contemporary, born of our own time and circumstances and intended to become significant statements in current debates, statements that serious Catholics cannot ignore, regardless of their prior views.

CRISIS Publications are classical, addressing themes and enunciating principles that are valid for all ages and cultures. Readers will turn to them time and again for guidance in other days and different circumstances.

CRISIS Publications are spirited, entering contemporary debates with gusto to clarify issues and demonstrate how those issues can be resolved in a way that enlivens souls and the Church.

We welcome engagement with our readers on current and future CRISIS Publications. Please pray that this imprint may help to resolve the crises embroiling our Church and society today.

Sophia Institute Press® is a registered trademark of Sophia Institute.
Sophia Institute is a tax-exempt institution as defined by the
Internal Revenue Code, Section 501(c)(3). Tax ID 22-2548708.